MEN IN WHITE SUITS

Also by Simon Hughes

SECRET DIARY OF A LIVERPOOL SCOUT
RED MACHINE

MEN IN WHITE SUITS

SIMON HUGHES

LIVERPOOL FC IN THE 1990S
THE PLAYERS' STORIES

BANTAM PRESS

LONDON • TORONTO • SYDNEY • AUCKLAND • JOHANNESBURG

TRANSWORLD PUBLISHERS
61–63 Uxbridge Road, London W5 5SA
www.transworldbooks.co.uk

Transworld is part of the Penguin Random House group of companies
whose addresses can be found at global.penguinrandomhouse.com

Penguin
Random House
UK

First published in Great Britain in 2015 by Bantam Press
an imprint of Transworld Publishers

A CIP catalogue record for this book
is available from the British Library.

ISBN 9780593074619

Typeset in Sabon 11.5/15pt by Falcon Oast Graphic Art Ltd.
Printed and bound by Clays Ltd, Bungay, Suffolk.

Penguin Random House is committed to a sustainable
future for our business, our readers and our planet. This book
is made from Forest Stewardship Council® certified paper.

MIX
Paper from
responsible sources
FSC® C018179

1 3 5 7 9 10 8 6 4 2

For Rosalind, who will now have to read this.

CONTENTS

FOREWORD

Alex Ferguson once claimed that his greatest achievement in football was knocking Liverpool Football Club off its perch at the top of the English game. The comment was accepted as an undisputed fact even though it isn't really true.

In the early 1990s, Liverpool went from champions to mid table in a few years and it had nothing to do with United's emergence. It wasn't as if Liverpool and United were going head to head for titles over a couple of years and United suddenly raced away over the horizon and into the sunset, leaving Liverpool behind.

Liverpool slipped away and United took advantage of the space at the top. Instead of beating Liverpool to titles, United finished ahead of unfashionable sides like Aston Villa and Norwich City. Liverpool's fall was self-inflicted.

Although in terms of results and league positions Liverpool's decline began under Graeme Souness, you could debate all day long where the problems started.

I joined Liverpool on the YTS a few months after Graeme left Liverpool in 1994 and Roy Evans was installed as his replacement. While training with the reserves, I could see there were a lot of issues with players who had been signed by Graeme and that Roy now wanted to get rid of. Players like Julian Dicks, Don Hutchison and Mark Walters had all been cut from the first-team picture but, because they were on big contracts, Roy was finding it difficult to move them out. He made them train with the reserves, and as they knew they had no real future at Anfield they were understandably demotivated and didn't always set the best example.

One pre-season, I remember Dicks attempting long-distance running around the perimeter of Liverpool's Melwood training ground and getting lapped. The perimeter is huge. He'd be cutting the biggest corner you've ever seen to try to catch up and nobody would say anything.

As a teenager, you don't know any different, so you laugh along with it all. You begin to think that this is what it must be like when you're a Liverpool first-team player: the allowances you are afforded. I'm not saying I wanted any of that but the management clearly could not afford to have disillusioned players at the club.

Around the same time, the young players in Liverpool's first team were given the 'Spice Boys' label. Lads like Jamie Redknapp, Robbie Fowler and Steve McManaman were unlucky and suffered as a result of the behaviour of other squad members who were focusing on going out and having a good time rather than trying to persuade the manager they were worthy of a place in the team.

In reality, those who were tarnished by the Spice Boys tag, including Jamie, Robbie and Steve, as well as others like Phil Babb and Jason McAteer, were not big drinkers who sat in a pub all day. They might have gone to a nightclub and met girls but that did not mean they were getting drunk. They were not the hell-raisers everybody on the outside thought they were. Lads of a similar age at other clubs were all doing the same thing but at Anfield it seemed to matter more because Liverpool narrowly missed out on the title in successive seasons. Look at Ryan Giggs and Lee Sharpe and others at United. They were in the same social circle but weren't judged in the same way as Liverpool's Spice Boys.

I was invited to pre-season training at Melwood for the first time aged sixteen. I'd only just finished my GCSE exams. Robbie was the player every lad in Liverpool wanted to be. Then there were John Barnes and Ian Rush – living legends. I was doing the same running as them, the same ball-work as them and playing in the same small-sided matches. I'd go home and tell all my mates about it. It was brilliant. During sessions, I wouldn't say much. I'd just listen closely to what everyone around me was talking about. There was lots of piss taking and you had to learn how to give it and take it.

It was a big jump to make. I'd always played twelve months ahead of my age group. When I was ten, I was playing with and against eleven year olds. When I was eleven, I was playing with and against twelve year olds. Suddenly, at sixteen, my teammates and opponents were often twice my age. I was competing with fully grown men. But we were all game. Nowadays, if you sign for Liverpool at sixteen you usually remain within your own age group, progressing into the under-18s then the under-21s. Then, it was a free-for-all. You had to get involved. Nobody made it easier for you because you were the youngest on the pitch.

I didn't know what to expect, because I was inexperienced and new to it all. What I could see was that Barnes was the best player in training every single day and had a fantastic attitude. Rush was different because he was a striker and strikers tend to save themselves for the game at the end of the week. You could never question Rushy's attitude but he didn't run around all day. That was just his manner and always had been. Both players set the right example.

I played with Rush in the reserves and he was ruthlessly efficient. He always did a shift and led the way. I later made my first-team debut in central-midfield with Barnes. What a player. Unbelievable. As an Evertonian, I had stood in the Gwladys Street end only a few years earlier, watching him bend one in for Liverpool during the 4-4 FA Cup tie that proved to be Kenny Dalglish's last match in charge before resigning as manager. Suddenly, I was running alongside him in midfield.

Liverpool's way of thinking was drilled into me by brilliant youth coaches like Steve Heighway, Hughie McAuley and Dave Shannon. The same attitudes existed at first-team level, where Roy, as the manager, was assisted by Ronnie Moran. The training was exactly the same as it had been since the days of Bill Shankly and Bob Paisley. The famous wooden shooting boards were there and every session finished with a five-a-side match. There was no suggestion that things should change, even though other clubs were going through big transformations at this time.

I remember Roy bringing in an extra coach with experience in rugby to help with aerobic sessions. His name was Andy Clarke. Ronnie was in charge of training but nobody had had the courage to tell him that Andy was coming in to try to improve our warm-ups. Although Ronnie would eventually agree it was a good idea, on Andy's first morning he was still none the wiser and you could feel the tension. Because things had been done a certain way at Liverpool with a lot of success over so many years, there was resistance to change. Ronnie had quite a temper and it's fair to say he instilled fear. Over the next few months, Ronnie called Andy 'Tippy-Tappy' because he liked to use a rope ladder for short sprints.

There is no doubt that Liverpool needed to move with the times and modernize. But some of the old ways still worked. If the first team had won on a Saturday and did not have another game until the following weekend, the players were given the Monday off. The coaches would still be at Melwood. Roy, Ronnie, Steve, Hughie and Dougie Livermore would team up and select the best reserve players to be on their side, along with the first-team fellas returning from injury. David Thompson and I would regularly be chosen alongside figures like Jan Mølby and we'd play against the rest of the YTS lads. There would be no positions. I'd find myself at right-back then suddenly at left-wing. The young players would do all of the running for the coaches but in turn they guided us. There would be nuggets of golden advice that I carried with me throughout my career. Ronnie had been a left-back and knew a lot about position-ing and tackling. While the game was going on, he'd help me understand what was happening in real-time. I've had manag-ers since who want to stop sessions every couple of minutes to explain how they expect football to be played. This was learning on the job and it made the development process a lot quicker than if a coach had constantly been blowing his whistle, breaking up play.

Immediately after my full first-team debut against Aston Villa in January 1997, I did an interview with a newspaper. I didn't want to come across as big-headed and so I said, 'I know John Barnes will be back next week as well as Michael Thomas . . . I'm sure they'll return to the team.' I was just trying to be humble and say the right thing. A few days later, Sammy Lee came over and asked me why I'd said that. 'Never make it easy for a manager to leave you out,' he told me. 'Make it as hard as possible – you've played, scored and performed well.' That always stuck with me. It was my first big lesson.

Deep down, I had confidence in my ability. I believed I should get selected more often. I remember going to Roy's office at eighteen telling him I should be in the team. I told him I was better than John Barnes, Jamie Redknapp and Michael Thomas. I wasn't being big-headed or cocky. That kind of inner confidence was necessary to get ahead. If you're a teenager and want to play for Liverpool, you need to have character. You need to embrace confrontation. I might have been kidding myself but you had to think like that to survive and progress. I was never nervous playing for the first team.

I wasn't the only player knocking on Roy's door. In the modern game, players seem to accept squad rotation a lot more. In that 1996–97 season, every Monday there would be five or six players queuing up outside the manager's office. I saw this happening and thought, 'Well, if they're doing it, so am I.'

It would always be a constructive discussion. Roy loved it. He wasn't a soft touch and wouldn't shy away from difficult conversations. It might have been different with senior pros but he gave me the impression he wanted players to come and talk to him. Initially, I'd tell Ronnie or Sammy that I was frustrated and they'd look at me as if I was daft – 'Go and speak to Roy.' It stopped resentment building up amongst the squad and helped morale. There is nothing worse than a player whingeing in the corner of the dressing room because he isn't happy but doing nothing about it when the person who can help change things is just a few feet away.

When most people think about Liverpool in the 1990s, three games spring immediately to mind. The first is obviously the white-suit FA Cup final, which I will come to shortly. The others are the 4–3 wins over Newcastle United at Anfield. Those latter games supposedly epitomized the Liverpool team: brilliant in attack and terrible in defence. Yet before the Newcastle games in 1996 and 1997, both of which fell in the final three months of the season, Liverpool held the best defensive record in the Premier League, conceding fewer goals than any other team. In those seasons, Liverpool completed their campaign with the second and third best defensive records – just behind the legendary Arsenal back four that was evolving under Arsène Wenger.

Liverpool did not have world-class defenders. But the defence as a unit was not as terrible as many make out. It was the manner in which they conceded goals that led to the dubious myth – David James flapping against rivals like United, or the team somehow losing matches they really needed to win. It suggests to me that at key moments there was either a lack of leadership or even confidence that they could see it through.

Had Liverpool beaten a major rival to a trophy in the mid nineties, giving the players that unique taste of victory, history might have been different. There is no doubt, in my opinion, that during the 1996–97 season Liverpool should have won the league for instance. That year, we played some of the best football seen at Anfield in the last twenty-five years.

I later played under Gérard Houllier and Rafa Benítez in teams that were more aggressive and dogged. They probably had a better understanding of how to grind out a victory. But Roy's side were unbelievable at times that season. Liverpool went to Old Trafford and Manchester United did not get a kick of the ball. Robbie Fowler would score hat-tricks, McManaman was unstoppable in midfield and Liverpool would be smashing opponents three or four nil quite regularly. After I made my debut, I was on the bench a dozen or so times, but I was always inside Anfield, watching whether I was in the squad or not.

Yet the breathtaking football was not enough to secure the title and the following season we fell away. It had been argued that the team needed a ball-winning midfielder in the mould of Paul Ince. So Roy went out and signed Paul from Inter Milan. It was seen as quite a coup, because not many players that have been a success at Manchester United join Liverpool even by an indirect route. His signing was seen as the one that would propel us to another level. But Paul had played 4–4–2 at both United and Inter. It was the way he liked to play. This Liverpool team was set up with three at the back, with Steve McManaman in a roving, attacking midfield role. When Paul came into the side, the formation switched to 4–4–2. Steve was shunted out on the left of midfield. Even though we managed to finish third, our performances were not the same. It was an average team. The centre-backs were not strong or powerful enough to operate in a two and the full-backs could not really defend. To accommodate Ince, the whole shape of the team changed and things were not the same. Soon, Roy was on his way out.

Houllier came in, initially as joint manager in July 1998 and was a lot more intense. He was very hands-on. He involved himself in every aspect of the way the club was run. Patrice Bergues was his most trusted lieutenant on the coaching staff and he was the nice cop. With Roy Evans and Ronnie Moran it was the other way around, with the manager being the good guy and Ronnie taking on the tougher role.

Both Roy and Gérard were desperate for the result but Roy wanted to play good football as well. For Gérard, it was solely about the result. Rafa Benítez was the same. If we had to play long to win, we'd play long. Roy was happy if we won 1–0 but not entirely satisfied. He wanted 3–0 or 4–0. Ultimately, however, Roy's approach did not win Liverpool the league title that everyone inside Anfield craved.

It frustrates me that there are some players who played for Liverpool in Istanbul when we won the Champions League in

2005 who were not very good but are defined by that success and remembered fondly. Unfortunately, a few brilliant players – Fowler, McManaman and Redknapp – are probably defined by the FA Cup final defeat to United in 1996, when the squad turned up at Wembley wearing those silly white suits. They can't escape from it.

If I had been a senior player at Liverpool at the time, I would have stopped this happening. As a senior player, you have to be thinking of the bigger picture. *What if we lose?* I can't believe nobody thought about that. It was not as if Liverpool were playing a Mickey Mouse team. You're playing Manchester United. You know about the rivalry. You know that every pass and tackle is going to be contested. Yet still you turn up looking like that.

I still can't believe it was allowed to happen. It was a massive mistake and it gave the wrong impression, feeding a reputation that still follows all of those players around today.

Jamie Carragher

INTRODUCTION

'Something has shifted; there's a new feeling on the streets. There's a desire for change.' Alastair Campbell, Labour Party Press Secretary, autumn 1996

ON SATURDAY, 13 JANUARY 1990, WHEN LIVERPOOL PLAYED THEIR first home league game of the new decade against Luton Town, 35,312 people turned up to watch a frustrating 2–2 draw. The Liverpool side that chilly afternoon included Alan Hansen, Peter Beardsley, Ian Rush and John Barnes, players that had contributed at different stages towards the collection of twenty trophies in the 1980s.

In the months that followed, Liverpool would suffer the indignity of dropping to second on two occasions thanks to the efforts of a bold Aston Villa side managed by Graham Taylor. From the start of April, however, Liverpool were in cruise control, securing the First Division championship easily with two fixtures to spare.

It says much about Liverpool's lore that even though there were no more titles, the final home game of the nineties against Wimbledon attracted a considerably higher gate of 44,107. A 3–1 victory over Wimbledon strengthened Liverpool's position in fifth, seven points off Leeds in top place. As had been the case in many of the previous nine seasons, Manchester United proved to be the only team consistently capable of chasing a lead and by May 2000 Leeds were toppled and United were champions by the huge margin of eighteen points.

An almost unbroken thirty-year cycle of achievement was over for Liverpool, a club where continuity had long been the key to success, where the management-selection system relied on promotion from within and teams were built on gradual evolution. It was a formula that had kept the club's most highly valued prize in seemingly permanent residence at Anfield rather than Old Trafford.

The 1990s was an era where there were three Liverpools, each one at odds with the last. There was the Liverpool of Graeme Souness, who inherited an old squad from Kenny Dalglish and quickly disbanded it, his previous success seeming to blind him to the fact he didn't know everything there was to know about management. There was the Liverpool of Roy Evans, who was just as quick as Souness to make changes but took the club back to its traditional values when those of the game as a whole were heading in a different direction. Then there was the Liverpool of Frenchman Gérard Houllier, another knee-jerk appointment, who represented an uneasy compromise between the Continental coaching technocrats who had flooded the British game and the older values of a different age.

It was ultimately a difficult period to be Liverpool's manager. Anfield remained buried in a traditional backstreet setting while the club tried to haul itself into the next century. Attempts at modernization included a financially beneficial merchandising agreement with Reebok, the lucrative sponsorship deal with Carlsberg and an in-house McDonald's complete with trashy-looking 'M' welded to the outside of the Kop. At Melwood, the training base in West Derby, a revamped facility eventually superseded the handwritten ledgers of Ronnie Moran, who was the club's oldest servant when he retired in 1998.

It was also a time of great transition for the players, courted not only by a different, more aggressive media but the jet set as well.

A new type of celebrity emerged. Managers and players operated in contradicting worlds but within the loose framework of a society bent out of shape by Thatcherite greed. Many see the nineties as both an inspiring decade and a scruffy clearing-house sale of British culture – the repackaging of Britannia, with added cool, for international distribution.

The global potential of football was spotted by Sky Television. In 1992, the Premier League replaced the old First Division, heralding a prosperous future and a move away from the hooliganism and stadium disasters that blighted football in the 1980s. There were fears that the English top flight had fallen a long way behind other elite European divisions in Italy and Spain, where clubs had more money and could attract the world's best players. Unhappy at the direction in which English football seemed to be heading, ten First Division clubs threatened to create a new breakaway competition, splitting from the Football League, which they'd been part of for more than a hundred years. It was this possibility that prompted the first steps towards the creation of a Premier League and soon a lucrative television deal with Sky, brokered by Rick Parry – a Liverpool supporter who would finish the decade as chief executive at Anfield – meant twenty-two Premier League clubs would share a pot of £304 million.

Manchester United used much of the bounty to develop Old Trafford, a stadium that today generates more income than any other in world football because of its size and merchandising opportunities. Elsewhere, the money encouraged those other clubs trying to catch up with Liverpool to be more ambitious in the transfer market. Exciting foreigners like Gianfranco Zola, Faustino Asprilla and Juninho signed for Chelsea, Newcastle United and Middlesbrough, while cheap players with European Union passports came to replace the dross at the bottom. It was good news for the Premier League's skyrocketing international fan base but bad news for players like Liverpool's Paul Stewart and soon enough, other-worldly characters like Zola, Asprilla and Juninho were skipping past English defenders like Neil Ruddock in a similar way to a sober man outwitting a drunken one.

And what of the actual matches? Well, they became soap operas where attractive and controversial figures secured the recognition of their names in the sport but also their notoriety in news headlines. Football became something entirely different.

All of this begs the question whether it should really be a surprise that the club built on comradeship and the strongest foundations of socialism fell the furthest when the free market began to eat voraciously into the game. Is it merely a coincidence that in 1991, the year the Soviet Union collapsed, the first cracks in Liverpool's domination over English football began to appear publicly for the first time? Liverpool's regression occurred when not just football was changing but the world itself. Perhaps Liverpool's decline was ultimately unavoidable.

Liverpool's simplicity before had been extreme. At Bill Shankly's behest, there had been no interference in football matters from boardroom level since the mid 1960s. Training routines remained the same season after season. A chain of managers acted as 'spokesmen' for the club, as Roy Evans put it; success was largely achieved through a collective spirit, instigated by the senior players. Everybody involved knew their role. Winning seemed easy.

Yet it is historically proven that, unless blood is spilt in morbid quantities, empires that are only prepared to peer inside their own souls for answers eventually come to an end. As Liverpool had achieved so much success, it was believed that the club's methods were infallible. At Anfield, the reaction to the general culture shift was unenthusiastic.

In the early 1990s, while other clubs became more professional and more competitive, at Liverpool the framework remained largely the same as it was before. Graeme Souness tried to make necessary changes only to be foiled by his own lack of diplomacy as well as resistance amongst a group he admits he could have managed better.

Under Roy Evans, some progress was made. Liverpool had the youngest average age of any squad in the Premier League, lower even than Manchester United. Yet United were always one step ahead of Liverpool and considered dreamy, a football imitation of *Beverly Hills, 90210*. Liverpool were crude, like *Men Behaving Badly*, a group of men, indeed, who were prepared to wear ostentatious white suits to the FA Cup final of 1996, a contest that featured their greatest rivals at a rare moment in history where there was not much difference in the quality between the teams.

After Souness's fractious reign, when morale was at a low, Liverpool's squad collective was rediscovered under Evans and, through an active social scene not too different to the one that had existed in the eighties, the players established a common bond. Unfortunately that clashed with the new expectations on footballers.

Following the bitter class war of the eighties, Britain had suddenly remembered how to enjoy itself again. Young people from working-class backgrounds were redefining social norms and this was reflected particularly in the music industry, with bands like Oasis and Blur storming the charts. In politics, Labour appointed their youngest leader since the Second World War and Tony Blair promptly won the next general election.

But it seemed that not everyone was welcome at the party. Footballers, with their new money, were often the target of resentment, especially those underachieving at a club with a history as rich as that of Liverpool. Players found their lives illuminated by the glare of the media spotlight and suddenly everyone had an opinion on their behaviour – good or bad. This, of course, was the birth of the talkSPORT age, which launched as Talk Radio in 1995. It seems normal now for callers to be in a rage by midday whenever Jack Wilshere smokes a cigarette on holiday, but back then an entire radio debate devoted to Steve McManaman's role in drinking games while on international duty for England before Euro 96 was a novel concept. It successfully tapped into the public's reasonably felt jealousy over disproportionate earnings while also redefining our beliefs about how footballers should act.

Liverpool's white suits merely confirmed the suspicions of

many: Liverpool were not serious about winning trophies any more. The FA Cup final felt like a big day out at the races, an opportunity to show off. Before the game, as Robbie Fowler and his best mate McManaman larked about on the pitch while being interviewed by Ray Stubbs, or 'Stubbsy' as they called him, live on BBC television, the sight of those white suits had the effect of pressing a mute button on Liverpool's support. On the terraces at least, United were delivered their gift-wrapped ammunition and travelling Merseysiders were forced to listen submissively as the other end took the piss before Eric Cantona shanked a late winner, with goalkeeper David James, who had a significant role in the selection of the suits in the first place, flapping initially at David Beckham's corner kick.

Patience ran out with Liverpool and probably Evans in the summer of 1997. It was at the same time that Labour got into power and invited Noel Gallagher – considered at the forefront of the social swing, definitely in musical terms – through the front doors of 10 Downing Street for a nauseating drinks reception. It killed Britpop. It killed Cool Britannia and the faith in the nineties as a time of cultural revival and pride. Enough was enough. Now it was necessary to prove that governmental change could represent real change. Evans' Liverpool, whose players were known as the Spice Boys because of their ability to sell newspapers on the basis of front-page headlines rather than back, similarly needed to grow up. It was time to prove something. The League Cup in 1995 was not enough. Where were the FA Cup-winners' medals? What about the Premier League – the stuff that really mattered? With those questions being posed, soon Evans was gone and Gérard Houllier, with his fist of iron, was enforcing a Souness-esque discipline and pushing through modernization that had been prevented from happening years earlier.

My involvement as a supporter ran in line with Liverpool's disappointments. Over the years, I've been at Anfield so often that if the notion took me I could find my younger self in any corner of the stadium. If I wait long enough in the Paddock, I can see myself two weeks before a birthday celebrating giddily after Ray Houghton lashed in a shot that flew beyond the hilariously named Coventry City goalkeeper, Steve Ogrizovíc. I was nearly eight years old. It was October 1991.

In the Kop, I can catch sight of myself standing there aged ten, right up against the crash barriers, struggling to breathe while watching Swindon Town, doomed to relegation yet inappropriately wearing the colours of the Brazilian national team, take an improbable lead through John Moncur and Keith Scott before Mark Wright headed in from a corner to equalize with just four minutes to go. I realized then that supporters are insignificant as individuals but as a collective they can become mighty, generating in a moment a level of noise that can affect the players and therefore the outcome of a game.

A mate of mine's father knew Joe Corrigan, Liverpool's goalkeeping coach. When he got us into the players' lounge in 1997, I remember seeing Liverpool's squad looking like they'd rather be anywhere else following an embarrassing 1–0 home defeat to Barnsley, who like Swindon would spend just one season as a Premier League team.

Three hours before the game, we had been invited for a tour, touching the mystical 'This Is Anfield' sign as we passed down the tunnel and on to the touchline of the pitch. I even peeked my head into the changing rooms and was told off by a steward for my bold intrusion. It was enough to establish that the space was small, spartanly decorated and reeked of Deep Heat. A medical table with slightly ripped brown-leather cushioning stood there solemnly waiting to treat the injured.

Following Barnsley's winner, scored by Ashley Ward, the lumbering journeyman centre-forward, the players' lounge had the feeling of an after-show party where the gig had been a real let-down. David James lay spread on a couch, a bottle of Carlsberg in hand, the top button of his shirt undone and his tie askew. Paul Ince had not played and was wearing an inappropriate New York Yankees cap. He had a lot to say for himself. Jamie Redknapp was there with his pop-star girlfriend Louise Nurding.

On the way out, we saw Roy Evans and Barnsley manager Danny Wilson chatting outside the new Boot Room, which had been relocated from its original position in order to create a press area. Evans was putting on a brave face. I wondered how he dealt with being a Liverpool supporter and leading the team towards defeat against dubious opposition like Barnsley. Did he just go home, turn the lights off and go to bed? Wilson, arms folded, could not stop smiling. He held the expression of a provincial army general after sacking Rome.

In the Centenary Stand – long after it had ceased to be the Kemlyn Road – I can watch myself as a teenager, punching the air triumphantly and swearing a lot when Ince appeared to halt United's charge to the title again by making the scoreline 2–2 as the game reached its conclusion. Ince had not, of course. United prevailed on the final day of the 1998–99 season, with Liverpool finishing out of contention once more.

I had not envisaged back then that I would soon be interviewing a lot of the players I grew up watching. Once I started work as a journalist, I quickly realized that while active, footballers are restricted in what they can say. This is not dissimilar to life in the outside world, where climbing the greasy pole is recommended and few people venture to say what they really think. Theirs are working contracts, which mean the thoughts of their colleagues and particularly their manager matter. Hundreds of interviews have taught me that speaking to retired players, those whose memories and passions remain fresh enough, always provides the most entertaining copy. They can look back over their careers with the benefit of both hindsight and greater life experience.

It is for this reason I did not pursue Robbie Fowler with the same enthusiasm as others in this book. Fowler was an exceptional talent and became a Liverpool legend thanks to his goals. Yet he has already released a reasonably candid autobiography and at the time of writing was employed as ambassador for the club, which I know from experience hinders the level of objectivity that makes a project like this worth starting. Steve McManaman was omitted for the same reason – he works at Liverpool's youth academy in Kirkby.

From the feedback to *Red Machine*, the book I wrote about Liverpool in the 1980s, I found that fans were more interested in reading about those with lower profiles: Howard Gayle over John Barnes, for example, two black players from different backgrounds and who had contrasting impacts.

Here, I wanted to showcase characters whose life stories were thought-provoking, largely untold and would knead together while simultaneously revealing the bigger picture of Liverpool in the 1990s. I wanted to establish whether Souness was solely responsible for everything that went wrong in the early part of the decade and whether Evans was too nice to reverse the trend, so while also getting players that were best placed to offer the most relevant insight, I made sure I interviewed the pair of them. Managers are usually better talkers, mainly because they have more to consider. Players tend to concentrate on their own role. Managers tend to set about trying to assume absolute control of the clubs they run and therefore have views on everything. From the encounters with both Souness and Evans I came away feeling excited and could not wait to start writing.

There were some surprises. John Scales probably spoke the most sense about what was happening at Liverpool during the Spice Boys period. Scales, whose intelligence did not sit comfortably beside the boorish attitudes in the dressing rooms of clubs he'd been at before Liverpool, reminded me of Michael Robinson from the 1980s, a closet intellectual who could not afford to let it all come out. Players had warned me that Scales was too polite for his own good and might not even be worth meeting. Yet now, after football, he was far more confident talking about his experiences and perceptive enough to analyse better than anyone else what was happening around him.

It is always better to do interviews in person, to shake your subject by the hand and look him in the eye. It pays to make the effort of travelling long distances, to treat them as people and get a couple of rounds in when necessary. Most of the figures that feature here had a negative view of the media, so I treated their initial caution with respect and hoped they might come to trust me.

Not enough has been written about the players from the nineties, a decade that prompts mixed emotions from Liverpool supporters. There isn't the romance or tragedy of the eighties, nor the success of the seventies. But it was an intriguing period of turbulence and ultimately endless transition, led by fascinating individuals who feel safe enough now to go on record because it happened a while ago.

I thank each of them for their time.

Simon Hughes

CHAPTER ONE

cultzeros.co.uk

MIDFIELD MAESTRO,
Jan Mølby, 1984–96

JAN MØLBY'S APPEARANCE HAS NOT ALTERED MUCH FROM THE player you once knew. He remains broad shouldered and substantially built, still with the unmistakeable, monumental thighs of a footballer. His blue eyes are piercing and when we meet I can imagine what it must have been like to be a goalkeeper facing him in the moments before a penalty kick. Him like a bull sensing blood; me like a *torero* on a losing streak. Him confidently staring; me undoubtedly trembling.

'I always took a long run-up, much longer than other players,' Mølby explains, nodding in a way that suggests I am the person he knows he is going to score past. 'The goalkeepers are more comfortable when there is no time to think, so they have to react instantly. A long run-up creates tension and fear. It also means you can kick it a lot harder in precisely the place you want to put it.'

27

He rises from a stool. He winds back as far as the patio doors that separate his kitchen from the back garden. Then slowly he ambles forward, recreating in his mind something he experienced for real forty-five times during his Liverpool career.

'I've always got my head up, see.'

I am observing Mølby side-on now. There is an illusory goalkeeper somewhere in the middle distance of his vision.

'I wouldn't charge in either. I liked to take as long as possible. The confidence to do this only came with time, after I'd scored on a number of occasions. They say the pressure is always on the taker, but I liked to put it on the goalkeeper, make him worry.'

Two or three steps before meeting the ball, Mølby would still be watching the goalkeeper's movement. Then came a swipe of the right leg. He preferred to strike with the side of his foot rather than the instep.

'Control over power,' he reasons. 'It was like in one of those western movies – who blinks first? He goes right, I'll go left; he goes left, I go right. If he didn't move, I'd always put it to the keeper's left. Always.'

In a League Cup tie at home to Coventry City in 1986, Liverpool were awarded three penalties: two at the Kop end, one in front of the Anfield Road Stand. They were all dispatched in exactly the same manner by Mølby, following the procedure just demonstrated in front of me.

In total, Mølby scored forty-two penalty kicks for Liverpool, which, until 2014 and thanks to the composure of Steven Gerrard, was more than any other player in the club's history. Remarkably, perhaps, Mølby never practised them in training. 'It was pointless,' he says. 'The pressure of the match changes everything.'

Mølby reiterates that the key to his success was confidence taken from the accumulation of truly important conversions. 'Once you were on a roll, there was no stopping you. I remember the surprise on Ronnie Moran's face when I insisted on taking the first one against Spurs in 1985. Ian Rush had missed in the weeks before, after taking over from Phil Neal, so I felt like it was my turn. I grabbed the ball; Ray Clemence was in goal. I saw it as an opportunity to make my mark. By the end of that game, I'd scored two penalties. It gave me a lot of self-belief.'

I sense, too, that Mølby trusted his eye for detail. He knew of a goalkeeper's diving habits. Following a pre-determined routine made it easier for him. Unlike some ex-footballers, Mølby's recollections are clear, almost pristine. Statistically, he is almost spot-on. He regrets not being able to take more penalties. He can remember the feelings of frustration when teammates were given the responsibility instead.

'John Aldridge took seventeen or eighteen and only missed one; John Barnes took fifteen; Mike Marsh took a few, as did Mark Walters. It's possible I could have taken 116 penalties if I'd played in every game. I'd have liked that. It would have been a world record, surely.'

He can also recall the games where he was not successful, mentioning the names of three goalkeepers who stopped him as though there remains a score to settle.

'I never hit a single penalty off target; the ones that did not go in were always at least saved. The first one was Martin Hodge of Sheffield Wednesday [also in 1986]. We ended up drawing that game, so there are some regrets.'

The second was against QPR a few months later. 'I think it was Paul Barron in a League Cup semi-final,' he suggests correctly. The last was during a 5–2 victory at Stamford Bridge at the end of 1989, a performance that prompted Chelsea manager Bobby Campbell to claim that the Liverpool team would stand 'a hell of a chance' of winning the World Cup if it were allowed to compete the following summer.

'That was the only time I knew I wasn't going to score,' Mølby reveals. 'We'd battered them, total obliteration. It was one of those party afternoons.'

The Liverpool squad was appearing at the BBC Sports Personality Awards the following evening and had planned a boozy weekend in London around the match.

'When Dave Beasant dived the right way, I was not surprised at all, because I wasn't concentrating as I should have been.'

Mølby was never denied again. Upon leaving Liverpool eight years later, he'd taken another eighteen penalties. All eighteen were scored.

But Mølby's penalty record is only part of the story of his time at Liverpool, which from the outside is easily summarized into two eras: the 1980s – good; the 1990s – not so good. As this seemed to match the story of the club as a whole over the period, I was keen to interview him at his home in Heswall, a wealthy area of private roads, towering oak trees and hidden family homes on the Wirral peninsula.

Mølby became the first footballer from his town to earn a cap for the Danish national side; when he was sold to Ajax aged nineteen, the transfer fee was the biggest ever paid for a Danish player to leave Denmark. On signing for Liverpool, he became the first Dane to play in three FA Cup finals, and after twelve seasons at Anfield Mølby was the first foreign player to be awarded a testimonial by the club. Whilst at Liverpool, he spent three months in prison for reckless driving. Football alone does not reflect the complexities of a human life.

There was also Mølby's size. No discussion about him passes without mention of this. Footballers now are turbocharged athletes, probably capable of competing in the Olympics as middle-distance runners. Mølby – the midfielder with a mysterious slash through the 'o' of his surname – was the heaviest player in the Liverpool team. He was different: a proper bloke, right at the top of his profession. Mølby drank. Mølby ate. He was not capable of covering every blade of grass. But he had vision, hypnotic technique and a rocket of a shot. He was also a considerable personality. Under pressure in his trial match against Home Farm in Ireland, following the departure of Graeme Souness – the midfield warrior he was supposed to replace – Mølby responded by tricking his marker using his thigh, running on to his own pass, beating another defender, before thumping a volley past a goalkeeper who did not bother moving because of the ferocity. Two days later, Joe Fagan offered him a contract.

Mølby's story begins in the summer of 1963 in Kolding, Denmark – a country that he says is markedly unspoiled by the pressures of modern life. A UN survey published in 2013 revealed that Danish people are the happiest in the world.

'I can see why,' Mølby says. 'The stresses that exist here [in England] do not exist there.'

Danes put their contentedness down to a dynamic economy and a pleasant work–life balance, with people leaving the office on time, jumping on effective public transport and heading off to pick up their delightful children from shiny, well-run kinder-gartens. But there are others out to savage the myth of the happy Dane, arguing that low expectations of life account for their unusually positive disposition.

'It is true that people have very basic aspirations,' Mølby continues. 'But this is not a bad thing. The best things in life are usually the simplest anyway: fresh air, open space and family. The term we use is *hygge* [it translates roughly as 'coziness']. We have time to analyse and interpret what life is about.

'Yes, taxes are high, but education is always paid for: daycare, school and university. We are taught from an early age that life is not about making as much money as possible. You go through school, head to university then enter a working environment that is quite stable. You become a banker, a solicitor, a journalist or join law enforcement. The majority have steady nine-to-five jobs. Your company looks after you. There might not be many opportunities for people to become millionaires, as there's not a lot of self-employment. But we aren't really influenced by the rest of Europe – we don't aspire to be American or British.'

Mølby speaks with a Scouse accent so thick you could spread it on toast. But he maintains that despite living in Merseyside for nearly thirty years, and raising a son and a daughter who are now adults during that time, he still feels emphatically Danish.

Although his father worked as a long-distance lorry driver for an oil firm, the Mølby family was from farming stock. He believes that this might account genetically for his distinctive powerful build.

'My brothers are almost identical,' he explains. 'I spent my summer holidays in between my grandfather's and my uncle's, who were both successful farmers. We were out every day at six o'clock in the morning, helping. We loved it. Most of the day was spent throwing bales of hay on the tractor, milking cows or picking strawberries. We did whatever we were told.'

Farming was all-consuming. The hours were long and tiring. There was no room for other interests in the lives of the Mølby elders. Yet Jan became obsessed by football. He believes it happened because the ground of Kolding's football team was less than eight hundred yards away from the Mølby family home. In the late 1970s, the team would rise from non-league football into the Danish second division, where previously improbable gates of more than 4,500 were regularly achieved.

'Every Saturday, I would see the crowd making their way to the game. The cars would park outside the house. I could hear whenever a goal was scored. A big roar went up. This fascinated me. My dad wasn't interested at all. His passion was pigeon racing. But when I got to seven or eight and I was still kicking the ball around the garden, I think he realized the obsession wasn't going to go away.'

It might be said that Mølby's aspirations were typically Danish. They began and ended with playing for Kolding's first team.

'I still insist that one of the proudest days of my life came when they recruited me within their youth set-up and handed over club membership, meaning I could attend all of the first-team games for free. An attacking midfielder called Frank Sørensen was my favourite player. He was a number 10. I've never forgiven him for joining Aarhus.

'Very quickly, I developed an adult game. At sixteen, I was calm – I already knew what to do. I played with some very good kids at Kolding. We were one of the top three teams for our age in Denmark. Yet only one of them aside from me played for Kolding's first team. If you'd asked me at fifteen, I would have said most of those guys had a really good chance. The difference was I developed quicker. I was always bigger than the other lads but the game in Denmark does not rely on physicality. It wasn't a case of me being able to muscle my way through games or being able to kick the ball further than anyone else. I was just able to get my overall game together a lot quicker.'

Mølby was training with Kolding's first team at sixteen. He made his professional debut at seventeen, then his international debut for Denmark at eighteen. Each year, progression was noted through significant landmarks.

'I remember looking around the dressing room at Kolding and there was a feeling that all the other fellas – guys twice my age – were looking right back at me as the missing link of the team. I felt a sense of responsibility straight away. But it never bothered me. I felt totally ready.'

Mølby's development was not recognized in Denmark's national press, however. 'Nobody knew who I was.' Halfway through his first season, Kolding played against a team from the outskirts of Copenhagen. 'A scout from Ajax happened to be there.' Afterwards, Mølby received a call from Danish international midfielder Søren Lerby. 'He said that Ajax had seen me play and that they liked what they saw, but they did not know anything about me aside from my name. I told him my age and the length of my contract.'

Ajax watched Mølby for nearly a year before finally making an offer. By then, he'd played forty times for Kolding. 'I was dominating games. I was ready again for the next step. You don't see that happen much now. A couple of decent games and, whoosh, the player moves on.'

Mølby demonstrates again his memory for detail when recalling his Kolding debut: 'Away from home – the crowd was intense,' then he remembers the day Kolding won promotion to the first division. 'It was in front of 9,500 people – unheard of in our town. When we scored the winner, the game wasn't finished but the lord mayor ran on the pitch. Afterwards, we were invited to the town hall and our neighbours and former schoolteachers were there. This was a big deal for Kolding. For me, it was right up there with winning the First Division championship in England and the FA Cup.'

Mølby did not want to leave Kolding, even for Ajax. 'I had the perfect life. I was working in a sports shop, InterSport, with my mate. I went to college twice a week, studying business. I was playing in the first division, I rode everywhere on my bike and had lunch every day at my mum's. It could not have been better.' Yet Kolding needed the money and Ajax offered in excess of £100,000. 'The club was quite keen for me to go. I would have done anything to help Kolding. So I went.'

Mølby says the first months in Amsterdam were the most difficult in his professional career. He'd arrived from a part-time background believing he possessed an adequate level of fitness. But he was wrong.

'It was the only time in my career when I didn't feel a sense of belonging. I struggled. I was tired all the time. We trained three times a day in the pre-season camp. At quarter past seven in the morning, we'd go for a long run. At half-ten, there would be football training. Then at half-two, we'd be doing specific sprint or weight training. Eight nights on the run at seven o'clock, we'd play a competitive match against an amateur team. We'd win each one by a minimum of ten goals. But the process was exhausting. I was awful. The players judge you, don't they? There was Ronald Koeman and Frank Rijkaard. We were all roughly the same age. I could see them looking over thinking, "This fella is crap."'

The person Mølby wanted to impress most was Johan Cruyff, one of the game's greatest players, who, nearing the end of his career, was rarely present during pre-season. 'We'd be running up fucking mountains but Johan did not join in at all. He was allowed to set his own schedule. Then again, he possessed a natural fitness that meant he did not have to.'

Mølby talks about Cruyff as if he is not a real person. There was an aura of otherness, as though he was perhaps superhuman, untouchable.

'You could not approach him. You were granted an audience.

It was like having the Pope as a teammate. He lived up to the legend and beyond.'

Mølby would usually be found with the other Danes at Ajax, Lerby and Jesper Olsen.

'Johan would come to us and never us to him. He could be a bit of a nuisance. He'd approach and ask what we were talking about. We'd tell him and he'd always start his reply with the same sentence: "Let me tell you . . ." He was very, very knowledgeable about everything. We'd play billiards after training. He'd tell us we were taking the wrong shots. "No, no, no . . ." Whatever you spoke about, he already knew. He was *the* oracle.'

Cruyff was a chain smoker. Mølby recalls observing him at lunch. As the light of a cigarette died, he used the butt before it was too late to fire a second cigarette. 'It was constant. He was a chain smoker. I could not believe any footballer – let alone one of the greatest – would get away with this and still be right at the top of his game. During a lunch break, he'd light ten then go and train, no problem. Over five metres, even at his age, he was the quickest player I've come across.'

Aged thirty-seven, Cruyff remained Ajax's most influential player at key moments during games.

'His presence helped us to win leagues in successive seasons quite comfortably. We scored lots of goals. Johan would celebrate his own but never if it was anyone else's. He probably created four out of five goals but whenever you turned around to celebrate, he wasn't there. He'd be walking back to the centre circle instead. It became the accepted thing to do to wave your hand in his direction to recognize his efforts. I don't think he meant this in an arrogant way. It's just the way he was.'

Mølby says the most significant thing Cruyff helped him with was his passing.

'Johan had this unique ability to understand a player's strengths and weaknesses after just a few training sessions. It would have been clear to anyone that I did not have a burst of acceleration like other Ajax players, so maybe he thought I needed to improve elsewhere to compensate for that.'

Cruyff offered Mølby tutorials in the art of passing.

'He told me that it is a misconception that the ball should be passed directly to a teammate's feet. Instead, it should be passed a yard or two in front of him. That way the ball is always moving forward and it gives the team momentum. It was also about the pace of the pass. He wanted me to drill it – the emphasis had to be on the first touch. If a player could not control a fast pass, he was not good enough to play for Ajax. Success and failure were determined by how graciously a player controlled the ball.'

One routine remains vivid in Mølby's mind. What an image this is – Cruyff showing Mølby how it's done on the chilly Dutch training fields next door to Ajax's brooding De Meer Stadium.

'He used to get me and Ronald Koeman together and ask us to hit the corner flag from the halfway line. We'd have our backs to whichever corner we were aiming for then he'd play the ball into us at speed. We were allowed one touch to bring it under control before pinging it towards the flag. You weren't allowed to float it. If you floated it and it hit the flag, it wouldn't count. We'd repeat this for more than an hour and it could become tedious. But we never argued with Johan.'

Mølby says this practice helped later on in his career when playing as a midfielder in front of Liverpool's back four.

'It was my favourite position because I was protecting the defence as well as myself at the same time. I didn't get dragged into areas of the field where my lack of pace would get exposed. I was right in the heart of the action. The more of the ball I saw, the better I became. I knew where to go. Critics would say I struggled to get around but I rarely got substituted. I could last ninety minutes.

'You were expected to pass. And I could pass. But it takes it out of you too. Drilling forty- and fifty-yard passes kills your thighs. But I never struggled with it. I had the stamina to carry on. I was able to ping those passes into injury time, the final kick. I've always had strong thighs but I only learned how to use them in relation to my technique at Ajax. For that, Johan must take the credit.'

When Mølby joined Ajax, his new manager Aad de Mos told him that for the first season he would operate as a sweeper, replacing Wim Jansen. Instead, Cruyff encouraged the club to sign Leo van Veen. The pair had spent a season together at Los Angeles Aztecs.

'Johan ran the team. If there was something he did not like, he would knock on Aad's door and, rather than ask him to change it, he'd tell him to change it. He always had a say on tactics.'

Mølby was switched to midfield. Ultimately, it proved successful, as Ajax swept aside everything that lay in front of them domestically.

Mølby was surrounded by a group of supremely talented teenagers. Despite being a defender, Ronald Koeman practised shooting for hours after the rest of the squad had left the training ground.

'He honed that technique of hitting the ball so hard and so sweet. That free kick he whacked in for Barcelona during the 1992 European Cup final against Sampdoria, it was a technique perfected at Ajax.'

Then there was Frank Rijkaard. 'A monster,' Mølby says. 'There was nothing he couldn't do. We used to do 150m runs on a slight incline. Our coach had trained the Dutch Olympic athletics team. Frank was my partner. Jesus Christ, I was absolutely flat out just to be ten metres behind him and he wasn't trying. He was so laid-back. Maybe it was his downfall as a manager. You see people like Guardiola on top of the players every day. Frank wasn't like that. He was relaxed.'

Marco van Basten was also there. 'He was sixteen and only allowed to train with us during the school holidays. In the second season, the club decided to sell Wim Kieft to Pisa. We were looking at each other, wondering who they'd sign to replace him. Marco came in and scored thirty-eight goals in the first year. He was a teenager. Cruyff had gone by then but I always remember him saying that Marco was as good as he'd seen. Cruyff wasn't a million miles off.'

It all started to unravel for Mølby in Amsterdam when he fell out with de Mos after a 3–0 defeat to Den Bosch.

'We were called in on the Sunday and fined 500 guilders. Then the following day we were sent out to the woods for a running marathon in the morning before another session in the afternoon. The coach walks in and reels off a couple of names: "Van't Schip [the Canadian-born winger], Rijkaard and Mølby – you're all playing for the reserves tonight." None of the first-teamers ever played for the reserves. In Holland, it wasn't the way: once you were in the first team, you never dropped down. They were part-time, training every day at five o'clock. We never saw them. But on this occasion, we were told we had to.

'Afterwards, there was tension. I was in the bath. The coach [de Mos] comes in and hangs up his towel. The reserve keeper decides to throw the towel at me and it flies into the bath. I move out the way and leave it there, floating. The coach walks through into the changing area with his soaking wet towel. He thinks that I have an issue with playing for the reserves. He looks at me and wrings the towel all over me. By this point, I was fully dressed with jeans on. The whole dressing room fell silent.

'The coach walks slowly back into his office. He's a big boy – 6 ft 3 and 15–16 stone, much burlier than me. So I got my own towel, threw it in the bath and chased after him. His suit was hanging over the chair. There was only one thing to do. After drenching his suit, I turned round and the vice president was standing there. The coach and I squared up to each other like two stags, head to head. Frank [Rijkaard] separated us. Although I get on very well with Aad now and we can laugh about it – he knows I wasn't responsible – it was the beginning of the end for me at Ajax.'

Mølby insists his departure was in many ways a natural exit. Only a select few players have remained at Ajax for their entire careers.

'The club never looked to keep young players for more than

two or three years. At that point, they'd sell them on then bring through another group. I also think it's impossible to play for Ajax for fifteen years because of the intense training demands. You can't keep it up. I think the only player who managed to do it was Danny Blind. They surely must have made concessions for him as he got older.'

By comparison, training methods at Liverpool were relaxed. Mølby says it is as much a myth that Ajax only focused on technique as it is that Liverpool trained harder than any other team in England.

'The sessions at Liverpool were short and sharp. The intensity was there and while you were in the midst of a five-a-side game, no corners were cut. But once the session was over, you went home. There were no designated fitness sessions like at Ajax, which sometimes went on for hours even during the season.

'I could not say one method was better than the other, because they were both designed for specific reasons. Liverpool's approach suited me more. But Ajax trained so hard because there were only thirty-four league matches a season in Holland. We'd cruise through the majority of them. At Liverpool, there were forty-two First Division games and usually a lot of cup matches. Although we regularly made it look easy, I can assure you it wasn't. Opponents would never give in, because their fans demanded the effort. If Liverpool had trained to Ajax levels, there wouldn't have been enough energy to see out a season successfully.'

There were other differences. Until Mølby joined Liverpool, he'd rarely drunk alcohol.

'I lived in an apartment block on the outskirts of Amsterdam, close to the De Meer Stadium. Seven of us were there. But we spent very little time socializing. There was no drinking culture. We only went fishing together. They were orange-juice-and-sandwiches sort of occasions. Alcohol was so far from our minds. There was never any drink on the coach coming home from away games. People thought we were running around Amsterdam partying all the time but it couldn't have been further from the truth.'

This soon changed. Mølby spoke to Howard Wilkinson about moving to Sheffield Wednesday in the summer of 1984. Then Liverpool approached. The call came from Tom Saunders, the club's youth-development officer. A ten-day trial was arranged.

'The directors put me up in the Moat House along with Paul Walsh and John Wark. After the uncomfortable introductions, we decided to go for a drink. It was Sunday night. I was on trial. I wanted to make an impression the following morning, so I asked for an orange juice and lemonade. Paul and John looked at me as if I'd fallen out of a tree. I wasn't judging them at all, but it was so foreign to me.'

The culture of match preparation at Liverpool was also different to Ajax.

'I made my debut against Norwich City at Carrow Road. As we filed into the dressing room, I asked Ronnie Moran what I should do. "Just get fucking changed," Ronnie growled. Then I asked him what time we go out to warm up. "We don't warm up. Save your energy." I was astounded by this; at Ajax we spent half an hour doing shuttles.'

Mølby then fell victim to a prank.

'The boys told me that the staff liked players to have a massage before the game instead. So I approached Ronnie for a second time. "Er . . . Ronnie. Can I have a massage?"

'"Fuck off!" he shouted. "You earn the fucking right to have a fucking massage. Go out and play some games and then maybe I'll think about it." I'd only been at the club for a couple of weeks and I started to wonder whether I'd come to the wrong place. Then I saw all the lads pissing themselves. That was my introduction to the Liverpool dressing-room humour.'

By 1990, Mølby had contributed to three First Division titles, two FA Cups and three Charity Shields. Had Liverpool not been banned from Europe after Heysel and had Mølby not spent time in prison for drink-driving, more honours surely would have followed.

As the eighties became the nineties, Mølby noticed that the young players Liverpool were signing were taking a lot longer to adjust to the standards at Melwood, although it did not seem to really matter initially, as the first team kept winning.

At face value, the new recruits were classic Liverpool buys: under the media radar, plucked from obscurity. In 1988, Nick Tanner, aged twenty-three, and David Burrows, nineteen, arrived from Bristol Rovers and West Bromwich Albion. In 1991, Jimmy Carter, twenty-five, was bought from Millwall. Meanwhile, those with more experience were also brought in. Glenn Hysén was a few months short of his thirtieth birthday when he moved from Fiorentina in 1989, while Ronny Rosenthal, aged twenty-six, came from Standard Liège a year later. Chelsea's David Speedie, nearly thirty-one, became Kenny Dalglish's last signing.

'It is possible that football was changing even before we realized it. Previously, Liverpool had been in a strong position; they'd been able to bring in totally unknown players, such as Rush, [Steve] Nicol and [Ronnie] Whelan, knowing they could watch them over a long period, safe in the knowledge that eventually, if you wanted them, they'd come to you, no question. Other clubs wanted Rush, for instance, but Liverpool could afford to wait and usurp everyone else's plans because of its history and status.

'That began to change as early as the late eighties. As players, we were hearing that other clubs were paying bigger wages. Liverpool missed out on Ian Snodin to Everton, for instance. There were others: Tottenham signing Gazza and Gary Lineker. Now, I'm not sure whether Liverpool ever went in for those players but I know they were getting paid a lot more than we were. I think that it possibly turned the heads of potential signings. Maybe they thought the higher wages elsewhere reflected the ambition of the club.'

Mølby believes Dalglish fell into the trap of overcomplicating the system at Liverpool. 'Post-1990, there was too much tinkering. He chose certain players for home games and others for away games. The inconsistency did not help us.'

Mølby was used to this strategy – different sides being picked according to the opposition – having been brought up like that at club and international level in Denmark and with Ajax. Others, however, were not.

'It was very different for any British team to do it, particularly Liverpool, who always followed the idea of letting the opposition worry about us. I've always believed that it's players that win you games rather than systems. The system should always be led by the players. If you don't have the players to fit a system, you don't play that system.'

Dalglish had thereby alienated several key players before his departure and Souness's arrival. Peter Beardsley – probably the least short-tempered player in the Liverpool squad – had asked for a move after being left out of the squad by Dalglish.

Beardsley departed under Souness and Mølby believes that in the position he played, Beardsley's best years were ahead of him. Beardsley was only thirty when he left for Everton. He continued a top-level career until he was nearly thirty-seven.

'For me, that's when the decline really started, when we lost that link-man,' Mølby says forcefully. 'For the previous ten to fifteen years, we had Kenny then Peter. They were essential between the lines of midfield and attack. Suddenly, we had Rush and Saunders: two goalscorers. It became a totally different game. We lost a lot when Peter left.'

By the end of 1990, Liverpool's future had begun to unravel. Despite starting the 1990–91 season fourteen games unbeaten with twelve wins and two draws, and although Arsenal had been docked two points by the Football League as punishment for a brawl at Manchester United, Liverpool headed into the Christmas period just six points ahead of George Graham's team after losing at Highbury in the first week of December. In a conservative move, Dalglish named defenders Gary Ablett and Barry Venison in midfield and the result was a 3–0 defeat. It was the first real indication of misdirection.

Quickly, problems were laid bare. In playing terms, Hysén was not good enough to replace Alan Hansen; Hansen's replacement as captain, Ronnie Whelan, was injured; Ablett and Venison continued to be used in midfield; then Carter and David Speedie were signed. Carter arrived for a considerable fee of £800,000 from Millwall and would play only eight games for Liverpool, while Speedie was most certainly a panic buy: a striker five years past his best, whose best was – at best – never greater than average.

Dalglish was regarded as Liverpool's greatest post-war player. He had made management look easy since his appointment in 1985. Yet the questions over his decision making were becoming more audible. A year earlier, he had briefly considered quitting the club due to the strain he had been put under following the Hillsborough disaster. There was a period where he had been attending funerals every day and, though he was always professional and dignified in public, Dalglish was beginning to show some of the symptoms of post-traumatic stress disorder. Before Hillsborough, he had witnessed the stadium disasters at Heysel and Ibrox. There is only so much human tragedy one man can take.

A classic symptom of mental stress is the inability to make simple decisions. This, perhaps, was reflected in some of his unusual team selections. As an FA Cup derby with Everton approached, Dalglish had made one decision that he was absolutely certain about. He was quitting football.

Against Everton, Liverpool took the lead four times before surrendering the lead four times – the only time this has happened in the club's history. After the final whistle, as the last of the players were trudging into the dressing room, an argument was brewing, ready to explode. 'It was the worst one I can recall,' Mølby says. Mølby remembers the showers being turned on only for nobody to go in. It was winter outside and cold. Steam enveloped the space quicker than usual.

'The defence was bearing the brunt of it. Both Ronnie and Roy were having a go about the conceding of two late goals. The forwards were doing the same. "How many goals do we actually have to score?" they were saying. Ronnie and Bruce [Grobbelaar] went eyeball to eyeball. It was getting out of control. I thought it was going to end in a fight.'

Dalglish was standing against a wall, staring at the floor. For fifteen minutes, he said nothing. Post-match inquests usually waited for a team meeting the following day. This was a Wednesday night. Mølby recalls Dalglish informing the group calmly that they'd speak on Friday morning.

'We got changed and went for a beer with the Everton players at the bar, where the discussions continued, only without any of the hysterics. Never in a million years did I reckon Kenny was about to walk.'

Mølby spent Thursday playing golf. He arrived at Anfield on Friday as scheduled. Liverpool were due to play Luton Town away on the Saturday.

Arrangements had been made to travel down twenty-four hours before the game to enable one training session on Luton's plastic pitch, a surface where Liverpool had previously struggled. Mølby spotted an unusual number of journalists in the car park. After the run Liverpool had been on, he figured that Dalglish had signed someone and therefore a press conference had been arranged.

'Every person I spoke to that morning thought the same, from the players to the receptionist. There had been some strange results but we were still there, fighting for the title with Arsenal. I was quite excited about the prospect of a new signing, because it usually helped kick all the players on.'

After changing, the squad gathered in the players' lounge, as they always did, waiting to be greeted by their manager for a debrief. Instead, Moran walked in. 'Dressing room,' he ordered. There was nothing unusual in that.

'We didn't wait very long. Kenny appeared and within twenty seconds he'd told us he was resigning and that was that. He looked like he'd had a rough night. His face was a bit swollen. Had it not been for his appearance, I would have thought it was a wind-up. There was shock. It was a bit like when Craig Johnston revealed on the morning of the 1988 FA Cup final against Wimbledon that it would be his last game. Nobody really believed him – that he'd walk away from Liverpool and a football career aged just twenty-seven. We all thought he'd change his mind and be back at Melwood on Monday. But he wasn't.

'We all figured that the board had turned down a request for funds towards a new signing. Surely there had to be more to it. Kenny couldn't just leave like that.'

Liverpool lost 3–1 at Luton with two goals by Iain Dowie doing the damage. In the short term, Ronnie Moran was placed in charge.

'Even though a lot of players were unsure about Ronnie because he was so aggressive, I thought his appointment made sense. You could never question his commitment. He was as unselfish as they come. Everything he ever did professionally was for the benefit of Liverpool. He had a remarkable ability to keep both feet of even the biggest personalities firmly on the ground. He wasn't impressed by status. It did not matter to him.'

Under Moran, the unusual results continued. There were four wins, including chaotic 5–4 and 7–1 victories away to Leeds United and Derby County. But they were offset by five defeats, one of which included the replayed FA Cup tie with Everton. Liverpool were shaking. Moran was unable to prevent Arsenal regaining the title.

Upon Dalglish's departure, the Liverpool board had hoped to install a full-time and long-term replacement at the end of the season. But on-field disappointments forced a decision to rush forward the appointment process.

'At one point, we all thought it was going to be Alan Hansen,' Mølby recalls. 'Before training one day, Jocky walked into the dressing room and told us that he was taking the job. Swiftly, he outlined all kinds of changes he was going to implement. There were going to be double training sessions, no days off on a Sunday, a ban on drinking ale after matches. It was all the stuff the lads hated. He even told Ronnie [Whelan] he was replacing him as captain. Ronnie was all red in the face, fuming.'

That Hansen was still at Anfield was significant. In the past, ageing players with an injury record like his would have been sold off and replaced. For sentimental reasons, he was still there. Moments after closing the door of the dressing room, the squad could hear Hansen laughing and it transpired his rousing talk had been a ruse. Instead, Hansen was retiring, and soon Graeme Souness – a European Cup-winning captain – was brought in and he attempted to impose the sweeping changes that Hansen had joked about.

'John Toshack was rumoured to be coming but I wanted Graeme,' Mølby admits. 'He'd tried to sign me for Rangers a few years earlier and he was a highly impressive individual.'

Souness's relationship with Mølby would illustrate just how impulsive he could be. Mølby was out of the team. Mølby was in. Mølby was out again. They would dine at restaurants together. They would not talk for months.

In Souness's first two games in charge, Liverpool beat Norwich and Crystal Palace at Anfield by 3–0 scorelines. Mølby was positioned as a sweeper in a back three that included the Garys, Gillespie and Ablett. Shortly before Souness's arrival, Mølby had signed a new four-year contract. Yet suddenly his place in the squad was under threat.

Two defeats in three days to Chelsea and Nottingham Forest prompted Souness to take the squad on a boot camp to Lilleshall.

'Graeme was having a pop at everyone,' Mølby remembers. 'Me, John Barnes and Peter Beardsley bore the brunt of it. He kept telling us that we were going to become one of the fittest squads in Britain. Yet if you look at the records, the squad's fitness standards were already very high. It was as if he was focusing on problems that were not really there.'

In the summer of 1991, Everton made a bid to sign Mølby. By then, his prospects had deteriorated at Liverpool.

'I wasn't originally included in the pre-season tour to Norway. But on the day we were due to leave, Liverpool sold Steve Staunton to Aston Villa and I had to take his place. It was clear I was only there to make up the numbers, because I was only ever named as a sub and hardly came on.'

Mølby was ready to leave. He was not given a firm reason for his omission. 'I was not the type of person to knock on a manager's door and ask.' Mølby believed it was the manager's responsibility to explain himself if he deemed it necessary.

In Norway, Jamie Redknapp, Don Hutchison and Mike Marsh were all selected ahead of him and when the season started, Mølby, at twenty-eight, was playing reserve-team football, often taking on extra training to keep on top of his fitness. Meanwhile, Liverpool struggled. By October, they were eighth in the league and on the verge of getting knocked out of Europe after losing 2–0 away to Auxerre in the UEFA Cup.

What happened next demonstrated Souness's unpredictability. Mølby was at Melwood alone, running round and round close to its perimeter wall. He could sense a presence getting close to him. He turned and there was Souness.

'He asked me to play against Coventry on the Saturday. Then he invited me to dinner to talk it through. You could see this as a weakness of Graeme's – that he was going back on an apparent decision to get shot of certain players. To me, though, in the single-minded world of management, it's not a bad thing if you can admit that you're in the wrong. He was man enough to do that.'

Mølby helped Liverpool to a 1–0 victory over Coventry. Dramatically, the deficit against Auxerre was overturned and the French side were eliminated with a 3–0 Liverpool victory, with Mølby scoring the first and assisting with the third. In the dressing room afterwards, Souness kissed each player on the forehead before pulling £1,000 from his pocket, offering the cash to Mølby.

'He told me to take all the lads out for a drink. That was the strange thing about him. Graeme could blow hot and cold. He had a bad side. But he also had a good side.'

Mølby remained in the team for the rest of the league campaign, where Liverpool finished a disappointing sixth – the lowest position for twenty-seven years. They were more successful in the FA Cup, reaching the semi-final, with Portsmouth the opponents at Highbury. Mølby regrets his role in what happened next.

'I was expecting to start. I thought I'd done enough to show Graeme I could be relied upon in the big games. We were walking around the pitch, watching the atmosphere build up, and Graeme sauntered over to explain that I was on the bench. "It's going to be end to end and it's really hot out there, Jan," he reasoned.

'I told him that wasn't happening. "You either start me or I don't get changed."'

'I wasn't budging. I'd been his best player since coming back into the team and now I felt like I was being messed around again. He wanted Ronnie [Whelan] in there but that didn't make sense to me as we were both a similar age and had similar running abilities. I felt used.'

Mølby didn't get changed that day.

Liverpool just about drew the game 1–1, with Whelan equalizing late on, before a path to the final was sealed in the Villa Park replay in a penalty shoot-out.

'It's my biggest regret in football, refusing to play,' Mølby says. 'Effectively, I went on strike. I was in breach of my contract. The club could have probably sacked me for it. If Liverpool had won comfortably that afternoon [at Highbury], there's no way I'd have been in the team for the final.'

Mølby insists he did not have a major problem with Souness, although some of his teammates did.

'If I could change one thing about his manner, it would be the way he chose his teams. It was very inconsistent, lurching from one extreme to another. Other people had an issue with his man-management. He could really lose his temper. I remember after one defeat he charged into the dressing room and chucked a bottle of smelling salts against a mirror and both smashed into a thousand pieces.'

Souness was not someone who would bear a grudge, however. 'By the time we returned for training on the Monday, he was prepared to move on if you were.'

Under Souness, Liverpool finished successive seasons in sixth place. At the end of the third season – during which he was sacked after more than half of it – they finished eighth. It was their worst sequence of placings since before Bill Shankly's arrival in 1959. In the meantime, Manchester United secured two league titles. Liverpool were behind. Over the next two decades, it was a position to which they would become accustomed.

'There's a lot of fingers pointed at Graeme for starting the rot and I think he has to take some of the responsibility,' Mølby says. 'This is based purely on the type of player he chose to sign. Any manager is defined by the players he chooses to buy and sell. Football boils down to transfers. It always has. Players are just the same as fans. When you hear of someone new coming in, you get excited. The most excited I've ever been at Liverpool was when we signed [Peter] Beardsley. We all recognized what a good player he was; Barnes, not so. It took two weeks for us to realize how good John was.'

Mølby cites the signings of Dean Saunders and Paul Stewart as misplaced because of the size of the fees involved.

'They were Graeme's first big moves in the transfer market and he spent more than £2 million on each. I'd played against Paul many times and I could not understand why Liverpool would sign him. He played a different type of game. He was only effective when it was a bit longer, picking up second balls off the centre-forward or becoming a nuisance in the penalty area. We never played like that.

'I think Graeme misjudged where we were. He thought the decline of certain players was further down the line than was actually the case. He overreacted. You can't blame him for making that decision. But you can blame him for the signings he made. They weren't good enough.

'Training certainly changed. Our tastes were very simple. We warmed up then we played five-a-side. It was all about creating angles and that served us well on a Saturday. Then we signed a lot of players from other clubs where there was a lot of coaching, clubs where players could lose and blame the standard of the coaching, as if they themselves were blameless. At Liverpool, that was never allowed to happen. As an individual, you only got out what you put in.

'Gradually, the standard of the five-a-sides declined. They became less and less competitive. It got to a stage where the staff team and the older heads like me, Ronnie and Rushy were beating the newcomers every day. The scorelines were embarrassing. You can't have that.

49

'I looked at some of the lads on the other team and realized that Souness's new Liverpool would have to play in a different way. Julian Dicks, for instance, was like a golfer. You'd give him the ball and he'd give himself a bit of space, then serve it in quickly to the front men, bypassing the midfield. I lost count of the times I'd show for the pass and he wouldn't see me from five yards away. He was used to playing that way. He wasn't capable of adapting to Liverpool. We were in danger of becoming a long-ball team.

'Paul Stewart was the same. When we were in possession, he went missing. He wanted to play off the front two and feed off the scraps. Dean Saunders was a good finisher but he was a poorer version of Rushy, so we had two players trying to do the same thing.

'Then we signed Mark Wright, who had a tendency to defend too deep. That wasn't the Liverpool way either. It all meant we had a defence falling further and further back and one that resorted to knocking it long to two nippy strikers. The midfield didn't matter. The proper footballers were exposed. I'll admit I couldn't play to this style. I played a short game. I wasn't one for a running match. But I wasn't the only one. There were too many gaps. The pitch was too big. It wasn't Liverpool.'

Souness has been accused of changing too much too soon. Those offering more of a generous appraisal claim he was ahead of his time.

'Maybe there were too many footballers who were just set in their ways,' Mølby concedes. 'If I'd have been him after arriving in April, I would have left things as they were to observe until the end of the season. The following season, slowly I would have introduced new methods one by one. Instead, from day one he was enforcing new ideas. Pre-match meals were an example. Ian Rush would always have a medium steak with beans. Suddenly, that wasn't available. Footballers are superstitious beings. We listen to the same music in the car and take the same route to the stadium every week. It makes us feel comfortable. The same applies to pre-match meals. Suddenly, Rushy stopped scoring.

'I don't think Graeme was ahead of his time entirely, because methods like his were being imposed at other clubs too. It's well documented. Football was heading that way. Yet if he would have done what he did in six weeks over a year, he might have got a more positive reaction.'

Mølby believed the reign of Souness was a blip. At the start of every season after his departure, it felt like Liverpool would return to the top. Players who knew what it took to win league titles remained at Melwood.

'Liverpool were watchers of situations. "Let's see how it works for them." At this time, though, so much was happening else-where. Other clubs were better prepared than Liverpool, certainly off the pitch, for the financial revolution. Peter Robinson once said that if Manchester United got it right off the pitch, Liverpool were in trouble. It proved to be true. With a good team and all the money being ploughed into the game, they were able to accelerate and leave everyone else behind.'

Roy Evans was appointed in Souness's place after the team reached a nadir, losing 1–0 at home to Second-Division Bristol City in an FA Cup third-round replay at Anfield. Again, the league form reflected badly on Souness. In January 1994, twenty-one points already separated Liverpool in fifth from Manchester United at the top of the table.

'I didn't think the club would go back [to the Boot Room]. Once the mould had been broken, I thought that was it. After all, Roy had been overlooked when Souness got the job. But when the announcement was made, I felt relief. I thought of Souness's spell as an experiment that didn't work out. It felt like things would go back to normal.'

Mølby says Evans returned to the tried and tested methods that had served Liverpool well in the past.

'For a long time, Roy was the sounding board. You did all your moaning to him. Then suddenly he was the manager. You couldn't go to him as much purely out of circumstance. But I thought he dealt with the transition well. He never lost himself.

'I remember on the first day of pre-season, the old coaching manuals from Shankly's time were out. Over the summer, Roy and Ronnie went through all the training sessions that had been practised and we followed the same process. Maybe I was naive but I figured that the results would get better. Most of the boys [Rush, Nicol and Whelan] were still there. Then the younger ones like McManaman, Fowler and Redknapp were making their mark. It did not feel like a terminal illness.'

Evans employed traditional Liverpool methods but he also introduced some of his own ideas and staff. Doug Livermore had been manager of Tottenham Hotspur only twelve months before and he was appointed as first-team coach.

'Liverpool wasn't famous for its coaching. You could not compare it to Ajax, for instance. Liverpool was famous for its simplicity. Roy wanted to change the shape of the team by switching from a back four to a back three. For a team that had played nothing but 4–4–2 for thirty years, this was revolutionary. Roy also realized that set pieces were beginning to play a more significant part in the game. We needed to score more goals from corners and free kicks, and defend against them a lot better. For years, a set piece had been a hindrance. We always wanted the ball in play. The centre-halves did not bother going up to the penalty box because we weren't aggressive in that kind of way. There was even a famous fanzine called *Another Wasted Corner*. Some things had to change, or certainly improve. And these factors all contributed to Doug's arrival.'

It felt like the good times would roll again. Liverpool were spending lots of money on transfers, even outspending Manchester United in the transfer market. A new defence was recruited. There was fluid, attacking football. Mølby was playing his part too. The 1994–95 season began with three successive victories. Mølby opened Liverpool's account for the campaign from the penalty spot in a 6–1 victory at Crystal Palace. Yet Mølby's body did not feel right. His decline had been relatively swift. Listening to him speak about that time is sobering. He talks in short sentences.

'I did not feel in control any more,' he says. 'I was injured in a game against United two years before. I trained really hard to get back – harder than I'd ever done. But I knew that I'd returned as an average footballer.

'Before the Palace game, I'd missed most of the games in pre-season. But I fought like hell to top up my fitness when I could in training. I was old enough to know when I was ready to play, so I told Roy that he had to start me against Palace. By his reaction, I could tell he'd previously decided to start Michael Thomas instead. In the end, Roy went with me. He was vindicated because the season started well. We went on a decent run. At the back of my mind, though, I knew it wouldn't last.'

This was around the time Mølby allegedly only reached level six on the bleep test, an exercise where players would have to run from side to side in time with the bleep, until the bleep outpaced them. Professional footballers were expected at worst to get to level twelve. Mølby says the story simply isn't true.

'We did a couple of bleep tests and there was never a problem. I got thirteen at Lilleshall. I was fit enough to play top-level football for nearly fifteen years without being superhuman fit. I never had a great deal of pace but I knew where to be.

'Liverpool players were great storytellers. That's probably where it came from. When I'm after-dinner speaking, I always leave a bit of grain on myself. Legends grow. Now I hear people say that I never misplaced a pass. Of course I did. In the same sense, the legend goes that I never used to run. But that's not true either. I'd always felt in control of what I was doing. I was comfortable. I could cruise through games and step up a gear when I really had to, like the FA Cup final of '86. But after Old Trafford [in '92], I only had one gear. There were no more great performances.'

Mølby recalls a later encounter at United when Liverpool lost 2–0.

'I was running the game and Roy took me off when it was 0–0. I knew I was only running the game safe. I never threatened to take what seemed like being a draw to a win. I played just inside our own half and controlled it. Had it been five years earlier, I'd have played fifteen yards inside their half and we might have won the game. But I could only offer us a safe option.

'I still had my moments where I could be a bit of a showman. I had my good days. I could execute a nutmeg or a back heel and the crowd would applaud. I was able to convert a penalty or a free kick. You'd get that adrenalin rush and feel like a real footballer again. But there were no more goals from open play. I could not help us win any more.'

Mølby believes it is a player's character that determines whether he is going to be a success at Liverpool over a long period of time.

'I look at the boys from the sixties, seventies and eighties. They were all huge personalities, with their own ideas about how the game should be played – hence the reason why a lot of them are in the media. They have things to say, big opinions. It was reflected by how they performed at the weekend. If something needed to be said, they'd say it.

'You learnt a lot about players away from home. Liverpool were there to be shot at. Teams tried to rough us up. But the best players never hid from anything. We never went looking for trouble, because we knew our ability would see us through anyway. But if it came, we could deal with it.

'In terms of the playing, it was very simple. You had to do it sixty times a season to the same standard. Later, this is where a lot of players fell short. I've always thought it was the hallmark of a great player, being able to play sixty times a season. Not twenty – sixty. It was in my make-up. It's all to do with desire. You finish a game and you want to do it again. In December 1986, I remember playing on the 26th and the 27th – one day after the next. We were ready for it. I was ready for it. There was no moaning. We lost to United on Boxing Day then went to Hillsborough the following afternoon and ground out a win.

'The self-policing was also an important part of the culture at Liverpool. The staff at Anfield were very clever, closing the dressing-room door and leaving us in there. Before matches and after matches. We knew how to deal with issues, you know? Players would take it upon themselves to have a word with other players.'

By the time Mølby left Liverpool to become Swansea City's

player-manager in 1996 after twelve years' service, he admits to being disillusioned with the culture that had infested the game.

'When you're winning, it's so much easier to sort problems out. When you're losing, it's doubly hard. Fingers get pointed everywhere. Maybe some of the younger players were going away with England and hearing about how things were done differently at other clubs. People started to think that Liverpool wasn't the be-all and end-all; what we had wasn't the greatest formula ever, although it worked for a long, long time.

'The celebrity thing was developing and people were becoming more precious and egotistical as a result. In the eighties, if you wanted a celeb to turn up at an event, you'd ask someone from *Brookside*. That changed in the mid nineties. You'd ask a footballer instead.

'Although we weren't the best team in the country by then, some of our players were among the bigger football names. The world was moving that way. People wanted to take a picture of footballers walking into a restaurant. There was never any call for that before, when we were winning things. We were only really media-worthy when we played football.'

In his management career, Mølby reached the old Fourth Division play-off final before winning promotion to the Football League with Kidderminster Harriers. He now lives comfortably with Mandy, his wife of nearly twenty-five years.

'The manager I learnt most from was probably Graeme,' Mølby says. 'He made me realize I did not want to be a shock-treatment manager. I never went in anywhere and attempted to make it oh, so much better in the first month. Everything takes time. It was a slow burner. I explained this whenever I went for an interview with a chairman.

'I really enjoyed being a coach and seeing the players improve, more than the results-orientated business of being a manager. I did Ajax pre-seasons and the lads hated it: out running at quarter past seven in the morning. The boys would curse my name under their breaths. But I didn't set out to be liked. Being from Kolding, I didn't set out to be anything.'

CHAPTER TWO

cultzeros.co.uk

WHOOSH!
Nick Tanner, 1988–94

BY THE SUMMER OF 1988, NICK TANNER HAD BUILT UP QUITE A reputation and it was unclear whether it would send him spinning to the top or the bottom of the professional game.

'Bristol Rovers wanted rid of me because I didn't get on with the manager, Gerry Francis,' he explains. 'Torquay United made an offer of £10,000 and the club accepted it. I spoke to Torquay's manager, Cyril Knowles, who was straight and to the point. I was a big shagger in those days, see, and he knew about it. "Come and live down on the English Riviera," he told me. "There are lots of young female students here. They'll be right up your street." I have to admit, it was very tempting, even though Torquay were in the old Fourth Division and it would have meant dropping a league.'

Tanner was still living with his parents in Bristol. His father, Dennis, who worked as a fireman at British Aerospace, did not have any interest in football, so he was none the wiser when answering a telephone late one evening shortly after Torquay's offer.

'My old man shouted up the stairs, "Nick, there's a bloke called Kenny who wants to speak to you."'

'The bloke went to me, "Kenny Dalglish here. I want to sign you for Liverpool." I thought one of the Rovers lads was winding me up. I wasn't even the best player there. Gary Penrice was. Then there was big Devon White.'

Tanner was on £220 a week.

'Kenny asked how much I wanted. Being daft, I wondered if he'd stretch to £300. "Of course, Nick . . . of course." I told my old man the good news but the significance of Liverpool didn't really mean too much to him. His first question was "What are they paying you, son?" Being a worker, he always knew the value of every pound. When I said that I was moving away from home for an extra £80, he was furious. "Ring that Kenny fella back and tell him you need more!" So I did and ended up getting £330 instead.'

Tanner had taken five years to jump ten leagues after starting out with non-league Mangotsfield. He spent the same amount of time at Liverpool before a back injury – which he believes may have been the consequence of the 'thousands' of sit-ups he'd do to use fitness to compensate for his lack of technical ability – forced him to retire aged just twenty-eight.

Tanner thinks he is the only Liverpool player since 1990 to have appeared in more than fifty games without earning enough money to retire on. His last contract – agreed in 1992 – would have tied him down for the next three seasons and at £1,500 a week was the most lucrative deal he'd ever sign.

'It was enough to buy a three bedroomed house down 'ere,' he says in a Bristolian accent so enthusiastic and croaky it sounds like it has swiftly been passed through a cheese grater. 'I was on £70,000 a year and made £50,000 off my testimonial against Yeovil Town. I'm not bitter about that, though. Money never motivated me. I'm happy-go-lucky, me; always have been. I was never a saver of money. You spend what you've got because you could die tomorrow. Live every day for what it is. Just crack on.'

It was this attitude that helped him reintegrate into a 'normal' life. Within six months, he'd taken an office job in accident management and personal-injury claims. His exit from football was not solely responsible for the separation from his wife, Sue, and Tanner claims he did not suffer from the type of 'meltdown' that many footballers experience when their careers are cut short in unfortunate circumstances.

'I've never smoked, don't do the drugs,' he continues. 'I drank a lot but if it wasn't for a lager I wouldn't have played football in the first place. When I first signed for Liverpool, they put me in a hotel for five months. All I did was go boozing and shagging. Nothing is worse than sitting there staring at four walls the night before a game. The tension is un-fucking-bearable. I started playing in men's leagues when I was fourteen and we'd go down the pub straight after games. It has been a part of my life since then and I'm not ashamed to admit it. I find it to be a relaxing agent. You see some footballers now drinking Coke without being told off. Surely the sugar can't be good for them.'

Winter has arrived when I meet Tanner near his home in Bradley Stoke, an uninviting cluster of housing estates in the most northern end of Bristol. The area is still recovering from a nineties collapse in the property market, which forced many households into negative equity, thus earning the town the nickname 'Sadly Broke'.

By 10 a.m., we are nursing real ale in a pub called the Three Brooks and it is early afternoon by the time we reach the almost identically modern Bailey's Court Inn, which is situated in a small retail park that includes a Tesco Express and a Chinese restaurant imaginatively named Beijing.

This is Tanner's local. He is a founder member of what he proudly informs me is called the Monday Club – a social gathering that holds liquid lunch meetings most weeks around this time. Tanner gives the impression he knows the names of all the customers within earshot, many of whom think it's acceptable to wear Diadora tracksuit bottoms, tan-coloured leather jackets and short-sleeved polo necks as one ensemble. Once they find out I have travelled from Liverpool, there are familiar jokes about stereos and hubcaps being pinched from the car park. Tanner looks on apologetically and wanders off to order another round while sharing flirtatious jokes with the buxom barmaids, who are familiar enough with him to play along.

Tanner is the smartest person in the establishment, dressed in a navy-coloured pinstripe suit jacket, jeans and black loafers. There is a goatee beard and his hair is swept behind his ears. He reminds me a bit of the housewives' television favourite, Trevor Eve. The blond highlights from the early nineties, which made me think of Pat Sharp from *Fun House* every time I saw him play, are long gone. 'That was Barry Venison's idea,' he smiles. 'The women liked it, didn't they?'

I decided to interview Tanner for two reasons. He is the only former Liverpool player currently alive to have represented the club at Wembley and now be doing a standard nine-to-five job away from football. I initially wondered what it was like to be back where he was aged sixteen, not really in control of his own financial destiny, especially with the personal-injury market struggling.

Principally, though, it intrigued me to find out what Tanner made of Graeme Souness – the manager that gave him and several other young players a platform to perform at Liverpool while alienating legends that had previously contributed towards a healthy collection of league and European titles. Jan Mølby had told me that Tanner represented the worst of all the average play-ers that Souness promoted. It was only fair to establish the other side of the story.

Tanner's climb into the professional game was not untypical of the time, despite sport not being in the family genes. 'My brother Martyn was more into motorbikes,' he explains. 'My dad was a grafter and worked like a Trojan to support the family. There wasn't enough time for anything else in his life.'

Home was in Kingswood, an enclave of Bristol Rovers support. 'I only went to away matches during the week if it wasn't too far, because I was playing every weekend for Frampton Rangers on a Saturday and Bromley Heath on a Sunday.'

The world of adult football beckoned.

'My mate's dad was nearly forty and playing centre-back for a Saturday team. I went down there and I was the youngest player in the league. I ran about on the wing and got taught all the ropes. The young 'uns would get kicked about everywhere and the old fellas would steam straight in, sorting it out. The beers after the game made me feel like a man. They were bloody good times. I think that exposure was one of the reasons why I got as far as I did. You don't play against men in these professional academies now, do you? It's a big jump playing against blokes. It teaches you teamwork and spirit. In kids' football, a little superstar can win a game on his own. That's not the case the older you get. You need everyone to stick together and pull the same way.'

Ralph Miller, a locally legendary non-league manager at nearby Mangotsfield, saw enough in Tanner to ask him to training. Miller was a builder by trade and a gnarly looking character who upon grinning revealed a single tooth hanging down from his upper gum like an upside-down cenotaph.

'I enjoyed playing under Ralph more than Bobby Gould, Gerry Francis, Kenny Dalglish or Graeme Souness,' Tanner beams. 'He loved players that got stuck in, and I was one of them. He was an old-school psychologist like Bill Shankly, a bloody clever bastard. There was a player that he desperately wanted to sign for Mangotsfield. Problem was, the fella lived the other side of Bristol. So he drove over in the car with a bicycle in the boot. He pleaded with the fella at his front door. "Look, I've cycled all the way over here." The lad looked at his bike. "Jesus Christ," he said. "You must really want me." So he signed the forms there and then. Ralph rode around the corner before driving home, the clever bastard.

'When I was eighteen, I came back from my first lads' holiday in Magaluf, where I'd gone out drinking every night and running on the beach every morning – sit-ups, press-ups, the lot. I felt as fit as fuck. After our first pre-season session, I got out of the shower looking all bronzed. "Fuck me," Ralph went. "You've got a body like Jane and a prick like Tarzan!"'

In the mid eighties, Bristol Rovers were, as Tanner puts it, 'in financial shit' and needing players that would play for practically nothing, so they scoured the Gloucestershire and Somerset county leagues for undiscovered talent.

'I could have earned more money staying at British Aerospace working on the planes and playing for Mangotsfield than I did going pro. There was a woman who supported Rovers. I could hear her most games, "Tanner! Earn your money!" There was a dog track at Twerton Park and one day I spotted her while warming up. I jumped over the fence and nipped it in the bud. "Excuse me," I said. "How much money do you think I earn?" She looked at me blankly. "I'm not on thousands of pounds, love." I explained that I'd sacrificed a reasonably secure future at BA to slug it out for Rovers every Saturday. From then on, she was as good as gold.'

Tanner had previously been part-time at Mangotsfield, earning a fiver a match plus fuel expenses.

'Rovers was an extension of playing non-league football to me. We were rag-ass, Rovers. We washed our own training kit every day and sometimes didn't even bother. There wasn't a huge jump in standard. The fact that I didn't have to go to work from six in the morning then train in the evenings meant I found the step up quite easy.

'My nickname became "Whoosh", because I'd knock a pass fifty yards down the line towards Gary Penrice or Devon White. The name stuck with me at Liverpool. As a left-back, that was my simple job: win it and twat it as hard as I could for the centre-forwards to run on to. The biggest difference was the levels of organization and discipline. Bobby Gould was our manager and he let everyone know what was expected. While he was manager at Coventry, Bobby had signed Stuart Pearce from Wealdstone, so he knew how to get the best out of non-league players like me.'

It frustrated Tanner that he was not always given the credit he thought he deserved for his efforts. When deployed in midfield, his partner was Gerry Francis, then on his last legs having made his name at Queens Park Rangers. Tanner claims he took a lot of Francis's buffeting, particularly when facing warlocks such as Brentford's Terry Hurlock, who was once described by *The Guardian* as 'An incredible bulk of a man', someone whose reputation prompted opponents to hire Sherpa guides to circumnavigate him in order to 'maintain a full set of limbs'.

'I'm not being funny but Gerry would get man of the match and I would think to myself, "He's only fucking passed the ball from side to side for ninety minutes – he hasn't been crashing into fellas like Hurlock." Hurlock was from the travelling community and you know what gypsies are like as fighters. I'd leave the pitch with my boots hanging off, my laces removed, my socks ripped, soaking in blood. All I wanted was a pat on the back. A lot of footballers are like that.'

After Gould left for Wimbledon, Francis was appointed as his replacement.

'Our relationship was never the best as players and it didn't get any better when he became manager. He dropped me to the bench one game and I told him I'd rather go and play for the reserves than sit on my arse. He couldn't believe it – told me he hadn't heard someone say such a thing in his previous twenty years as a footballer. Later that afternoon, he told me to go to Tottenham the following morning with the reserves on a minibus. The reserve-team manager told all the boys he'd give us a tenner each if we kept the score below a 5–0 defeat. Somehow we won 2–0.'

Tanner describes himself as a 'Jack of all trades but master of none'. Often used as a left-back, he was spotted by Liverpool running up and down the left of midfield, despite naturally being right-footed. His ability to use both feet must have alerted Liverpool's chief scout, Ron Yeats, while watching Penrice, who like Tanner had began his career with Mangotsfield. Years before, Yeats's predecessor Geoff Twentyman, whose son with the same name was also curiously playing for Rovers at the same time as Tanner, was renowned for recommending players with the ability to 'go both ways', meaning they were two-footed. Tanner seemed a classic Liverpool signing: cheap, underrated and versatile. Similarly, nobody thought much of Northampton's Phil Neal before, like Tanner, he moved to Anfield aged twenty-three.

'Gerry decided to play Vaughan Jones at left-back and shifted me further forward. We went seven games unbeaten and narrowly missed out on promotion from the old Division Three. I couldn't run past anyone, though. It was just a case of getting it out of my feet and whipping it in. I'd cut back inside and aim for big Dev. It was predictable but very effective.'

Tanner admits he was not ambitious. Had he ended up at Torquay, it would not have been a problem. 'I'm happy-go-lucky, me,' he reiterates. 'Easy come, easy go.' Suddenly, for the grand sum of £20,000, he was a Liverpool player.

'I thought I'd be at Rovers for my whole career then maybe drop back into non-league football as I got older. Being a local lad, Rovers was all right for me, you know? Within a couple of months, I was running about at Melwood with Phil Thompson screaming and John Durnin telling me I was crap. It was a big shock. It was a tough school, lots of hard knocks. I don't think anybody knew I'd played football to a decent standard. At Rovers, we beat Leicester City 3–1 in the FA Cup and Gary McAllister was in their midfield. What a player he was. Alan Smith and Mark Bright were up front. We gave them a roasting that day. It was probably my best-ever performance: hunting them down, getting stuck in and causing mayhem. Maybe if some of the Liverpool lads had seen that game, they'd have realized I had something about me.

'I knew other players were more talented at Liverpool but I never had a negative syndrome – no, no, no. That goes all the way back to the beginning of my story with football. If someone had an advantage, I'd crash into them. It was cynical but you had to be that way to survive – give 'em a good hiding.'

To play regularly for Liverpool it was not merely enough just to display energy and unhinged spirit. Tanner appreciated he needed to improve other areas of his game in order to progress.

'I got taken on by Liverpool because I was a fit lad. I could run up and down all day after a heavy night on the beer,' he says. 'In pre-season, I'd be miles ahead of everyone else, thinking it was easy. Then the balls came out. That's where I struggled.

'At Rovers, we'd play five-a-side for a bit of fun on a Friday afternoon. At Liverpool, it was the routine. It was all two-touch and if you messed it up, Bugsy [Ronnie Moran] would stop the play and single you out, giving you a right bollocking. On the outside, people hear of the five-a-sides and think of what happens in your local gym. This wasn't a load of fat blokes knocking it round. It was done with intensity. Jamie Redknapp used to say to me, "Fuck off, will you?" because I'd go in and nail him every time. Everyone was nailing each other.'

Moran had filled every role imaginable at the club from player, to physio, to coach and trainer, through to caretaker manager in a career at Liverpool that lasted almost fifty years. Bruce Grobbelaar described him as the staff's 'barking dog'.

'Bugsy would go mental these days, with the conservative passing that takes place around the back. At Liverpool, you never passed for passing's sake. Everything was done for a reason, a purpose. His football knowledge was frightening. After games, he'd pick up the kit off all the players. One by one, he'd get the shirts, the shorts, then the socks. If he felt it was needed, he'd have a quiet word in your ear – it was never in front of the other lads, unless you'd done something really bad. His memory for detail was unbelievable. "I saw what you did in the fourth minute there," he'd say. "Nobody else saw it but I did." At the beginning, I thought he was being a bastard but over time I realized he only bothered with me because he knew I was willing to learn.'

Tanner waited almost eighteen months to make his first-team debut and in that period became a central defender for the reserves under Phil Thompson, Liverpool's former European Cup-winning captain.

'I remember being on the bench at Rovers and watching people like Mick Harford drifting out towards the full-back while the goalkeeper took his kick. He'd charge across the pitch and bang into the centre-half. It was frightening. I didn't really fancy dealing with that. I was crap in the air too, so it surprised me when Liverpool started playing me in the middle, even though I had the pace to recover in a race. I'd ask Phil to try me out in midfield but he kept telling me I didn't have the football brain to play there for the first team, so it was pointless.'

When Graeme Souness was appointed as Liverpool's first-team manager in 1991, one of his first big decisions was to sack Thompson. Souness had replaced Thompson as Liverpool's captain a decade earlier and there was bad feeling between the pair. When staff informed Souness that Thompson was being too harsh with players, who did not enjoy working under him, he decided to act. Tanner can understand why.

'Some of the stuff Thommo used to try was baffling,' Tanner says. 'It amazes me that we managed to win any games. If we were playing Leeds away at two in the afternoon, he'd have us at Elland Road doing sprints around the cinder track by midday as a warm-up. It only stopped when Jan [Mølby] came down from the first team. Jan was never going to take part in that, was he – the size and reputation of him? There were lots of fights and arguments. Eventually, I plucked up enough courage to tell Thommo that if he kept hitting me with a stick, he wasn't going to get anything positive back. Man-management is about knowing when to crack the whip and when to ease off. Thommo rarely eased off.'

On trips away, Thompson would relax a little.

'The pre-season tours to Cornwall were fantastic. We played the United team of Beckham, Scholes, Butt and the Nevilles and wiped the floor with them. We'd have a few drinks and, to be fair to Thommo, he'd encourage it. The United boys were staying in the same hotel and they'd be sitting there with protein shakes, watching Mike Hooper stumble across the bar with a round of sixteen beers on a tray.

'One evening, Wayne Harrison dived off a boat and the coastguard had to rescue him. The lads knew that Wayne had swum to a safe place but everyone was shouting, "Man overboard! Man overboard!" When he emerged from the water and crept up behind Thommo, you can imagine his reaction.'

Tanner's closest friends were Hooper and Mike Marsh. Marsh had joined Liverpool from non-league Kirkby Town around the same time as Tanner, while Hooper, a goalkeeper, was also from Bristol and had signed from Wrexham in 1985.

'Hoops was crazy. Boy, I could tell you a few stories about him,' Tanner says. 'Love Hoops to bits. I bought a house in Cressington, which backed on to the garden of Holly Johnson from Frankie Goes to Hollywood. Next thing is, Hoops buys a gaff opposite me in the same cul-de-sac. He just rocked up one morning without saying anything beforehand. I thought that was a bit weird.'

Hooper was interested in wildlife.

'He was big into twitching,' Tanner says. 'He'd disappear into the Lake District for days at a time with his binoculars. Hoops had a silver XR3 and he'd put the seats right back. I figured he'd been out shagging. But one morning, he gave me a lift to work and in the cassette player he had a tape of birds whistling. He proceeded to tell me that he'd lie there in his car listening to these tapes because it helped him relax.'

The peculiar behaviour did not prevent Tanner from accompanying Hooper in successive summers to El Arenal, Majorca, a concrete jungle built in the 1960s, popular with Brits and Germans for cheap holidays.

'He could eat for England, Hoops. There was a greasy spoon that did fry-ups. The sign outside was advertising six English breakfasts for the price of five. So Hoops went in, put a big order in and ate them all.

'The last I saw of Hoops was a few years back at Cheltenham races. He was working then as a nightclub doorman in Durham, which again was a bit strange, because he wasn't really the confrontational type. The only time I saw him lose his temper amongst the lads was on the trip to Limassol in Cyprus during a Cup-Winners' Cup game, which we won 2–1. It all kicked off in the tunnel because one of their players messed with Paul Stewart's curly hair. Hoops was right in there.'

Tanner's relationship with Marsh was built on different foundations.

'Me and Hoops were thrown together because we were from the same area: two bumpkins was probably the idea. With Marshy, it was more natural. To be fair to Marshy, he was a Scouser and would tell players like Steve McMahon and Jan [Mølby] if he thought they were being out of order. After a couple of beers, he'd have a right go. He was a proper little terrier.'

The pair would start their nights out in either the Kingsman on Aigburth Road or the Mariners Inn, close to Marsh's home in Kirkby.

'Then we'd head to Yates' Wine Lodge opposite Central Station and meet the other young 'uns, like Alex Watson. I'd prefer to get pissed in the grotty spots rather than stand posing all night with the big heads in places like the Continental, looking important. I've always been outgoing and I've never struggled with women. I didn't use that terrible line: "Do you know who I am?" It wasn't the case with some of the others.'

The Conti, as it was commonly known amongst Liverpool's squad, was the club where most nights out wound up. Before even reaching there during a Christmas get-together one year, Tanner had a fight with Steve McMahon at a restaurant in Chinatown.

'I've been on a couple of the Liverpool legends tours to Scandinavia and he's all right now, Macca. But back then he was a pain in the arse. His best mate was Ronnie Whelan. Maybe Ronnie was the only one that knew how to deal with him.

'We were in this restaurant and Macca confronted a kid I was talking to who was a supporter and just asking me a few questions about Liverpool. "Who the fuck are you?" Macca kept saying. I thought he was being out of order and I told him so. "Just jog on, Macca. Stop being a dick." He wouldn't stop, so I lamped him. He lamped me and we started a big old scrap. Macca turned up to training the next day and Bugsy was straight on to it, asking what had gone on. I'm not sure whether Macca could remember what had happened or whether he just didn't want to admit that it was me that had cracked him one and caused the cut above his eye.

'Wayne Harrison, bless his cotton socks, told me a story about a time he ended up going back to Macca's house. Macca had him playing pool until six o'clock in the morning. Because Wayne was a kid, he went along with it.'

Of the other established first-team players, Tanner got on best with Bruce Grobbelaar.

'In my first month at Liverpool, we went to La Coruña in Spain for a pre-season tournament. Bruce asked me to go for a walk and we ended up in a bar and had two beers each. When we got back to the hotel, Bugsy was fuming because there was a game the following day. Kenny knew about it and was apparently fuming too. I'd only spoken to Kenny twice before – once on the phone when he called to say he wanted to sign me and then again briefly on the first day of pre-season training. There was nothing down for me if I'd pissed him off already. I didn't play against Atlético Madrid but unfortunately everything went to shit. Bruce conceded five, making two mistakes, and Alan Hansen got carried off with a serious knee injury. There were no stretchers, so me and Steve McMahon had to help him into the changing rooms. Later, Kenny went ballistic. He rounded on all the boys then came to me. "You!" he said. "On your first fucking trip, messing about." To be fair to Bruce, he stepped in and took the blame. He could see I was a bit overwhelmed by the telling-off I was getting. Kenny grounded me for the rest of the tournament. I wasn't allowed to leave the hotel.'

Tanner says he only had three meaningful conversations with Dalglish, who kept his distance from the other players too until the Hillsborough disaster, which drew him closer to those around him who were suffering. On one of the rare occasions the squad, wives and management all socialized together, Tanner 'messed up' again.

'We went to see Wet Wet Wet and Kenny was busy talking to

Marti Pellow. I got chatting to Marina, not knowing she was Kenny's wife. The lads were going, "You're in there, Worzel! Go for it!" I was called either Worzel or Whoosh at Liverpool. They all knew who she was, of course, then Kenny shows up. "Give us a sec, boss, I'm in here." Kenny wasn't happy. "That's my fucking missus!"'

Tanner played just four games for Liverpool under Dalglish in two and a half seasons, appearing as a substitute during a 4–1 victory over Manchester City in December 1989 before making his full debut towards the end of the same campaign at Charlton Athletic, a 4–0 win. Tanner says that although he was playing regularly for the reserves and included in first-team match-day squads, he felt like an outsider intruding on someone else's victory parade when the old First Division championship was secured in April 1990. Tanner needed, indeed, to be reminded that he was involved in Liverpool's last title squad. 'I didn't play enough to win a medal, so it's no achievement of mine,' he reasons.

When Dalglish announced his surprise resignation in February 1991, Tanner saw it as an opportunity.

'I was twenty-five and I needed to either kick on at Liverpool or go somewhere else. I'd been on loan to Norwich and loved it there. We lost just one in six. I played centre-half with Andy Linighan and we roomed together. The night before games, he'd reach into his sports bag and pull out a four pack of Carlsberg with a big smile on his face.'

Graeme Souness was viewed as an exciting appointment.

'I was delighted because it was a fresh start. It gave people a big kick up the arse. I used to watch him play as a kid and think, "Fucking hell – he's a real man." I wanted to be him. In the first few weeks, he told everyone in a meeting that he would reward effort. It was a fair day's pay for a fair day's work. It's the way it should be. You couldn't afford to be in cruise control.'

It quickly became apparent that Souness wanted to dispense with the old guard.

'In working man's terms, it was like going into a pub where regulars have sat in the same seat for years but the carpet's smelling and the place is going down the pan,' Tanner says. 'The landlord encourages the new clientele because he realizes the pub needs the income to flourish. But his changes are met by resistance. The old 'uns even complain when he tries to redecorate, because the walls have been cream for years.'

There are other chapters in this book that outline the changes Souness made at Liverpool. Tanner concedes that the club's younger players were more receptive to his ideas because they didn't know any better.

'If Graeme asked us to do something, I'd do it. I'd always been like that, ever since Mangotsfield. Ralph used to say that if he asked me to run into a wall, I'd run into a wall. He also said that I was quick to learn lessons. If I put my head through a hole in a wall and got punched, I wouldn't do it a second time.

'The old 'uns gave the impression they thought the young 'uns weren't fit to lace their boots. If that was the case, they should have focused on earning a new contract by playing well rather than arguing about it with the manager. The attitude was: "We've won five league titles" and anyone who thought differently could get to fuck.'

The poisonous atmosphere made Tanner realize that it's not always just the players in the team that define the results. He uses the relationship between Dean Saunders and Ian Rush to illustrate this. The pair formed a partnership in the Welsh national team but were not always selected together by Souness due to Rush's injury problems.

'He was alright, Deano. Cost a lot of money from Derby County but he scored a decent number of goals when Rushy wasn't about. As soon as he returned to fitness, Rushy was niggling whenever Deano didn't score, saying he should be back in the team. It was there in the background all the time.

'It can be the players on the sidelines that ruin the morale of the squad. Big characters like Rushy and Ronnie Whelan would get together over a few beers and slag everyone off. Maybe they were a little bit worried about getting back in because we trained harder and took Graeme's fitness programmes more seriously than they did. They'd argue that league titles had been won eating pie and chips. But in those times, everyone else was eating pie and chips.

'I'll stick up for Graeme until the cows come home because he gave a lot of young players a chance. There was Marshy, Steve McManaman, Jamie Redknapp, Don Hutchison, David James, Steve Harkness, Rob Jones and me. I'll admit I was the least talented of all those players. Maybe they all thought I was crap. But most of the others proved later on in their careers they were pretty good.

'Graeme helped improve the diet of the team. There was no more pie and chips. There were no more buses from Anfield to Melwood and back with us all being freezing cold. You probably think I'm only backing Graeme because he trusted me. But the tradition at Liverpool was that the manager always had the final say. Some of the players had become too big for their boots and did not help him when they should have done.'

Souness met resistance because many of the older players were teammates of his and were there when he stretched the boundaries as Liverpool's captain. Souness would lead the team off the pitch as much as he would on it and was a chief organizer of nights out. Suddenly, he was imposing his own rules, which could have been deemed hypocritical.

Yet some of Liverpool's players simply did not like Souness, whose confrontational style was often crushing. One of them was David Speedie – Dalglish's last signing. In an interview with *The Scotsman*, Speedie recalls hearing about Souness's arrival at Anfield as manager, a moment that prompted him to turn towards Bruce Grobbelaar in the dressing room and say, rather perceptively, 'That's me, I am history.' The enmity with Souness could be traced back to Speedie's full Scotland debut, in the 1–0 win over England at Hampden Park in 1985. Speedie told *The Scotsman*:

The ball's been thrown in, and the full-back Viv Anderson has gone straight through the back of me. Souness was like,

'Give it to me quicker, you should be giving it to me quicker.'
I just said, 'Shut it, you muppet.' You don't want that from
one of your teammates. I was making my debut, with my
whole family in the stand, and he is giving me stick. I was only
twenty-four years old. You want to be encouraging people
– I got more encouragement from Butch Wilkins, who was
playing for England against us.

When Souness became Liverpool's manager, Speedie was in form
and scoring goals, having moved from Coventry City at a late
stage in his career when other players his age were more likely
to be transferring the other way. Whilst on a pre-season tour
in Germany, however, Souness and Speedie's relationship broke
down completely. During a gruelling two-week training camp,
Souness banned the squad from drinking alcohol. By the end of
the trip, Speedie, Gary Gillespie and Ray Houghton flouted the
rules and went out anyway. On returning to base, Speedie found
Souness at the bar of the hotel nightclub.

'You know something, you are a cunt,' Speedie said. 'He didn't
say much back. He never gained respect as manager of Liverpool.
He was brilliant as a player, I could not say enough about him as
a player. But as a manager, no.'

Speedie was allowed to join Blackburn Rovers in August 1991,
the fourth sale sanctioned by Souness in just ten days. Peter
Beardsley was the first player Souness got rid of. Although there
was an impression that Souness and Beardsley did not get on,
Tanner sees Beardsley's exit differently.

'Peter did not drink and a rumour went around that he was
telling the staff what all the players were up to during nights out
because he could remember everything clearly. Peter was being
forced out of the door before Graeme arrived, because the moan-
ers had persuaded Kenny that he couldn't be trusted as one of
the lads. It was a shame, because I think anyone will tell you that
Peter was one of our most important players.'

I ask Tanner about Mølby, who had also admitted to a fraught
relationship with Souness.

'Jan was the one who you'd give it to if you wanted to keep hold of the ball, because he was so strong, nobody could knock him about. Although we roomed together, Jan slagged me off, saying I was the worst player he'd ever seen play for Liverpool. I told him that if we merged my fitness with his ability, you'd have a Liverpool captain right there. Jan turned round and said, "Yeah, but you're fucking crap." Jan's one of the great under-achievers in football in terms of the impact he had on the pitch. If Graeme offered him a million pounds to lose five stone, he wouldn't bother. He just wouldn't get fit enough.'

Tanner was selected alongside Mølby at centre-half when Wimbledon won 3–2 at Anfield in April 1992, a game where Tanner split his nose after being elbowed full on in the face by the human cyclone that was John Fashanu. Tanner's only full season at Liverpool corresponded with the club's worst in decades. His personal statistics read reasonably enough: forty-five appearances – all from either centre-back or left-back – fifteen clean-sheets (conceding more than two goals just twice in the games he played in) and seven defeats. Some of those defeats were of the embarrassing kind, however, the type that underpinned arguments against Souness's management. Tanner was in the starting eleven during the 2–0 loss in Auxerre, at Peterborough United when Liverpool exited the League Cup, and when they suffered a 4–0 hammering at the hands of Arsenal. He also struggled upon returning to Bristol Rovers for an FA Cup match that Liverpool could only draw. 'I got loads of stick that night. I played so badly, I wondered whether I'd be able to set foot in Bristol ever again.' In the First Division, Liverpool finished sixth, eighteen points off title winners Leeds United.

'I didn't have many bad games but I had a few bad moments,' Tanner insists. He talks about the occasion when Luton Town, doomed for relegation, led at Anfield after his own goal in front of the Kop – the result of an excruciating back-pass and a misjudgement of Bruce Grobbelaar's positioning.

'I should have just put it in the stand. That was my natural instinct. If I was playing for Rovers, that's what I'd have done.

But because I was playing for Liverpool, the crowd would get on your back if you booted it. It's better to give it long than give it away and concede a goal, isn't it? The options got inside my head. Remember, though, I cost £20,000. I made a high-profile mistake in a game that Liverpool still won. There were fellas around me that cost £2.5 million. They were making more mistakes. I think I offered greater value for money than someone like Torben Piechnik, who cost half a million quid. Then there was István Kozma [the Hungarian midfielder signed for £300,000 from Dunfermline Athletic].'

Liverpool's problems with back-passes continued the following season when an FA ruling decreed that from then on goalkeepers were to be punished from handling them by the awarding of an indirect free kick. Tanner believes the law affected Liverpool more than other teams.

'Under Kenny, whenever we went away from home the first rule for the opening twenty minutes was to make sure Bruce had plenty of touches. It would frustrate the crowd and we'd feed off that. Liverpool were really cynical. We'd kill games all the time. So long as we won, nobody was arsed.

'In 1992, I played in the Charity Shield against Leeds at Wembley. It was the first time we couldn't use Bruce as an out-ball just to relieve a bit of the tension. Eric Cantona went on the rampage, scoring a hat-trick. The tradition of Alan Hansen knocking passes backwards and forwards to the full-backs was over because the risk became greater. We didn't adjust at all well.'

There were some lighter moments during the 1991–92 campaign. Tanner scored Liverpool's goal during a 1–1 draw in the Merseyside derby at Goodison Park. As with his own goal against Luton, the ball trickled over the line. This time there was also some confusion about the identity of the scorer due to the scrum inside the box from a corner at the Gwladys Street end. 'I'd rather we won 1–0 and someone else score,' Tanner says. 'Goals aren't the be-all and end-all. It would be fairer if there was a definitive list of defenders who have contributed towards the highest number of clean sheets. Maybe then us defenders would get a bit more credit than we do.'

Tanner enjoyed European games the most. Liverpool were in the UEFA Cup following a six-year ban, the penalty for the hooliganism that led to the Heysel disaster in 1985.

'They were easier, less physical. At the back, you could get your cigar out. It was more about concentrating. The foreign teams would play one up front. It was a doddle. We came unstuck against Genoa because they were very English, the way they played. Tomáš Skuhravý, the Czech centre-forward, was a beast. We didn't get to grips with him.'

Tanner says the improbable victory over Auxerre in an earlier round was a career high. 'I never really felt like I belonged as a Liverpool player but after this game, I did. The feeling only lasted for a few days. We lost 2–0 over in France and everyone expected us to go out. We were terrible. Alan Hansen slated us in the press. But at Anfield, we won 3–0 and went through. It was a defiant performance, really emotional. It felt like an achievement because we'd come through a fair bit of adversity. Unfortunately, Anfield was only half full that night in a period where Graeme was getting lots of abuse. So the game isn't remembered. It was unfortunate for Graeme that he was also dealing with European football at a point when the club hadn't been involved in it for such a long time. People expected Liverpool to romp away and win the UEFA Cup because of the club's history. It was never going to be that easy.'

One of the real positives was the emergence of Steve McManaman, a teenage winger from Bootle.

'I was great at running long distances, me,' Tanner says. 'Rob Jones was pretty good at it too. When Macca came in, he cleaned us both out. He was as thin as a rake but his endurance levels were unreal. I played with him before he reached his peak but even as a kid he was winning games for us. He gets a lot of stick for leaving Liverpool but he didn't cost the club any money in transfer fees and he was quite open about being an Evertonian. It never stopped him putting a shift in.'

Tanner's performances prompted Souness to offer him a new three-year contract. Tanner remembers his naivety in discussing terms with Peter Robinson, Liverpool's chief executive.

'Graeme told me to go and see Peter because he wanted to speak to me about something. He was standing at the end of a big table in the boardroom. I'd scored the own goal against Luton the week before. "What have I done wrong now?" I asked him. Peter pushed a contract towards me. There were no agents involved. I just signed it. I didn't even realize I was tripling my wages from £500 a week plus a couple of signing-on fees. Peter seemed surprised that I didn't want to negotiate. Apparently, some of the senior players were haggling. I don't know what John Barnes was on. But £1,500 was good enough for me. I was bloody delighted.'

After tearing his ankle ligaments in a tackle with Coventry City's Robert Rosario, Tanner struggled to regain what he describes as his 'six or sometimes seven out of ten' form of early season and ended up missing the FA Cup final in May.

'It fucking killed me, still does to an extent,' he says, emphasizing that he was fit but not selected in the match-day squad because only two substitutes were permitted. 'You see football now and it seems like the lad on work experience that does all the secretary's photocopying gets a medal whenever a team wins a trophy. That's not good for the soul of the game. It should fucking hurt when you get left out, as it did for me on countless occasions. Barry Venison picked up a piece of chalk, threw it across the room and stormed out of the dressing room when he found out he wasn't playing against Sunderland.'

Tanner joined Venison and Ronnie Whelan, who was injured, in the players' bar rather than join the rest of the squad in the pre-match walk around the pitch.

'We all got pretty drunk. I wanted to forget about it. I wouldn't have felt a part of it even if I was one of the subs and didn't get brought on. Imagine being a third-choice keeper now. You must be laughing your fucking cock off. It's the easiest job in the world: lots of money, no pressure, no scrutiny. Yet the Premier

League has twenty of them. If I died, I'd want to be reincarnated as a third-choice goalkeeper.'

Goals from Michael Thomas and Ian Rush helped Liverpool beat Sunderland, an achievement that compensated slightly for the poor league finish. Yet morale amongst the players was on the floor and attitudes were reflected the following weekend when the squad gathered at Manchester Airport bound for Tenerife in the traditional end-of-season booze-up.

'Fifteen of us were meant to go. Only five showed. There was Phil Boersma, Barry Venison, Marshy, McManaman and me. That tells you all you need to know. These used to be important social occasions. But the spirit wasn't there. Macca spent the week hanging round the pool wearing his jeans. His legs were so white.'

This was not a bright new dawn for either Tanner or the club. Tanner was soon diagnosed with colitis after passing blood in the changing rooms before a reserve game. 'One of the lads used the toilet immediately after me and came out going, "What the fuck has happened in there?" I didn't even notice the blood. The doctor told me it was a result of stress, which had been disguised a long time by drink. Deep down, I felt the pressure of football – performing in front of a crowd and trying to meet expectations, not letting anyone down.'

Tanner trained harder in order to get back to a supreme level of fitness, something he always prided himself on. There were hundreds of sit-ups and press-ups every day. He felt a pain in his back and it did not go away. There was a second diagnosis, this time sacroiliitis – inflammation of the joint between the lower spine and pelvis.

Medical solutions at Liverpool were not much more advanced than at Bristol Rovers.

'At Rovers, we didn't have a physio. They used a mega-pulse machine to treat injuries. After a few years, it was serviced and we found out that it wasn't even working. At Liverpool, there was an ultrasound that was originally designed to treat horses. Bugsy [Ronnie Moran] and Roy [Evans] acted as physios but had no real medical expertise. If there was a major problem, Liverpool would pay for a private doctor to come out but that only happened in extreme circumstances.'

After everything else failed, Tanner was subjected to acupuncture, different injections, a course of CT scans lasting five hours at a time and was sent to a chiropractor.

'Twelve months later, I still wasn't able to sit down at Anfield and watch the team play for ninety minutes without suffering pain. I'd had enough of having needles stuck in my back. You can't replicate the buzz of playing football but it was time to pack it in. Not facing the rehabilitation every day was a relief. The back's OK now but it flares up every now and again.'

The decision Tanner regrets most is leaving Liverpool and returning to Bristol almost straight away.

'My son, William, was born and the missus at the time was homesick. She wanted to be closer to her family with the little 'un. If we'd stayed in Liverpool, it would have been better for all of us. There would have been more opportunity to remain in football, with so many clubs being based in the north-west. Down 'ere, there are only three or four in a 150-mile radius. I jumped without thinking.'

Tanner tried scouting with Forest Green Rovers in the Conference and eventually management even lower with Almondsbury Town, where there was no budget, then returned to Mangotsfield with a budget 'but not as much as other teams' in the Western League, where he balanced part-time duties with his office-based job.

He finds it frustrating that qualified coaches are fast-tracked towards the top at the expense of those with practical experience. 'The FA charge thousands of pounds to teach you how to put cones out. There's nothing in the manual that tells a coach how to deal with a player that knocks on your door telling you their wife and kids have left them. How do you give that lad the confidence to get out on the pitch and do the business for you?

'Listen, though. Football don't owe me nuffin'. I started really low and finished really high. I'm still the only player to score in both Bristol and Merseyside derbies, even if the Bristol one was in the Gloucestershire Cup.

'I'm just a fella on the street. I'll talk to anybody. I've been married, divorced and don't want to get married again. I've worked for five or six different companies since retiring. I'm always looking for different ways to support myself. Like anyone else, I could be made redundant next month. The only difference with me is, I'm going to make sure it reads on my gravestone: *Nick Tanner – once cost twenty grand.*'

CHAPTER THREE

cultzeros.co.uk

THE ROCKET,
Ronny Rosenthal, 1990–94

RONNY ROSENTHAL IS TALKING ABOUT HIS CAREER AS A FOOTBALL consultant with a great deal of enthusiasm. 'I have discovered many, many players – players you will recognize,' he beams, moments after I set foot in the kitchen of his home in West Hampstead, north London. He points towards a cork notice-board pegged proudly on the wall, where there are photographs of him and his two sons posing with footballers, some of whom are more illustrious than others. There are Vincent Kompany, Dimitar Berbatov, José Bosingwa and Aly Cissokho.

'Five years ago, Aly was standing just where you are now,' he tells me. 'He was playing for Gueugnon in France and struggling to get into the team. They were in Ligue 2. He was going nowhere. I suggested to Vitória Setúbal in Portugal that they sign him and within twelve months he'd gone to FC Porto and then Olympique Lyonnais for around £15 million. His starting value was £150,000. It was quite a mark-up for a left-back and a lot of money was made. That's impressive, don't you think?'

Rosenthal claims Bosingwa was a defensive midfielder before being converted to a right-back on his say-so and that Berbatov was on the brink of joining Liverpool from Bayer Leverkusen in 2005 only for the teams to draw one another in the Champions League, leading to a collapse in the agreement. 'I watched Dimi ever since he scored sixteen goals in thirty-four games for CSKA Sofia,' Rosenthal continues. 'I see players and recommend them to clubs. It's up to the clubs and the players' agents to complete the transfer.'

Over the next three hours, it becomes apparent that Rosenthal is a private scout with his own network of watchers. His company Interfoot is registered in Belgium and operates out of Liège. His most recent deal involved his own son, Tom, who left Watford's youth academy after Rosenthal was asked by Zulte Waregem boss Francky Dury to suggest a young and cheap midfielder.

'Clubs will call me and say, "We need a striker and we need a defender. We have a budget of so much; can you help us, Ronny?" There are a lot of directors at football clubs with business experience only. I understand football better than them. If they are intelligent, they develop a good relationship with me and the club benefits by increasing the value of the player and selling him on for a nice profit. It is no different to understanding where there might be a property boom – you need to appreciate the potential of the apartment.'

I quickly get the impression Rosenthal sees our meeting as a business opportunity to advertise what he does. Yet his observations about the industry are revealing and his comments about what was happening around him during his time at Liverpool are quite thought-provoking when related to what he has learnt about the game since.

Rosenthal uses the word 'discovered' a lot when describing his work, as if he's landed in a world not previously inhabited. As he has lived in Liverpool then London for nearly a quarter of a century, his English is very impressive. He speaks six languages fluently and has a decent understanding of another two. Yet I find his claim to have 'discovered' Cristiano Ronaldo and Nemanja Vidić far-fetched. He surely could not have been there before each player was signed to a club.

Soon, he is illustrating what he means on a desktop computer inside his personal office at the front of his home. He has compiled his own database, which charts almost fifteen years' work. There is a spreadsheet that seems to go on forever, including players in every position. It can also be manipulated to reflect price range, a rough estimate of wage, length of contract and age. Another page reveals he was in Čačak, Serbia, in September 2001, watching Vidić play for Spartak Subotica while he was on loan from Red Star Belgrade. Rosenthal spoke to the Serbian FA and contact was established with the player through a high-ranking member who was later assassinated by Serbian nationalists. 'I met Vidić at a hotel near Heathrow Airport. But all the English clubs told me he was not for them.'

Around a year later, Rosenthal was in Lisbon, looking at Portuguese midfielder Hugo Viana before recommending to Bobby Robson and Newcastle United that they should sign him. 'The fee they agreed was too big,' he insists. On the same trip, Rosenthal saw Ronaldo play for Sporting Lisbon. Both Vidić and Ronaldo later moved to Manchester United for considerable fees via different routes. 'If the United people had listened to me, it would have been a lot cheaper,' Rosenthal says, before finally conceding his work is maybe not so pioneering as he first implied.

'There are players who start to dominate from a very young age. But there are also those who learn to dominate and become top players with a little understanding and patience. I identify players when they have made their first-team debuts at lower clubs and let the other clubs know early. They are seventeen, eighteen or nineteen, maybe twenty. I told Liverpool to sign Samuel Eto'o at this age. Kompany was the same. Belgium is my second country because my wife is from there, so I saw Vincent play a lot. Liverpool said no on both occasions. But, OK, maybe 'discover' is too extreme. I go; I see; I recommend.'

During this interview, Rosenthal disappears to take long telephone calls with directors from different European clubs on at least half a dozen occasions. 'This game never stops for anyone,' he explains on the third return from another room, this time accompanied by his Belgian wife, Nancy, who is wearing a velour tracksuit and has an appointment at the hairdresser.

Rosenthal has a muscular body, too restrained in his neat turquoise T-shirt and tight stonewashed jeans. He has a heavy Hebrew accent that shoots into an upper register at the end of certain words. '*Look*, everything is documented,' he sighs. 'You meet a lot of people in football who claim to have done this, to have done that. But *look*, the number of Vidić is right here. *Look*.'

In his study, as well as framed shirts from each of the teams he represented as a player, there are hundreds of VHS videos and DVDs on a set of shelves, although, because of new technology, there is no need to record matches any more. 'Everything is one click away on the Internet.' There are newspapers, some less reputable than others, scattered on his desk and piled high in the space underneath. There is a large satellite dish outside and a plasma television connected to a system called Wyscout, which means he can watch any game of football from anywhere in the world at any time, day or night. Rosenthal informs me it has revolutionized the way clubs operate when recruiting. 'It's harder than ever to unearth the big player,' he says. 'But it's also harder to trust the right person who understands what it takes to be a success. I like to think I do. You notice only certain things when watching on TV. You need to see also in the flesh.'

Rosenthal's interest in the movement of players stems from personal experience. During twenty years as a professional footballer, he played in Israel, Belgium and England. He would have also played in Italy had Udinese not reneged on a contract in the summer of 1989, leaving him in limbo. The uncertainty eventually led to a transfer worth more than £1 million to Liverpool, where in 1990 he helped the club to its last title before his open-goal miss at Aston Villa two years later earned him enduring notoriety. 'I think I have enough experience to know how this business works,' he says. 'You have highs, lows and a lot of frustration. It resembles life, which is why we all love it so much.'

Rosenthal was one of the first generation of children to be born in Israel after the country was partitioned into Jewish and Arab sectors in 1948. His father was born in Romania and moved there in 1951. His mother came from Morocco a decade later.

'My father knew a lot of people who were sent to the concentration camps during the war but he hid in Bucharest and somehow remained safe,' Rosenthal says. 'My parents met in 1962 and I was born in 1963. We now live in a materialistic world but my childhood was not like that in Israel. My parents were pleased to be there and made sure we understood the sacrifices of our forefathers.

'Football was not in the education programme. School was 8 a.m. until 1 p.m. six days a week because the heat was too great in the afternoon and Saturday was left for Shabbat [the Jewish holy day], where nothing happened but religious practice.'

The Rosenthals lived within five hundred yards of the nearest Mediterranean beach in the Kiryat Eliezer neighbourhood and their apartment block overlooked the old football ground of Maccabi Haifa. Rosenthal's father worked as a taxi driver.

'It was a very friendly place. It was not posh but not poor. Young families, a long promenade and lots of green – which is unusual for Israel because the landscape is very dry. There was grass to play football. I would watch Maccabi games for free because there was a small supermarket on the side of the stadium and my parents were customers, so the owner would let me enter the stadium through his back door and I'd support the team. There would be ten thousand people screaming and I would join in.'

Two days after Rosenthal's tenth birthday, the Yom Kippur War started between Israel and the alliance of Egypt and Syria. It lasted for twenty bloody days. The summer before, eleven Israeli athletes were murdered by the Palestinian group Black September at the Munich Olympics. Israel was always in the news.

'Of course I remember,' Rosenthal says. 'But I cannot remember feeling under threat during those uncertain times. For example, Haifa is an hour or so from Damascus in Syria by car – or maybe a military vehicle. But my parents were very good at making me feel protected. Jewish people had long been persecuted and I think the first people to move back to Israel wanted the next generation to live in safety and also without fear.'

Rosenthal used his afternoons and evenings away from school to practise football. He trained with Maccabi Haifa for the first time when he was eleven years old. 'My dream as a kid was to leave Israel and play for a top club somewhere, you know?' He took a crucial step on that path when he made his professional debut aged sixteen and ten months.

'We played a club from near the Lebanon border and they had a lot of problems hosting matches because of the political situation. I was still in school, so to score in an official game was unbelievable. The game was not on TV, so my friends only read about it in the newspaper. It meant that I could tell them what I wanted. I told them they were the greatest goals ever scored, of course.'

Maccabi were promoted from Israel's second division during Rosenthal's first full season as a professional and have not been relegated since. They finished seventh and sixth before leaping into a title race.

'I was the smallest player in the team. I was probably the smallest player in the league. But at twenty, I became Maccabi's most important player. I was fast and strong. I would run straight at the defenders and they did not know what to do. Some players become men early. I see players now aged sixteen who look twenty-six. I was twenty but looked sixteen. That gave me an advantage, because everyone else underestimated me.'

Rosenthal says he had developed an impressive physique by the time he joined Liverpool but only achieved it by training hard and using the gym. Although he was barely out of his teens and talked about as an important player for the Israeli national team, an English coach of Maccabi had previously tried to release him on a free transfer.

'Jack Mansell was from Manchester. He'd played for Brighton

and Portsmouth before becoming a coach. He moved around Europe – to Galatasaray – before landing a job with the Israeli FA. After some bad results, he left the position but wanted to remain in the country, so Maccabi appointed him. He did not like me very much. I had played for him with the national team. I was in and out. I could not find the consistency that he wanted. He wanted experienced players and I was very young. Mr Mansell went to the president and said that the club was wasting its time with me. But the president was intelligent.

'He [Mansell] made me realize very quickly how ruthless football can be. It is all about opinion. The world is fragile. You think you are doing well then suddenly you vanish. That could have been me. It taught me to ignore people who doubt you and be single-minded. If you want something so much and you try hard to make it happen, it will. You focus. There are a lot of good players who become distracted easily. I did not. I wanted to stay at Maccabi Haifa. So I did.'

Rosenthal likens his own situation then to that of some of the players he works with now.

'A lot of managers only understand the moment – what is good for them as individuals rather than what is a long-term investment for the club. They cannot see how a player will develop in the future with the right guidance. I took Didier Zokora to Harry Redknapp at Portsmouth and to Alan Pardew when he was at West Ham. Didier was a central defender with [Racing] Genk in Belgium but I thought he was perfectly suited as a defensive midfielder. He had all the qualities: the discipline, the leadership and the positioning. He was available for €400,000. After the trial, both Harry and Alan said the same thing: "Not for me." The bottom line is, both managers could have bought the player for peanuts and paid the player's salary, which was also peanuts. Instead, Didier moved to Saint-Étienne for two seasons, where they paid this kind of money – really, really cheap. Saint-Étienne then sold him to Tottenham Hotspur for €11 million. Of course, Harry gets the Tottenham job. One day Harry called me and said, "Ronny, you offered me Bosingwa for €100,000. Now he is worth €20 million. How did I not see it?" I said, "Harry, but what about Zokora?" He did not realize the player in his midfield was the same player I took to Portsmouth three years earlier. So Harry called Zokora into his office. "Boss, I was with you for three days." It was an embarrassing situation for Harry.'

Mansell was soon replaced and his successor, Shlomo Scharf, thought rather more of Rosenthal. In May 1984, Maccabi were on the verge of the first championship in their history.

'Beitar Jerusalem were contenders on the final day with us, which meant we needed to win against a club from the outskirts of Tel Aviv who were trying not to be relegated. The coach took us to a hotel at the top of Mount Carmel, which stands above Haifa. I could see the stadium in the distance and five hours before kick-off it was already full, with twenty thousand people packed together. I realized then that we were talking about a historical moment. Nobody wanted to miss it.'

Rosenthal recalls a nervous day, which even affected Maccabi's groundstaff. 'They laid a fertilizer that killed the pitch. It was really shit. I could not even describe it as a pitch.'

Maccabi just about got the result they wanted: a 1–0 victory. 'The fans jumped over the hoardings and joined us. It was so, so hot and I was desperate for some water, maybe a beer. One guy poured whisky down my neck from a hip flask.'

Rosenthal won another league-winner's medal and would have helped secure a third had it not been for a final-day defeat to Hapoel Tel Aviv in 1986, a game where he was scouted by Club Brugge from Belgium. Twelve months earlier, a week-long trial in Germany with Nürnberg was successful only for a deal to fall through because he needed to complete military service.

'In my mind, I was not ready to leave anyway. The military was important. In the morning I'd be in the barracks and in the afternoon they would let me train with the team. It helped that the boss in the army was a fan of Maccabi Haifa. I wanted to do more but the corporal always said no.'

Brugge had been alerted to Rosenthal's potential by an Israeli agent based in the city.

'Brugge agreed a deal with Maccabi for around £200,000. It was a record fee for Maccabi. It was the perfect move for me. It was the right step at that time. You see players now making the big move earlier and earlier because clubs offer a lot of money. They get swallowed in by the club then spat out. This was not the case at Brugge. I'd waited until I was mature enough to live abroad. I trusted myself. Belgium was halfway between Israel and England in terms of culture and the style of football. It was the intelligent thing to do.'

Brugge or Anderlecht were reliably Belgian champions and both did well in Europe. In his second season, Rosenthal helped Brugge reach the semi-final of the UEFA Cup, where they lost narrowly to Espanyol, letting a two-goal first-leg lead slip.

'We were a very competitive team. In the eighties, the gap between the top team in Belgium and the top team in England was not so big. Now, because of TV, the power is centralized. The TV money allows the English clubs to hoover up all of the top players. Thirty years ago, if you were a club like Brugge, which had a stadium that could hold thirty thousand spectators, plus a little bit of commercial income here and there, you are not too far removed from a club like Liverpool that has maybe more commercial income but not ten times the budget to operate with because the TV money was not there. It might be two times the budget instead. So Brugge could attract international players from Israel, the Netherlands and Denmark. It could keep top Belgian players like Franky Van der Elst, who was a wizard – a brilliant footballer – in Belgium. Now, this is impossible.'

After two years, Brugge – under new management – wanted to sign a promising striker from Standard Liège called Dimitri MBuyu but could not agree a fee. Standard would only agree to a deal if Rosenthal was sacrificed in exchange.

'Standard offered me a better contract, so I went,' Rosenthal says flatly. 'The money was good. It was less than in England but not much less. If a club wants to sign you and they offer more cash and a long-term future, you have to go. I became Standard's top goalscorer and the team finished third, qualifying for the

UEFA Cup ahead of Brugge, which gave me a lot of satisfaction.'

His performances led to an offer of more than £1.5 million from Udinese in Italy.

'Serie A was the best league in the world. Everybody went there. The money was there. Italy was hosting the World Cup in 1990. The stadiums were there. The weather was also good. When Udinese came in with the offer, I was dancing around the room. We agreed the deal and my contract was due to start on 1 July. Then I went on holiday to Israel for the summer and was watching TV when the news station said that I had failed a medical and Udinese were cancelling the deal. Apparently, they preferred the Argentinian striker Abel Balbo to me. I was twenty-five and he was twenty-two. Balbo also had an Italian passport, which meant he would not be considered a foreign player in Italy.'

Rosenthal returned to Standard to find Urbain Braems had been replaced by Georg Kessler as coach. Believing Rosenthal was already another club's player, Kessler had made alternative plans and it became clear that Rosenthal's future lay elsewhere.

'A representative from Luton Town got in touch with me. They'd won the League Cup against Arsenal a few years before and I'd read about it in the newspapers. So I went there for a trial. They had a plastic pitch and the ball was bouncing really high. The manager was Jim Ryan, who later became Alex Ferguson's assistant at Manchester United. He explained that my pace would be an asset on this surface. Luton played with two wingers and I was tempted. While Luton made a financial proposal, I went to Hibernian in Scotland, where Alex Miller was the coach. I have to say, I was very surprised when Liverpool were the next club to make an approach.'

Ron Yeats, Kenny Dalglish's chief scout, had seen Rosenthal score four goals in a friendly match for Luton against Cambridge United. During a ten-day trial at Liverpool, Rosenthal played in three reserve games, scoring against Manchester United, and it was enough for Dalglish to sign him until the end of the 1989–90 season.

'It was the beginning of March and the contract was only

short. I did not have an ego and Liverpool was *the* biggest club, so of course I was going to accept any offer they made me. Kenny explained to me the club believed in me as an impact player but wanted me to develop a level of consistency that meant I could start games.'

Rosenthal was introduced as a substitute for the first time when Liverpool were losing 2–1 at home to Southampton.

'I changed things around. I didn't score but made the corner for the equalizer within three minutes and really added something to the game. Ian Rush scored the winner. I was feeling the pressure but the other players were so relaxed. They knew Liverpool would score late, as they always did. I was naive. I thought I did enough to play the following week but I didn't get off the bench against Wimbledon then was left out of the squad for the FA Cup semi-final with Crystal Palace. This was strange for me because whenever I'd played well before, like I did against Southampton, I was rewarded by the coach.'

The defeat to Palace, which is seen as a watershed moment in Liverpool's history, triggered changes three days later when the squad travelled to London to face Charlton Athletic. Rosenthal was selected in a starting eleven that also included another debutant in Nick Tanner and left-back Steve Staunton wearing the number 7 shirt.

'Kenny was disappointed with Peter Beardsley and told me an hour before the game I'd be playing. After twenty-five minutes, I scored with my right foot, then again immediately after half-time with my left and finally with my head after combining with John Barnes. It was the perfect hat-trick.'

Four goals in the last six games followed and Rosenthal's contribution to Liverpool's last league triumph was marked. His form saw Standard's asking price rise considerably but that did not deter Liverpool from securing a permanent deal in the summer.

'I was one of the most expensive foreign players to join an English club from abroad at the time,' Rosenthal says proudly. 'The fee did not bring an unreasonable pressure. I think I gave back to Liverpool what they paid. When I analyse my career, I would admit that I was not a prolific goalscorer. But I was some-one who could change the game at any time. Now I see things from the other side [as a scout] and I would say that if I was a manager, I would pay a lot of money for an impact player like me. You need one or two: players that will find solutions when the game is tight. Every manager wants this but there are not a lot of them around.'

In many of the photographs taken in the dressing room after the 2–1 victory over Queens Park Rangers at Anfield that sealed the First Division title, Rosenthal is pictured sitting there with his short red shorts, his socks around his ankles, with beers in both hands, flanked by Kenny Dalglish and Roy Evans.

'We had some champagne also and there was a bit of singing. But there was not a night of massive celebration. We had a meal with our families. Hey, we were expected to win. Had I known then that it was going to be Liverpool's last title, I would have made more of it.'

Rosenthal enjoyed the culture of English football. He would choose to drink white wine over lager but 'would act like one of the boys when I needed to'. He also relished playing in the atmos-phere of the stadiums, where the stands were much closer to the pitch than in Europe.

'I'd never experienced anything like it before. In England, the crowd is very powerful. It can have an impact on the result of a match. Most games, there was a capacity crowd and the energy it created was unbelievable. I had played against Panathinaikos and Red Star Belgrade for Brugge with seventy or eighty thousand inside the stadium. In England, half that number of people could make the same noise.'

Rosenthal insists he never suffered racist abuse in his career. Yet he feels that foreign players in England were blamed when results were not meeting expectations.

'When the team is not doing well, the first players that suffer are always foreign, although it's not xenophobia,' he explains. 'It's a natural reaction of managers. They think it is easier to correct a problem by passing their message on to players who speak the same language. It happened at Liverpool. It happened at Tottenham. But it also happened at Brugge.'

Rosenthal was frustrated when Dalglish omitted him regularly from match squads the following season, especially when results were indifferent and he could not 'help the team get back on track to the levels of before'.

One of Dalglish's last tricks as Liverpool manager was to sign David Speedie.

'We had the same attributes: strong, direct, aggressive and quick; only I was quicker,' Rosenthal says. 'I was disappointed because it felt like Kenny had lost faith in me. I realize now, though, that maybe his judgement was not correct. He resigned soon after because of the stress.'

Under Graeme Souness, Rosenthal's role was a continuation of before: best used from the substitutes' bench when other teams were tiring. Yet results for the team were not of the expected standard.

'Graeme had absolute control of the transfers, so he bought his own players,' Rosenthal continues. 'Liverpool did not win enough. Sure, some players wanted to leave. But he was given the finances to replace them. The players he bought were like him. As a player, Graeme was one of my favourites to watch. He had everything: technique, he was aggressive and a leader. But as a manager, this is not enough. You can have a few players like this but not every player. If you have eleven players doing the same thing, it does not work.'

Rosenthal noticed that a lot of Souness's signings were not quick enough to implement Liverpool's traditional passing game.

'Liverpool always had fast players – dynamic right-backs and left-backs. Barry Venison and Steve Nicol were like this. Not many teams in England wanted the full-backs to attack but Liverpool did. It was the same in midfield. There were players who could do a bit of everything: passing, tackling and moving. Suddenly, we had Paul Stewart, who was a good player but not a good

Liverpool player. Paul was not the only problem, though. It was a combination of all the transfers and the jigsaw not working.'

Rosenthal does not solely blame Souness for Liverpool's decline.

'I liked Graeme then and I like Graeme now. I sometimes worked with him when he was manager of Blackburn and I offered him Peter Odemwingie for £150,000 when he was playing for La Louvière in Belgium. Graeme rejected the opportunity and Peter instead moved to Lille for the same fee. Within two seasons, he'd signed for Lokomotiv Moscow for £10 million.

'Graeme understands better than anyone that a manager lives and dies by his transfers. When he was at Liverpool, I believe the structure around him wasn't as stable as it should have been. The club was naive in thinking its methods would be successful forever. The game remains the same but everything around football was changing. Scouting was improving at other clubs, who were looking a lot closer at Europe for new signings. At Liverpool, there was one scout – Ron Yeats. Other clubs – Manchester United, for example – were appointing full-time scouts in Scandinavia and northern Europe. Liverpool missed out on these players.'

In Souness's first full season, Rosenthal played in twenty-seven games and scored just three goals. One came during a victory over Notts County in the League Cup and the two others could not prevent Liverpool from losing at home to Chelsea and Wimbledon.

'I remember this game against Wimbledon because the attendance inside Anfield was very low [26,134]. It was April and it became my last game of the season. When the team won the FA Cup a month later, I was not even in the squad. We won the cup but it was the minimum we should have been achieving. There was no sense of celebration.'

Rosenthal's goal ratio improved in the next campaign, with six being registered in twenty-seven league appearances. Yet it is his miss at Aston Villa that is best remembered. From a David James kick, Villa's centre-back Shaun Teale misjudged the ball's flight and Rosenthal nipped in to round goalkeeper Nigel Spink. Free of any opposition player, Rosenthal took another touch and honed in on the Holte End. With his left foot, Rosenthal struck from nine yards out but just as the connection was made, he leant back. With Jan Mølby fifteen yards behind and turning, veering off towards Liverpool's supporters in anticipation of the goal, the shot crashed against the crossbar, allowing Teale to clear. Mølby realized nobody on the terraces was celebrating. Rosenthal would later score but Liverpool lost 4–2.

While Danish defender Torben Piechnik struggled on his debut and would not improve, Dean Saunders – who Souness had sold to Villa just two weeks before, after listening to teammates who did not want to play with him – scored twice to compound a miserable afternoon. The pressure on Souness was telling and he cancelled a planned dinner with Villa's manager, Ron Atkinson, and drove home up the M6 in tears, wondering whether it was time to resign.

'I get asked about this game a lot,' Rosenthal says, offering an ironic smile. 'With pleasure, I always answer,' he continues, although not too convincingly. 'I always say, you need to have the confidence to miss otherwise you should not be playing. I am not making excuses but there was a little bounce. Teale was getting closer and closer, so I put a little bit more power into the shot than usual. Instead, it lifted. I have seen this happen in training before with other players and everyone laughs. Of course, this is not acceptable in a real match. I can say, though, that it never affected me in the way you might think. When people ask, I say, "Hey, I am happy that I am still on the map." It even helps with my work now. When I speak to struggling players, I tell them it could be a lot worse. They could be me! This cheers them up.'

A sixth-place finish and early exits in all cup competitions represented one of Liverpool's worst seasons in living memory. It was made worse by the fact Manchester United won their first title in twenty-six years, with Liverpool's future chief executive Rick Parry presenting them with the trophy at Old Trafford. Rosenthal, though, could see some positives. While several of the United youth team that won the FA Youth Cup in 1992 made their first-team debuts, Souness was promoting from within as well. Jamie Redknapp and Steve McManaman had emerged as first-team regulars, while Rosenthal was feeling the pressure from a seventeen-year-old Robbie Fowler.

'In training, this player [Fowler] was ruthless,' Rosenthal recalls. 'It seemed like he scored with every single chance. He had a lot of confidence and mixed well with the boys. There was the swagger of a typical Liverpool lad. I remember him telling me he wanted to replace Ian Rush as Liverpool's number 9. This is quite a thing to say when you have not made your debut. Graeme must have been very tempted to use him. The fans might have been more patient. But I think Graeme realized if things went wrong, as they did, it might kill the player's progress. So he was quite selfless in that respect.'

Liverpool began the 1993–94 season by securing three wins in a row. Within a month, however, Souness's team failed to score in four successive games, a run that included defeat in the Merseyside derby where McManaman and Bruce Grobbelaar started fighting on the pitch.

It was enough to make Souness use Fowler, and against Fulham in the League Cup the striker scored all of Liverpool's goals in a 5–0 victory in front of just 12,541 people – the lowest attendance at Anfield in decades, another marker of attitudes and fortunes. Fowler remained in the team and was swiftly ordained by the Kop as 'God'. Yet even divine intervention could not prevent Souness's exit, which finally came in January 1994, and Rosenthal was the last player to be sold before his departure.

At Tottenham, Rosenthal would partner German centre-forward Jürgen Klinsmann in attack – a World Cup winner. Rosenthal believes Klinsmann was the profile of player that Liverpool needed to revive their flagging fortunes, though the management and board would never have sanctioned such a deal.

'Liverpool was still a very conservative club, which only really wanted to sign the best British players,' Rosenthal explains. 'But by 1993–94, they had a lot of competition for these players. Leeds came. United were becoming stronger. Arsenal were there. Liverpool lost its domination of the league. For a long time, the club could get away with paying lower wages for players because of its history of success. Then – now, even – it wasn't there to fall back on.'

Between 1992 and 1997, Manchester United, whose directors realized the potential of brand-management in the Far East at a time the club was becoming successful on the pitch, generated an income of £249 million, of which £66 million was reported as profit. Meanwhile, the London clubs were attractive to players because of their location. 'Arsenal, Tottenham and Chelsea could all offer bigger wages because it was London. It's like anything else, if you work in London, you earn more money than if you work in Liverpool. The rule applies to football as well. I left Liverpool for Tottenham and earned more money. This meant foreign players like Klinsmann would choose Tottenham over Liverpool too.'

Liverpool's record in recruiting players from outside the British Isles was poor between 1990 and 1995 and has never been as good as rivals like United and Arsenal. Rosenthal believed it was initially down to an absence of cultural understanding when all aspects of football were changing quickly, particularly in the way clubs operated in the transfer market. He uses his own situation as an example.

'Liverpool had a secret and that secret was very simple: everybody was working the same amount all of the time. It was relentless. But I was an explosive player – maybe I should have been a hundred-metre sprinter. I needed time to recover. I could not run like a maniac for ninety minutes non-stop. There were periods in the game where I was quiet. Maybe the coaches did not realize that I was more influential when I came into the game in the last thirty minutes. I was lethal. When I started the game, slowly, slowly I would fade. Instead, they thought I was resting – taking it easy, because of a different mentality. People at the club from the very top were slow to understand the foreign player.'

Although Liverpool later appointed Rick Parry as its first modern chief executive, Rosenthal thinks it came too late. He also believes that the idea of a football manager being 'all-controlling' is a dated concept and thinks it would be beneficial for a club's long-term stability if it appointed a director of football with a specialist knowledge of recruitment and football finance.

'Manchester United's chairman Martin Edwards was a visionary and he could see the way football was going,' Rosenthal says. 'Liverpool did not want to admit that football was becoming a business. The board was focused only on football and it missed out. This is a decision that the club still suffers from.

'Football is a business now whether you like it or not. For a football club to be successful it needs each person to be able to function in his strongest position. Some people are better at training the players. Some people are better at negotiating. Why not leave them to operate at their strongest?

'The days of a manager being able to see everything are over. They need help. They need specialists who can analyse specifics. When the manager is the only person who can say what is good, this is a problem and it explains why so many clubs have gone bust. The majority of managers only want to buy for now. You must also buy for the future.'

Since retiring as a player under Graham Taylor at Watford in 1999, Rosenthal has been offered interesting positions at a variety of clubs, although he is reluctant to tell me which ones.

'To be honest, I think I have the skill to be a perfect director of football at any top club. I am skilled at identifying and understanding the value of the player commercially. I speak many languages and I have the football experience that many directors do not have. But I have a good life: good wife and kids. The focus should be on my son, Tom, and his career, not me at this stage.'

For the time being, Rosenthal will continue to operate in the shadows.

CHAPTER FOUR

cultzeros.co.uk

THE GOOD-LOOKING ONE,
Jamie Redknapp, 1991–2002

'IT WAS THE BIGGEST FUCKING MISTAKE WE MADE,' SCOWLS JAMIE
Redknapp in an interview where swear words are used almost
exclusively when discussing this particular subject. 'If we'd have
won the match,' Redknapp pauses, readjusting his body, pointing to his right. 'I'd probably have that white suit framed on my
living-room wall over there.'

Redknapp is referring to the FA Cup final of 1996, an occasion where it was suggested by goalkeeper David James – a model
with Armani – and agreed by the senior Liverpool players, that
the squad should complete its pre-match amble around Wembley
Stadium wearing attire that, at best, made them look like a team
of turf accountants at the wrong sports event, or, more realisti-
cally, as Redknapp admits, 'a bunch of idiots'.

Redknapp remembers being presented with the suit at a
Melwood photo shoot before the meeting with Manchester

United. 'My first reaction was to say, "Wow!" But everyone was focused on the final; it didn't seem to matter. We all went with it. Nobody stopped it happening.'

The previous Sunday, Liverpool had let slip a two-goal half-time lead at Maine Road to draw in the final game of the Premier League season. It was a curious occasion, where Manchester City believed they had escaped relegation only to find out they'd gone down on goal difference, with Southampton benefiting. It was also a classic Liverpool collapse. A month earlier, Roy Evans' side remained in contention for their first championship in six years by beating Newcastle United in the first of those famous 4–3 games, only to lose hopelessly at Coventry a week later, gifting United with a clear run to the title.

'We were finishing third no matter the result at City, so it was understandable we eased off in the second half,' Redknapp reasons. 'At half-time, Roy [Evans] told us not to do anything stupid, because he didn't want anyone getting injured for the FA Cup final. City also had everything to play for, so it was no surprise they ended up getting something from the game.'

Back to the hideous suits, which to the critics confirmed that Liverpool's pretty young things were more concerned with how they looked off the pitch than how they performed on it. The football media considered them a team that lacked the bottle to turn their slick passing game into a realistic title challenge.

'It was typical of the flak we received,' Redknapp says. 'Yes, we had a young team but you wouldn't catch any of us out on a Thursday or Friday night before a game. If one of us had been out – and we weren't – we would have deserved to be in trouble.'

Redknapp was confident of a victory over United.

'The spirit was really good, better than it had been at any other point in my Liverpool career. That season, we'd played United off the park at Old Trafford, with Robbie [Fowler] lashing two goals past Peter Schmiechel. A couple of refereeing decisions went against us and they managed to scrape a draw on the day Eric Cantona returned from his long ban for kung-fu kicking the Crystal Palace fan at Selhurst Park.

'Then, at Anfield, we did them 2–0 with Robbie on fire again. On a level, we had the measure of them. In my eyes, we could have walked round Wembley wearing flip-flops, never mind white suits. It wouldn't have mattered, because we had confidence that we'd beat them.'

Redknapp, a former Liverpool midfielder and captain, is now a seasoned pundit with Sky Sports. I meet him on a bright midsummer afternoon at his home in Oxshott, Surrey, the most expensive village in England and the premier address for top footballers. Oxshott is one stop on the South West railway line from Cobham, where Chelsea's training ground is situated. Redknapp can count John Terry amongst his neighbours as well as tennis player Andy Murray. It is to the south of England what Wilmslow or Alderley Edge is to the north.

Redknapp greets me by offering a lift from the nearest station in his top-of-the-range Mercedes Benz. He winds down the smoke-tinted window on the passenger side and, leaning over, removes his sports cap in an act of courtesy, introducing himself. His face is smooth, tanned and unshaven. His smile reveals two rows of excellent white teeth. His inky brown eyes remain deep enough for a swim. The car roars with pleasure as Jamie switches on the ignition before settling at a gentle speed, coolly using one hand to steer the wheel, easily negotiating the country lanes.

Sandwiched between the A3 and M25 and known as the country's 'wealth corridor' according to Savills estate agency, Oxshott is thirty-five minutes from Waterloo in central London. Not a single family house on the Crown Estate where Redknapp lives is for sale for much under £2.5 million.

It has not always been this way. In 1885, Oxshott was, as it had been for centuries, a hamlet of pig farmers living on ancient hunting land owned by the Crown. The arrival of the railway led to the development of a high street that contained three shops – a draper's, tobacconist and set of tea rooms – as well as a rapidly growing community of comfortably well-off commuters living in new-build mock-Tudor homes.

Today, the high street has twelve shops that include four estate agents, three interior stores and the Clay Salon and Spa, which describes itself as a 'blissful sanctuary of tranquillity'. They serve rows of homogeneous multi-million-pound houses, commonly owned by twenty-something footballers and thirty-something fund managers, mostly sited on 'The Crown', as the main patrolled estate is locally known.

Here, each property is built on half an acre or so, separated from the others by red-brick walls and swathes of evergreen foliage. In 2011, a report in the *Sunday Telegraph* revealed that there are no listed properties in the area. Currently, the old manor houses built in the fifties are falling down faster than Didier Drogba in the penalty box. So too are the detached houses from the sixties, seventies, eighties and even the nineties, making way for neo-Georgian stone pads, like Redknapp's home, which is safely tucked behind an electric wrought-iron gate.

'We've been here for nearly seven years,' Redknapp tells me as he parks on the block-paved drive, where there are already five other cars, including a mandatory large black Range Rover Sport. 'I lived in north London when I was at Spurs. But for some reason, I never took to it. I like it more down here.'

Redknapp removes his Adidas training shoes as he pushes through the huge front door and steps on to a wide marble-floored entrance hall that opens into a guest sitting room on the right and a kitchen to the left, where his wife and former pop star Louise Nurding is waiting.

Wearing a pair of cotton tracksuit bottoms and an oversized woollen jumper, Louise briefly discusses secondary-education options with Jamie for their ten-year-old son Charley. 'I'd like Charley to focus more on school than I did, because I didn't focus and it's a bit of a regret,' Jamie says, while a kettle of water boils in the background as he offers me a selection of flapjacks and caramel shortbreads from Waitrose, to accompany the steaming mug of tea that follows shortly.

We leave Louise filling in forms and move into the aforementioned guest sitting room, a space that, despite its size, I suspect is used rarely. There is a clinical opulence: sophisticated French-style bay windows affording shards of natural light through the towering Monterey pines outside. There are cream walls and carpet, a two-tone grey-fur rug and a glass table. We sit on two comfy black-leather couches and the interview begins.

Financially, football has served Redknapp better than any of the other characters in this book. Football is the family business. There is his father, Harry, who has managed teams for four decades; Harry's brother-in-law is Frank Lampard senior, who played for England and West Ham United, and his son Frank Lampard, who followed the same path before becoming a legend at Chelsea. When Jamie was Liverpool captain, he faced his father and the Lampards when they were all involved at West Ham.

'I caught Frank with a late tackle on the ankle and he had to go off,' Jamie remembers. 'Les Sealey was my dad's goalkeeping coach, God bless his soul. He ran over to Frank on the touchline and I could hear him shouting, "Go back and do him, Frank. Go back and do him good and proper." My dad was standing behind him in front of the dugout shaking his head. He was saying, "Hang on, Les – that's my son!" It was a really weird feeling. I suppose that's football for you.'

I suggest to Jamie that football must be in his DNA. He believes it is more to do with 'obsession' and necessity colliding. Harry entered management when his playing career was over because there were no other options. Football was all he knew. He was not qualified to do anything else. To tell Jamie's story is also to tell Harry's.

'My grandfather was a dock worker in the east end of London,' Jamie explains. 'He was crazy about football and used to go to Arsenal a lot. He was a grafter and my dad was the same. After he finished playing, his only immediate path was into coaching or management. I'm sure he would have found another way eventually if that hadn't worked out, because he's a survivor.'

Jamie was three years old when the Redknapps moved to the United States after Harry accepted a player-coaching role with the Seattle Sounders in the North American Soccer League.

'My dad had to go where the work was, like any other regular family in the seventies, because he hadn't made enough money out of the game to sit on his bum for the rest of his life. The difference was, my dad would take me to training most days. I fell in love with the game very quickly. When we moved back to England, I have more memories of training at Bournemouth than I do of being at school. I'm not saying I'm proud of that. Without knowing it, my dad was subconsciously making me a footballer.'

Aged eleven, Redknapp was allowed to take part in full-scale training matches with Bournemouth's professionals.

'They were adults, good players. Ian Bishop was there and he later signed for Manchester City. Shaun Teale progressed his career with Aston Villa. My dad wanted me to play and compete. If I gave the ball away, it would mess up the session. It made my touch so much better than it should have been.'

Jamie played for a Sunday-league team in Bournemouth. Harry watched every match but stood quietly.

'He never interfered. He later told me that Ron Greenwood, West Ham's manager, wouldn't allow any parent to shout from the touchline. Ron thought that players should think for themselves. Although my dad was in a position to give the best advice, he was the one who said the least and just let me get on with it. The rest of them would be screaming, "Get rid of it." Of course, they were wrong.'

Although by then comfortable enough, Harry made sure Jamie took on a paper round as a teenager – to learn the value of money.

'I was the spare boy and covered for my brother Mark if he was unavailable. Mark was three years older than me and a decent footballer. He would have had a career if it wasn't for an ankle injury that left him in pain for days after games. The paper round meant I had to learn all of the routes. Bournemouth is hardly *The Wire* but my dad didn't really like me being out alone on my bike. He just wanted me to experience the discipline of working for a wage. If the call from the newsagent came at short notice, he'd whizz me around in his car and help me deliver the papers to the door.'

Harry was regularly recognized.

'"Harry Redknapp . . . what are you doing?" one season-ticket holder at Bournemouth asked. "Yeah, yeah," he'd say. "Times are hard, I'm not getting paid much by the chairman that runs your club." Then he'd walk off, laughing to himself.'

Management in the football league's lowest divisions was stressful for Harry, even with twenty years' experience behind him as a player.

'My mum [Sandra] never went to watch my dad. She's a very quiet and unassuming lady. We're very protective of her. She doesn't ride a bike; she can't swim. She's very gentle. To be able to put up with us being obsessed with football, it's probably best that she's very relaxed. Even now when we're having dinner, the conversation will be based around football. She's very patient and always has been. My dad could get stressed at work but it's all he's ever known. People tell me that at his age [now in his late sixties], he shouldn't be managing. But I think it's the best thing for him. He likes stress. Whenever Bournemouth lost, it was horrible because I knew how much he cared. If he won, on the Saturday night he'd treat us to a Chinese takeaway. All I cared about as a kid was Bournemouth winning, because I wanted to see him happy. I'm like that now. Of course I've got a soft spot for Liverpool, because my kids support them, but the first result I look out for is whichever team my dad is managing. It was the same whenever I was a Liverpool player. If we won and he won, the weekend would be complete.'

During the course of this interview, it is clear that Jamie and Harry share more than just an average father–son bond. A friendship exists. The pair were brought closer together when Jamie was seventeen, a few months before he joined Liverpool. While visiting Italy during the 1990 World Cup, Harry was involved in a road accident with Bournemouth's managing director Brian Tiler. Travelling near Rome, their minibus collided with a van containing several Italian soldiers and Harry's vehicle was flipped on to its roof and skidded fifty yards along the road. Tiler was killed, while Harry was doused in petrol and pulled clear of the accident, suffering a fractured skull, a broken nose, cracked ribs and a gash in his left leg. Ambulance services arriving at the scene believed him dead and placed a blanket over his head. Unconscious for two days, Harry was flown home two weeks later in a special air ambulance paid for by Bournemouth. Though he recovered, the physical scars remain, with Harry developing a facial tic and losing his sense of smell.

'It was a terrible time,' Jamie remembers. 'It made me realize, maybe a bit earlier than it might have, just how important family is. I know he'd do anything for me. He's like a best mate. I'm a parent myself now but I still speak to him two or three times a day. I just want to make sure he's OK. We protect each other.'

Harry's presence in the stands at Anfield would have an effect on Jamie's performances.

'It gave me a lift. I'd walk off at half-time and I could see him sitting there just to the left of the tunnel. I'd look at him and I could tell by his expression how I was doing. It could be a subtle thumbs-up that said, "Yeah, you're doing great," and I'd feel ten feet tall. Then there'd be other times when I'd see a glare and him standing there gritting his teeth as if to say, "Come on, liven up." A lot of the time I didn't worry about what the managers or the coaches said. That's not being disrespectful to them, because Roy Evans, for instance, got on very well with my dad, as they saw the game the same way. Ultimately, though, I only wanted to please my dad. If I did, it meant so much to me.'

There were periods when Harry was preoccupied by his duties as West Ham manager, so other family members watched Jamie instead.

'My granddad would go to a lot of matches. Say we were playing United, I'd be nervous getting off the bus. I'd be reminding myself of what I was about to do, playing in front of thousands and thousands of people for Liverpool. Then I'd see my granddad standing in the Main Stand car park waiting for me with two cheese-and-pickle sandwiches. At the beginning, he only brought one for me. But after games, me and Macca [Steve McManaman] would drop him off at Lime Street Station. Granddad felt bad that he only had one roll, so after a while he made my gran make a second one for Macca too. She made sure there was extra butter on Macca's because he had spindly legs and she thought he needed feeding up.'

It wasn't always easy being a manager's son. Jamie played thirteen games for Bournemouth over the course of eighteen months.

'Some people might have thought that I was only getting a chance because my dad was the manager. They didn't realize that it's harder, really. If things went wrong, I'd be the first one to be dropped. I felt I should have had more games. We'd have that conversation over breakfast. But I realize now, my dad had to be careful with me.

'I had long hair and didn't really look like a footballer. In the lower leagues, there were real men, guys that could get away with kicking you. Most of the players were in their late twenties or early thirties. Clubs didn't really have youth systems. Football was different. You could tackle. You could injure someone else and get away with it. Tony Pulis was my partner in midfield and he was an absolute animal.

'My league debut came at Hull and they had Billy Whitehurst up front. We won 4–1 and I came on with fifteen minutes to go. I remember playing the ball out to our left-back, Paul Morrell, and it was a bit short. Billy notoriously had a short temper and his head was boiling because we were beating them easily. Billy went and whacked Paul high in the air. Then he got hold of Paul and lifted him off his feet by the throat. I thought to myself, "Jesus, that's my fault."'

Word of a lank-haired teenager in Bournemouth's midfield spread north. One of Ron Yeats's southern-based scouts recommended to Kenny Dalglish that he should take a look.

'My dad was at a football-league managers' dinner in London. It was a bow-tie affair. The story goes that towards the end of the night, my dad was having a dance with my mum. He must have had a drink, because he never dances. My dad realized that Kenny was following him around the dance floor with his wife, Marina. Eventually, he caught up with him and said, "Listen, I want to sign your son."

'Dad came home and woke me up in the early hours of the morning. He said, "You won't believe this, son, but Kenny Dalglish wants to sign you for Liverpool." Liverpool were the biggest club in the world. They were my favourite club other than Bournemouth. Kenny was my favourite player. Can you imagine my reaction? After that, Kenny would ring my dad every Sunday morning for an update on my progress.'

Eventually, a trial was agreed.

'Kenny made a real fuss of me. It couldn't have gone any better. Then he explained that he was going to put me in the youth team. I'd only left Tottenham [aged fourteen] for Bournemouth because I wanted to experience first-team football sooner. The path at Tottenham was blocked because they had some very talented boys in the reserves. It seemed daft to go from league football to youth football again. Liverpool felt like a backward step.'

There were also reservations about working with youth-team coach Steve Heighway, Liverpool's legendary former winger.

'I didn't really hit it off with him to be honest. It was difficult. I think he thought my signing was being forced upon him. When I decided not to jump at the offer straight away, he got the impression that I was trying to skip the youth-development phase at Liverpool. That wasn't the case. I knew that staying with my dad and playing in front of crowds would give me a better experience. I was also a baby in football terms. I would have been the only southerner in the youth team at Liverpool and I was happy at home living with my mum and dad. I didn't see why I needed to rush, because I was in a good place.'

Within six months, Redknapp was ready to move and the night before signing he stayed at the old Moat House Hotel on Paradise Street in Liverpool's city centre with his father. The Moat House was the place where the Liverpool squad gathered before getting the bus to Anfield for home matches and a favourite watering hole amongst the players.

'At 3 a.m., you could hear police sirens. Someone had been shot dead outside. We heard the bangs. The next morning it was like a scene from *Police Squad*, where they make a cordon and draw an outline of the body on the floor. My dad looked at me and said, "Listen, son, do not tell your mum about this . . ." I was a Bournemouth boy, you know?'

The Redknapps were told to make their way to Anfield.

'Ronnie Moran greeted me at the door, as he did every morning, shouting really loudly, "Och aye the noo." To this day, I have no idea what he meant. I was petrified.'

Redknapp changed with the reserve team in the away dressing room.

'It was a lot quieter than the first team in the home dressing room. Nobody said much to me. I found it hard with a couple of the boys. Alex Watson had gone to Bournemouth as part of the deal that brought me to Liverpool. That upset one or two of his mates in the reserves. They were cold with me. I felt as though a few people weren't on my side. It felt like I had more to do to win them over than other newcomers might have. When Kenny left, I had a bit of a struggle. They were quick to have a dig. It wasn't easy. I felt lonely for a while. That's when you've got to hang in there and be strong.'

On his first day, Redknapp struggled to find a seat on the bus to Melwood.

'I went to sit down somewhere only to be told by Steve McMahon that it was Alan Hansen's place. So I chose another space and Jan Mølby chirped up, saying it was Bruce Grobbelaar's. It felt like the first day at school. They had me on a piece of string. I had John Barnes to thank because he invited me to the back of the bus. He looked at me and went, "Hello, pretty boy, do you like the girls?" I smiled like a geek. I had pictures of Barnesy on my wall at home. He was another hero. I didn't know what to say. I was a fresh-faced-looking lad with long hair. I think he thought I was gay. "Sure, I like the girls," I responded nervously.

'The journey to Melwood seemed to take forever. It was snowing and we did a session on the cinder pitch. We were warming up and as I've gone to pass the ball, I've slipped up in the ice. I went arse over tit. I nearly broke my back. I could hear the shouts, "How much? How much did we pay for him, Kenny?" Then everyone laughed.'

During his first week as a Liverpool player, Redknapp was invited to stay with Dalglish and his family in Birkdale.

'Kenny was amazing with me. I'd only just passed my test but he asked me to drive his car. Marina made us a lovely dinner. We were playing Wimbledon at the weekend and he told me I was in the squad. I couldn't believe it. I figured I'd be the fourteenth man, as there were only two subs. On the morning of the game, Marina made us both breakfast: eggs and beans. Kenny kept talking to me like I was a senior player – someone important, someone ready to play for Liverpool. In my head, I thought, "Surely not – he's not going to include me in the thirteen."

'I entered the dressing room and sat out of the way, next to where the coaches sit. Seventeen or eighteen players were in there. Kenny reads the team out: Grobbelaar, Ablett, Burrows, Nicol, Staunton, Gillespie, Carter, Mølby, Rush, Barnes and McMahon. The subs were next. I heard him say Ronny Rosenthal. I was still in awe of my surroundings, watching John Barnes get changed. Then everyone started shaking my hand. Because I wasn't listening for it, I didn't hear. Rushy went, "You're thirteenth man, congratulations." What a feeling that was.'

Redknapp remained on the bench during a 1–1 draw, secured by a late equalizer from the visitors' right-back, Warren Barton.

'At half-time, Ronny didn't want to go out and warm up but I was desperate to experience the atmosphere – to see the fans and be out on the pitch kicking the ball around. There was a big cheer because there'd been a bit of fuss about the fee Liverpool had paid for me.'

Redknapp became the most expensive seventeen year old in football when Liverpool paid £350,000, with the fee later rising to £500,000. Yet he would never play for Dalglish, who resigned within a month.

'Kenny must have been going through some personal torment on the day he decided to walk away but it didn't stop him from ringing me. He was very calm and assured me that I'd be a big part of Liverpool's future. It meant an awful lot.

'It was a tough environment anyway but the uncertainty made things more intense because I was the new boy. It felt like Ronnie Moran [who'd been made temporary manager] was having a go at me all the time. For a few weeks, he was relentless. He'd give me stick, shouting, effing and blinding. I couldn't understand it. I didn't realize why at the time but Ronnie was trying to be consistent with what had gone before. It had always been Ronnie's way. You had to roll with the punches at Liverpool. I spoke to Steve McManaman about it. I couldn't figure out why Ronnie was always having a go at me but never Steve, for instance. The thing was, Macca was more established, whereas Ronnie knew he had to work on me – beat out all the insecurities. Macca promised me that, soon enough, Ronnie would leave me alone and start on someone else. And he did. Eventually, Ronnie just called me "Harry".'

Redknapp was placed in digs with Don Hutchison, a midfielder who later became the first player sold during Roy Evans' reign as manager after being pictured by a tabloid newspaper exposing himself during a drunken night out.

'I stayed with Mrs Sainsbury for a while on Anfield Road as a lodger in her big terraced house. Unfortunately, she didn't cook like Sainsbury's; every night she'd serve up powdered Smash. A young Irish player called Mark Kenny was in there with me. It was difficult because you'd wake up every morning, open the curtains and the Shankly Gates were there. You never got away from it.

'The club then moved me in with Don on the Brookside Estate where the soap opera was filmed, just around the corner from Melwood. We'd see characters like Jimmy Corkhill and Ron Dixon driving to work. It was a good laugh, quite a few parties. Don had got a place of his own and it became one of those gaffs where everyone in Liverpool ended up going back to at the end of a night out. It was known as the place to go and it's not how it should have been. Don had his problems with the management and I was pulled out of there by Graeme [Souness]. It was the best thing he ever did for me.'

Redknapp went to live with Alan and Janet Collier and their two young kids in Sandfield Park, closer to the training ground.

'I was going to buy an apartment and Graeme told me, "No chance – you're meeting this family." Lodging with two old folks was the last thing I wanted to do, even though they had a beautiful house with an indoor swimming pool. But I was still there in 1995 when I made my England debut against Colombia. I'm probably one of the only international footballers to have been living in digs. They were great with me. If I ever wanted to bring a girlfriend home, they were cool with it. Alan was a bit of a boy, to be fair. He knew everyone, so if I ever got myself into silly scrapes he knew the right people.'

In the early days, McManaman became Redknapp's closest friend.

'Before signing in the January, I watched Liverpool's victory over Blackburn in the FA Cup replay from the stands. Macca was eighteen years old and he was on the bench. I could see his touch and passing range in the warm-up. He only got on for the last five minutes or so but he had an impact, dribbling past opponents like they weren't there. I was sitting with my dad and both of us were open-mouthed. What a player. I realized there and then that his was the standard I had to get to. Macca was only twelve months older than me. So it was a huge step up.

'In the summer holidays now, we go to Mallorca with our families. Macca's the nicest guy you could meet. Very generous. Never has a go at anyone. I've got a lot of time for him.'

It might not have been the case for Nick Tanner but Redknapp says he received a lot of support from Liverpool's senior players.

'They were brilliant with me, considering I was coming into their world – people like Ronnie Whelan and Steve McMahon. We played in the same position and they might have thought I was there to take their place. But it never showed. John Barnes couldn't help me enough. I'd watch him in training and he'd never give the ball away. He was calm in possession and treated the ball as his friend. If the team was struggling, he'd go hunting and take responsibility. I tried to take that attitude into my game.

'Ian Rush was such a clever player too. He had this ability to always pounce on a defender's mistakes. He'd toe the ball away from you and score within seconds. He did it to me ten times in the first two weeks. Fucking hell, he was brilliant. You didn't see that kind of craftiness with Bournemouth in the Second Division.'

It took Liverpool's board nearly three months to appoint a full-time replacement for Dalglish.

'Graeme [Souness] didn't say a word to me for months. The first time he said something was before I made my debut [in the defeat at Auxerre in the UEFA Cup the following season]. Nobody owed me anything but I signed as a kid at seventeen and maybe I needed a bit of guidance. I suppose I wasn't Graeme's signing, so I had to win him over. We got on great in the end but had a few run-ins at the start.

'I love Graeme,' Redknapp continues, speaking about their current relationship while working for Sky. 'But when he came into Liverpool, he was a different Graeme to the one I now know. He was very aggressive. He was having wars with everybody when he didn't need to, really. If he had his time again, I'm sure he'd have been different with the players. He would have been a bit more relaxed. He's a legend, Graeme, and he knows it. He has an aura. He's intense. If he'd gone in there with a feather rather than a sledgehammer, he might have been more successful. He tried to take on too much too soon.'

Souness tried to change the players' lifestyles by cutting down on fatty foods as well as alcohol.

'The problem was, the older pros still at Liverpool from Graeme's time as a player remembered him and what he was like – someone who loved socializing, someone who was a bit of a glamour-puss. His nickname was "Champagne Charlie", wasn't it? Graeme used to be one of the lads and got away with a lot – being the captain, supremely confident and strong-willed. Suddenly, he was laying down the law to people like Bruce Grobbelaar and Ronnie Whelan, who thought it was hypocritical.

'There was lots of moaning and bickering behind his back, and even as a kid I could see that everyone wasn't pulling in the same direction. The worst thing about it was that nobody would pull up Graeme to his face. Everyone was too scared. It created a negative working environment. It spilled on to the pitch. Individuals weren't performing to their potential and the team was suffering.'

Redknapp probably benefited from the uncertainty. He might not have shown it but Souness regarded Redknapp highly, issuing him with the same number 11 shirt that he'd worn as a European Cup-winning captain a decade earlier.

Aged just nineteen, Redknapp played forty times for Liverpool during a 1992–93 campaign where the team finished sixth in the league, were knocked out of the European Cup-Winners' Cup early by Spartak Moscow and also suffered humbling exits in the League and FA cups to Crystal Palace and Bolton Wanderers. Souness was given until January 1994 and may have stayed longer but decided to resign following another FA Cup third-round exit at home to Bristol City.

This time, chairman David Moores and his board waited just four days to make an appointment, with Roy Evans promoted from the role of assistant to manager.

'Compared to Graeme, Roy was a bit more personable but I wouldn't say he was nice,' Redknapp says. 'At Liverpool, you never got told, "Well done." I can't remember being given praise once. At the beginning, I asked Macca about it and he told me I'd have to adjust quickly or I'd sink. I'd been brought up by my dad, being praised and told off in equal measure. At Liverpool, nobody ever said anything positive to you after a good performance, especially when Roy was there. I think that was the environment of many years gone by. It was a case of winning the league, putting the medals away and forgetting about them before starting afresh the next season.

'I don't think you can be like that with everybody. I reacted well to praise. It motivated me. If I knew I was pleasing someone, it made me want to do it more. My dad knew Bobby Moore really well. They managed together at Oxford City. Bobby told him that the biggest kick he got in football came at the end of a match when someone told him, "Well done today, Bobby." This is the great Bobby Moore, England's World Cup-winning captain. Apparently Ron Greenwood [West Ham's manager] never did it once. Even legends need a pat on the back.'

Evans never tried to be friends with the players, according to Redknapp. Yet he did not instil discipline either. Again, this was the Liverpool way. Evans had been at the club since the late fifties in a variety of capacities. It had been standard practice for the senior playing staff to govern the squad day-to-day, with management interfering only when it was really necessary.

'There were one or two things Roy could have nipped in the bud sooner – things the players couldn't deal with,' Redknapp continues. 'Like when Stan [Collymore] went back to Cannock every day and started missing training sessions. The boys felt like he wasn't pulling his weight and he'd stopped making an effort with people, becoming distant. If Roy had stopped me going down to London every now and then, I would have done exactly as he said, no problem at all. We needed the iron fist a little bit more.'

Collymore had arrived at Liverpool in the summer of 1995 after Evans asked Redknapp about the striker's ability and character.

'We'd played against each other a few times and he was a right handful. Stan had the lot: pace, power and a ruthless finishing ability. In terms of talent, signing him was a no-brainer. I'd met him on a few nights out too and he seemed all right. I'd spoken to the Forest lads and they said he'd been as good as gold. So I said to Roy that he'd be fine with us. With hindsight, he was a bit difficult. I wouldn't have liked to manage Stan.'

There were other personalities. Evans had the courage to change Liverpool's formation from a standard 4–4–2, as it had been for thirty years, to 3–5–2. He signed Jason McAteer and converted him from a central-midfielder to a right wing-back. He also brought in John Scales and Phil Babb to play in defence. Babb became the most expensive centre-half in British football by signing for £3.6 million from Coventry City following a World

Cup where he'd managed to shackle one of the tournament's best players in Roberto Baggio during Ireland's opening game.

'Babbsy was the boy about town. He knew everybody. He treated everybody as his friend and no one differently. He could be hanging about with Robbie Williams or the kit man. It did not matter. Babbsy had a lovely left foot and struck the ball really well. I always knew as a midfielder that if he was fizzing the ball into me, it was going to be a good one and it would allow me to get things moving quickly. Unfortunately for Babbsy, he's probably remembered more for crashing into the post when we drew with Chelsea at Anfield, nearly cutting his ball-sack off. I still wince when I see that.

'Scalesy was different. He was quieter than Babbsy. Some of the lads called him James Bond, because he was well spoken and knew how to conduct an intelligent conversation. There was a bit of mystery about him, because on nights out he'd just disappear.

'I think Jason wanted to be super famous but because he played right-back nobody was that bothered. Unlike some, I thought he was a sharp lad.'

In the autobiographies of a number of Liverpool players it is claimed that Redknapp, Babb, Scales and McAteer became regulars on the London club scene between 1995 and 1997. With Evans granting Sunday as a day off when games were played on a Saturday, it was common practice for the quartet to fly to Heathrow from Manchester Airport immediately after the end of a 3 p.m. game at Anfield. They would stay at the plush Halkin Hotel in Knightsbridge, where bags would be dropped off and by 9 p.m., they'd be in Soho, taxiing between Chinawhite, the Emporium, Ten Rooms and Browns. This was a brave new world. From Conservative to Labour. From synthesizer to Britpop. Footballer to celebrity. Small time to big time. It was socially intoxicating.

'You'd turn up at a lot of places, you didn't have to say anything and they'd be on to you,' Redknapp says of his experience of women on occasions in the capital, though he insists he was not out as much as the critics believe. 'If I had my chance

116

again, I probably wouldn't have done it as much,' he admits. 'But my dad was West Ham manager and my brother lived down there, so there was more of a natural pull for me. Don't get me wrong, I enjoyed a night out, and which young lad doesn't get a buzz out of female attention when you're single?

'In the same places, I'd see Ryan Giggs and the United boys. In fact, Giggsy'd be out a lot more than me. My friends would tell me. I'd be tucked up in bed and Giggsy would be out. The difference is, nobody cares when you're winning. If you're just falling short, everybody wants to let you know about it. When you're winning, everybody wants to buy you a pint and indulge in the glory. It says just as much about society as it does about footballers.'

Redknapp insists that Robbie Fowler, Steve McManaman, Dominic Matteo and Steve Harkness only accompanied the group on 'a couple' of occasions. 'Neil Ruddock was thrown in with our crowd in the press because he was a Londoner,' Redknapp continues. 'But Neil was a pub man. He preferred finishing a match, going home then heading to The Grapes in Formby.'

Redknapp can't remember the first time he read about the 'Spice Boys', a moniker given to Liverpool's supposed hedonistic party animals, a group of which he was allegedly a founder member.

Liverpool may be a city of storytellers, a place where taxi drivers present gossip as undisputed fact. Yet there were some undisputed facts. Rob Jones, for instance, the unheralded right-back signed from Crewe Alexandra in 1991, became friends with Robbie Williams in the months before he left pop band Take That. Williams integrated into the Liverpool squad's social circle seamlessly and was invited on the team bus for an away game at Aston Villa in May 1995. Later that month, Williams accompanied a group led by captain John Barnes on an end-of-season booze-up in Magaluf. Jamiroquai's Jay Kay, who had no interest in football, was also invited by Phil Babb but did not turn up at the airport. Within twelve months, Robbie Fowler was going out with Emma Bunton, better known as Baby Spice. Whiston-born

Melanie Chisholm, Sporty Spice, was a Liverpool fan and regularly seen at Anfield. While Jason McAteer started a relationship with Donna Air, voted the fifth sexiest woman in the country in 1996, Redknapp dated Louise Nurding from Eternal, the four-piece R&B girl group who preceded the Spice Girls as the most popular band in the UK. It all contributed towards a general impression about the priorities of Liverpool's players.

'It progressed quicker than anyone could comprehend, when you consider players were having beers and fish and chips on the bus after games just a few years earlier,' Redknapp says. 'We were focused on what we had to do as professional football players and what happened on nights out had nothing to do with what happened when we took to the field. Look at Robbie [Fowler], for instance. There were all kinds of rumours about him [taking drugs] but they were all absolute rubbish. Robbie's a great lad. He could be a bit of a rascal and he liked a night out, although he probably came to London only twice, because he, Macca and others like Dom and Harky preferred drinking with their own mates in Liverpool. They didn't even like London. Robbie said on a number of occasions that he considered it too flash for him and Macca particularly. Robbie's attitude on the training pitch and during matches was spot on. He scored more than thirty goals in three successive seasons. He wouldn't have achieved that if the focus and drive to do well hadn't been there.'

Redknapp concedes his relationship with Louise did him no favours with the media.

'I met a pop star. Then I married a pop star. And we're still together all these years later. I didn't like her because she was a pop star. I liked her because she's a lovely person. It goes without saying that I liked the look of her. It's very simple: we fell in love and now we have two kids. Yet it added to the whole Spice Boys narrative. People thought image meant more to me and the other lads than football. That was rubbish. The only people I speak for are myself, Robbie and Macca, because they're the ones I was closest to and the ones I still see now. Football meant everything to me. I never did anything that would stop me training well, never mind playing well.'

When Redknapp did interviews back then, the line of questioning became predictable and his answers were almost spat out.

'It used to frustrate the life out of me,' Redknapp says. 'I wanted to talk about football. Most of the journalists wanted to talk about the Spice Boys. I became resentful. Maybe that wasn't the right way to deal with things. Rather than laugh about it, I got angry. I remember doing interviews and being really prickly. It might have given the wrong impression: that I was too defensive about it. If the papers knew it wound us up, maybe they went for it even more.'

On the pitch, Liverpool faltered at crucial times. In three successive seasons, there were mystifying results just when it seemed Liverpool might progress in a cup or win the league.

'We'd play some great stuff one week and be awful the next,' Redknapp admits. 'I can understand why people might figure that we'd dine out on a victory by going out partying, therefore losing our focus. But it was as frustrating for us as it was for them. We didn't have that figure on the pitch who'd guide us through games when things got really tight.'

Solid leadership was absent in the build-up to the FA Cup final of 1996. From the team's Sopwell House Hotel base in St Albans, Liverpool made their way to Wembley in a bus sponsored by Soho's Emporium nightclub, a venue that had been hired by the players for a party after the final was over – win or lose. Draw, and the event would have been cancelled due to the impending replay. It was another occasion where Liverpool were not necessarily unprofessional – just not professional enough. There was also the issue of the white suits.

'If I'd been twenty-nine or thirty in that situation, there's no way we'd have worn those suits,' Redknapp says. 'I think Rushy was the captain – it was his last game. If I was Rushy, I would have said, "Lads, I don't care what we do but we're not wearing them." The manager should have done something too.

'Jamo [David James] got the blame because he was an Armani

model and knew the people there. I got a bit of the blame because I was dating a pop star. Everybody took a fair bit of stick. But the truth was, I was twenty-two years old and still learning my way in the game. It should have been the top people sorting it out.

'When I work with Graeme [Souness] on Sky, he always talks about senior players. In our team, they should have said, "Listen, no fucking way." We had two club suits anyway, one black and the other navy. Why not go to Wembley in them?

'As it turned out, it was a shit final. United were shit. But we were shit too. It was a terrible game. The football was poor. Maybe the pressure got to everyone. Gary Neville [United's right-back who is also now employed by Sky] said years later that Alex Ferguson didn't need to do a team talk after he saw our suits. He claimed that Fergie told them to target crosses into the box because Jamo would be too busy focusing on waving to the Armani people in the stands. Fuck off. That's rubbish. You were shit, we were shit, you nicked it. If Jamo catches that corner, Cantona doesn't volley it in. It wasn't as if we were diabolical. It should have gone to a replay.'

Instead, by around midnight, the Emporium was a who's who of celebrities, all of them there to celebrate with the losers. Not for the first time, Liverpool's players were partying with nothing to party about.

Redknapp believes the result of the final was more significant, as it had far-reaching consequences for the rest of the decade.

'Had we won the FA Cup that year, I honestly think we'd have gone on and dominated for a long time, like Man United did. It was a pivotal couple of weeks because it was the first time the Nevilles, David Beckham, Nicky Butt and Paul Scholes experienced success with the first team. They got the taste for it and carried on. It gave them the confidence to grow.

'We had the potential to be a really great side too, but we never experienced that taste. We beat Bolton in the League Cup final a year earlier but we were expected to win that one. We needed that experience of beating one of our rivals to a trophy. But it never happened. It's a frustration of mine, even talking about it now. It makes me angry. We were close.'

Within a month, Redknapp had broken his ankle playing for England at Wembley against Scotland during Euro 96. He'd been introduced as a half-time substitute by Terry Venables with the game scoreless and was pivotal in securing a 2–0 victory before falling in a heap.

'That summer I went away with my mates to Ayia Napa. The right thing to do would have been to head straight to Melwood to start rehab. But nobody at the club suggested that to me. I was twenty-two years old and didn't have all the answers. If I was a manager and I knew a player had an injury like mine, I would have been straight on the phone telling him to come in.'

It was the beginning of an eighteen-month period where it seemed that Redknapp appeared in women's magazines more often than in Liverpool's first team. It took him until January 1997 to break up the John Barnes–Michael Thomas midfield axis and regain his place. He was then injured on England duty again during a friendly with South Africa.

'The thing some fans never understand is that it takes a while for a player to regain his sharpness after an injury. They presume that as soon as you pull on a red shirt, that's it, you're fit. I had spells with the fans where I wasn't the most popular. Ronnie Whelan had similar periods even in the eighties when the team was successful. I'd talk it through with my dad. It felt like I'd give one ball away and they'd be straight on to me. Other players would give three or four away and nothing would be said. These times seemed to coincide when I'd just returned from injury and I wasn't as confident with my body as I should have been. It affects everything: your movement, judgement. My dad gave the best advice. He told me that as long as I made tackles and chased the opposition, putting them under pressure, the Liverpool crowd would respond positively. And he was right. The Liverpool crowd were educated football people. They weren't doing it to be nasty. I had to realize I was playing probably the most important position on the pitch. I had to do more to impress people. I remember scoring one against Birmingham, sticking it in the top corner. I ran over to the crowd screaming. They realized it was frustration on my part. The next week, they really backed me.

'Then there are other times when it's going badly. You're a goal down and you're giving the ball away. The crowd are on you. Individuals in their seats wait for a moment when it's quiet inside Anfield to give you a bit of stick. Each match is like a life in ninety minutes because it encapsulates all the extreme emotions you feel as a human being: the happiness, the sadness, the frustration, feeling fortunate. It's a pressure cooker. You have to be tough to survive.

'Then there were times at Liverpool when life felt so, so good. There were games when everything went right. You had forty-five thousand people roaring your name or celebrating a goal. When the ball hits the back of the net, you don't hear a sound. It's like a silent explosion. When you spray a pass thirty yards and it meets the target and everyone applauds, you feel a million dollars.'

Another nugget of advice Redknapp received from his father was to speak to the manager as soon as possible if he was ever left out.

'Roy Evans will tell you I carried that with me throughout my career, because he wasn't afraid to drop me. On a Sunday or Monday, I'd be straight into his office. My dad's thinking behind that was from his own experience. If he had a player banging down his door every time, he'd think twice about doing it in the future. It wasn't always easy with Graeme Souness, because I was scared stiff of him.'

When he regained full fitness and had persuaded Evans his name should be on the teamsheet, Redknapp became a scapegoat for some poor performances. The Anfield crowd, fed up of watching players like Roy Keane and Nicky Butt power Manchester United towards trophies, decided it wanted midfielders with the aggression of a Graeme Souness, Jimmy Case or Steve McMahon, midfielders who could pass but also win possession back quickly.

'I was sensible enough to realize I wasn't everyone's cup of tea,' Redknapp admits. 'I used to think that the way I looked was my biggest problem, because I had long hair. It was easier to have a dig at me because I looked like I didn't fancy the rough stuff. But that wasn't true. There are different types of bravery – being able to put your foot on the ball when everyone inside the stadium is telling you to move it quicker is brave.'

Nevertheless, Roy Evans must have agreed that Liverpool needed brawn as well as brains and soon enough Paul Ince had become a part of the midfield, arriving for £4.5 million from Inter Milan. Despite more rumours, these linking Redknapp with a move away from Anfield, he never came close to leaving.

'Roma made a bid for me when I was twenty-one. Their captain Giuseppe Giannini had retired and they were looking for someone to play as their number 10 in midfield. My agent felt I should go but I didn't want to. The club rejected the offer and I always felt wanted at Liverpool. In terms of contracts, if you were doing well the club would always look after you. There was no messing around or haggling. I realized that when I went to Tottenham, because there they would haggle all evening even if it meant pissing off the player.'

Redknapp became Liverpool's captain in 1999 under Gérard Houllier after it was decided that Ince should be sold. Ince had an annoying habit of doing little for eighty minutes before trying really hard in the final ten, prompting fans to leave the stadium all saying a similar thing, 'At least Incey put a shift in.' Houllier was on to him straight away and sold him to Middlesbrough.

'When I see the TV and it describes me as a former Liverpool captain, I still can't believe it,' Redknapp says. After scoring against Derby County, Redknapp sustained the knee injury that he says finished him as a Liverpool player. 'I could hear clicking. I knew I had a big problem. That's what upsets me most. I never had the opportunity to lead the team from a position of strength, where my body allowed my mind to take a proper leadership role on the pitch. I could see Steven Gerrard developing into a world-class player. The club were also trying to sign Didi Hamann. I wanted to be a part of that midfield. The way I played, it would have been perfect.'

Instead, Redknapp's relationship with Houllier deteriorated after the pair disagreed about the best way he should recover, with Redknapp feeling that the advice given by eminent American knee specialist Dr Richard Steadman wasn't heeded entirely. Redknapp retired from the game aged just thirty-one, three years after leaving Liverpool. His last club was Southampton, where his father Harry was manager during a season that concluded in relegation from the Premier League. 'I didn't want it to finish that way but when your body is saying "no", you have to listen to it.'

My time with Redknapp is at an end. Louise breezes into the room, reminding Jamie of a home-gym session which had only been sprung on him that morning. It starts in quarter of an hour.

'I'm sorry but we'll have to wrap it up there,' Redknapp tells me, raising his eyes as if to suggest he has no influence on the matter. He explains the best way back to the railway station on foot.

'I'd have given you a lift but there's a one-way system here and some of the roads are shut. When Louise tells me to do something, I go along with it.'

CHAPTER FIVE

cultzeros.co.uk

DAVE,
Jason McAteer, 1995–99

JASON MCATEER IS DESCRIBING THOSE MONTHS AS A TEENAGER
when he'd reach the doors of Birkenhead's Wirral Council offices,
see the dole queue snaking outside and join it.

'It was fuckin' shit, mate, and I mean really fuckin' shit,' he
starts. 'I wasn't alone. A lot of lads from round our way were
joining the line. I honestly didn't know what the fuck I was going
to do. When you're young, you don't think too deeply. But now,
looking back, fuck me – it was desperate. It was like being in a
funeral procession.'

Soon, McAteer is revisiting a period three and a half years later,
standing somewhere very different, with a collection of famous
international footballers, while representing Ireland in the 1994
World Cup. Twelve months after that, he signed for Liverpool.
Hollywood films have been made about less dramatic changes
in fortune.

'It was literally going from playing on a dogshit park against a gang of scallies smoking ciggies to the Giants Stadium against Maldini, Baresi and Italy in front of one hundred thousand people for a game being watched on telly by millions. Then I was at Anfield, being able to call John Barnes – who was my hero – a teammate. The odds must have been a billion to one.'

McAteer is in his forties now but when listening with closed eyes he sounds like someone half his age. He speaks with a rising inflection, which means he concludes most sentences leaving an impression of optimism. He is unshaven and there is less hair than before but the youthful facial features remain: dark brown eyes, high-set cheekbones and a grin that borders on flirtatious, emphasized by the way he occasionally purses his lips when stressing a point.

At Liverpool, McAteer's reputation was set – the daft one, *the* butt of the jokes – although he clearly doesn't mind. A natural raconteur, McAteer stumbles through stories with laughter of his own, drawing you in as if you're somehow part of it all, like you were there too, in the background. He appreciates the art of using bad language to humorous effect. Our conversation begins with one of his favourite tales.

'I used to get asked all the time: what was it like playing for Ireland? We had no right to get to European Championships or World Cups but we did. Stripping it all down, people couldn't believe how we'd managed to get a result here, get a result there. It was down to the way the team was, the camaraderie we had and the closeness – playing for each other. We used to go out as a group, eat together. For friendlies, everyone would turn up whether you were injured or not.

'At the '94 World Cup, we were playing Norway. Beforehand, the teams and the officials were waiting. The national anthems were being sung. I glanced across at Andy Townsend, who was our captain, and saw him whispering into Packie Bonner's ear. Usually it was instructions: don't give the ball away, keep it tight for the opening twenty, that kind of stuff. I was thinking to myself, whatever he's said, I need to take it on board, because I was the youngest there. I was keen as mustard.

'The message reaches Aldo [John Aldridge], who's standing to the right of me. Aldo leans over and whispers, "Row F, can you see the bird in the Viking hat? Look at the size of her tits. Pass it on." I've turned to my left and the next person is Roy Keane.'

Keane had the fiercest reputation in British football, a midfielder with a glare that could liquefy ice caps. But there was no going back.

'I plucked up the courage after half a minute or so and went, "Roy . . . don't give the ball away and don't do anything stupid for the first twenty minutes. Pass it on . . ."'

With that, McAteer is unable to contain himself, wriggling about in his seat at a well-known Liverpool city-centre hotel. He is wheezing with laughter. And so am I. It is like spending time in an ale house with a mate you once knew, reminiscing over old tales that are still funny no matter how many times you recall them.

McAteer had two unflattering nicknames. With Ireland, it was 'Trigger', after the gormless character from *Only Fools and Horses*. At Liverpool, it would also have been Trigger, had Rob Jones not taken the title already. Instead, McAteer was known as 'Dave', Trigger's mistaken name for Rodney from the same show.

'Rob wasn't switched on at all – a brilliant lad but totally stupid at times. Before away games, we'd drive past the ground. You could see the sign clearly: "OLD TRAFFORD". Then one of the lads at the back of the bus would shout, "Hey, how long is it until we get there? I'm sure it's round here somewhere . . ."

'Rob would fall for it on each occasion. "Look, *there's* the ground," he'd emphasize. "We're here now." Then everyone would start pissing themselves. A few weeks later, we'd be near Highfield Road. "Where's the ground?" Rob, as ever, would be the daft navigator. "Look, it's there!"'

Other players tell similar stories about McAteer. There is the one where Neil Ruddock asked for a coat hanger to help open his jammed car door only for McAteer to return eagerly carrying a wooden one. On another occasion, McAteer was ordering a takeaway and when asked whether he wanted a standard ten-inch pizza cut into eight slices, he replied, 'Only four, thanks. I'm not that hungry.' According to Dominic Matteo, when filling in his passport application McAteer wrote 'Right-back' in the occupation section.

McAteer reasons that his own reputation was self-cultivated in a deliberate attempt to fit in.

'I was thought of as not being the brightest and being on the other side of thick,' he admits. 'But when you're making your way in an industry and you're trying to fit in, having arrived late into the game, you try to find a place, a way of being accepted. I always had the ability to make people laugh because I never took myself seriously. I liked to have fun. I wouldn't be afraid to do or say something that was silly. I've got quite broad shoulders when it comes to stick and I have the ability to give it back too.

'It started in the early days at Bolton. I twigged that people used to enjoy my company. It was like, "Get him to come out with us . . . get him to come in our car . . ." I liked it. I was everyone's mate, the funny, happy chap of the team. It was my niche. Eventually, it stuck and it was easy for people to say, "Dave? We love him but he's a thick bastard."'

McAteer is dressed in a navy-coloured velour J. Lindeberg tracksuit. On his feet are a pair of maroon Adidas original Gazelle training shoes. He also wears what might be Davidoff's Cool Water. He looks, sounds and even smells Scouse. Yet McAteer grew up in Birkenhead, a town that is separated from Liverpool's city centre by less than half a mile of river. Although Birkenhead has much more in common politically, culturally and demographically with Liverpool than it does with other more affluent areas of Wirral like Heswall or Caldy, the Mersey has long been considered a boundary between two very different locations linked only by two road tunnels.

It is claimed that Birkenhead, with its Viking heritage, and Liverpool, Anglo-Saxon, are like oil and water. The two have proud and discrete histories. In Lewis's *Topographical Dictionary of England*, Birkenhead's right of 'ferryage across the Mersey, granted by charter in 1318' was the political hot potato of the nineteenth century, as Liverpool sought to claim the shipping channels that led out towards the Irish Sea. Resentment lingered.

Today, separate councils administer Liverpool and Birkenhead. Followers of Tranmere Rovers regularly inform other supporters through the medium of song that they are not Scousers and, instead, are from Birkenhead; while to older residents of Liverpool, Birkenhead is a 'one-eyed city', in the same way Mancunians view those from Salford; and Newcastle, Gateshead. It's a term of derision, meaning that those from Birkenhead are wannabes; they have some of the gear but no idea.

What Birkenhead does have is the cheapest housing on Wirral, located on a sink estate known ominously as 'The Jungle'. It's an area where survival is a serious business. Unemployment runs at nearly twice the national average, long-term youth unemployment rose by 100 per cent in 2012, and the town's shopping centres are little more than a parade of discount stores and payday loan sharks. It is no wonder The Boo Radleys from neighbouring Wallasey referenced Birkenhead in their song 'Everything Is Sorrow'.

McAteer was a teenager by the time the decline had really taken a grip. He was fourteen years old when, in 1985, the cutbacks began at the nearby Cammell Laird shipyard. Among the famous vessels to slide down the old dock's great slipways on to the Mersey were the cruise liners *Mauretania* and *Windsor Castle*, the *Alabama*, an American Civil War Confederate raider, and the aircraft carrier *Ark Royal*. The yard provided jobs for tens of thousands of working-class men at any one time over a number of generations after opening in the early nineteenth century. Many still believe a secret clause in a deal between the British government, led by Margaret Thatcher, and the European Commission reduced British shipbuilding capacity in return for £140 million, helping to sink the yard and employment levels.

McAteer grew up with his brother, sister and parents in a

small two-bedroomed terraced house on Town Road, a winding thoroughfare on a steep gradient near Prenton Park, the home of Tranmere Rovers, a team that had toiled in the lower leagues of English football. The club's financial difficulties mirrored those of Birkenhead – on several occasions in the eighties insolvency was only forestalled through a series of friendly fixtures, contributions from fans and a £200,000 loan from Wirral Council. 'I'd be lying if I said Tranmere was *the* place to be seen,' says McAteer, who remembers his teenage years as a time where his significant elders worked long hours. Income was uncertain.

'My mum was a cleaner but she did loads of odd jobs,' he continues. 'Then my dad was an electrician by trade and he was doing "foreigners" all the time, a bit of enterprise [in addition to his nine-to-five job]. It was Thatcher's era, wasn't it? You had to do whatever it took to put food on the table. She didn't give a fuck about the working class. We were left to rot.'

By the time McAteer became a semi-professional footballer, he was running out of ideas. His career progression had been limited to promotion from glass collector to barman at the sizeable Sportsmans Arms public house not far from his home. He considered enrolling on a football scholarship at Tiffin University in Ohio 'but didn't have the bottle to move away'. Instead, he began a graphic-design course at a college on Withens Lane in Wallasey, 'only because it was a bit trendy and there were a couple of nice-looking girls'.

'When I was in school, I wanted to be a footballer. I came out of school and still wanted to be a footballer. Then the reality struck: there were YTS schemes but if you don't get taken on, you're knackered. It was a bad time in terms of getting jobs and trades. What do you do? I was decent at art, so I started a BTEC National Diploma. It was a means to an end. I didn't really know what I wanted to do but I knew I didn't want a life on the dole. I was a bit lost.'

One lunchtime after playing five-a-side in the college yard, McAteer was approached by the facility's caretaker and asked to represent a Sunday team run from another pub, the Royal Oak.

League and cup success there led to a move to Poulton Victoria in the West Cheshire League – a higher standard. Like many of his teammates, his whole weekend centred on football. After a game on the Saturday with the Royal Oak, he'd roll out of bed the next morning to represent Parkside, a team that boasted players with professional experience. Amongst them was Joey Craven, a midfielder who'd played more than a hundred games for Tranmere before signing for Caernarfon Town in the Welsh Football League. There was also Paul Meachin, a well-known non-league striker with Marine, a club based over the river in Crosby.

'Paul was one of Marine's stalwarts and a person I really looked up to. I was one of the youngest lads at Parkside and if I ever ran into problems with any of the aul arses from other teams, he'd sort it out. He saw enough potential in me to ask whether I'd fancy giving it a go at Marine. I was only working in a bar and Paul said if I did well I might get some expenses in my back pocket. I didn't drive – I didn't have enough money to learn to drive – and Paul offered to give me lifts Tuesdays, Thursdays and Saturdays. I thought I might as well try. It was only twenty-five minutes away.'

Marine were in the Northern Premier League, a competition as glamorous sounding as the company that sponsored it: HFS Loans. Although it has since seen improvements, their College Road ground was (and remains) three-sided. There was a shed behind one goal, an old wooden stand behind the other and a single-stepped covered terrace down the side. Opposite, only tall netting separated the back gardens of old Victorian houses from the touchline of the pitch.

McAteer did enough in training sessions to be asked to join Marine's reserves. This was an era when non-league football teams were populated by real men and the outcomes of games were determined by earth, muscle, leather and bone. 'At Marine, we had Keith Johnson, Jon Gautrey, Peter Smith and Kevin O'Brien. They were all tough as nails. Then there was me, the scrawny daft kid from Birkenhead trying to fit in.'

Marine's reserves were a part of the Lancashire League, along with A and B teams from Football League clubs as illustrious as Liverpool, Everton, Manchester City and Manchester United. Marine were reliably mid table, admirably finishing above the juniors of Crewe Alexandra, Preston North End and Bury.

'It was the best league I could have been playing in,' McAteer insists. 'We were up against really good kids – some of the best in the country. The reserves opened your mind to a quicker and more technical style of football than the first team because we were playing against full-time professional footballers one or two times a week. With the first team, it was a lot of kick and rush; with the reserves, the football was on the deck – quick, fast and skilful. I played against Barnesy and Rushy when they were coming back from injury. It was their first game on the road to recovery. After that, they'd have a run-out in the reserves and the first team. They'd only be going at 20 or 30 per cent but they'd still be miles better than anyone else on the pitch.'

Marine's first team were managed by Roly Howard, a legend of the non-league scene and someone who was recognized by Guinness World Records as the longest-serving manager in football on his retirement in 2005 following thirty-three years and 1,975 games in charge.

Howard, a brusque Lancastrian, combined his part-time role with a job as a window cleaner and Kenny Dalglish was one of his clients in Southport. Howard had a fierce reputation. On one occasion, he slammed the home dressing-room door in anger at half-time and only the opposition, the referee and the linesmen appeared for the second half. 'I'd bust the lock,' Howard told *The Independent*. 'We had to shout for help until someone came and smashed the door in from outside.'

Under Howard's stewardship, Marine enjoyed its most successful era. Having already beaten Halifax Town of the old Fourth Division by a 4–1 scoreline, his team reached the third round of the FA Cup and might have faced Dalglish's Blackburn Rovers in the fourth round had they not lost to Crewe. Despite being a league below the Conference, Marine were one game away from Wembley on two occasions, only to falter in second legs of FA Trophy semi-final ties. Howard secured five league titles and fifteen cups.

Howard built his teams around experience and was mistrustful of youngsters. McAteer admits his mistake in attending an end-of-season awards ceremony wearing a tracksuit, even though he didn't earn 'enough money to buy the real thing'. He recognizes now that Howard would have seen this as youthful disobedience.

'Roly was strict, hard and very difficult to deal with,' McAteer remembers. 'In some ways, I was happy to be with the reserves because the manager there was a good guy, Dave Ramsden – an arm-around-the-shoulder fella who took an interest in the welfare of the players. I never reacted well with characters like Roly, whose personality was aggressive and unforgiving.'

McAteer only played five times for Marine's first team across three seasons, scoring once at Witton Albion.

'I'd get selected quite a lot and travel away on the bus. But when it came to naming the match-day squad, I wasn't in it. After the game, Roly would order me to pick up the kit and put it in the bag. There were shitty undies, jockstraps and sweatbands. I'd come home crying, telling my mum he'd taken me all the way to fucking Goole for nothing, getting in at 2 a.m. midweek. But these are the things that shape you, make you determined.'

McAteer's fortunes began to shift after impressing Bolton Wanderers' coaching staff during a Lancashire League reserve match.

'The phone rang and my mum answered. The fella on the other end of the line said, "Listen, this is the deal. We want to sign Jason and we've approached Marine. We know he's not on a contract, so we know he's available. When he goes to training on Tuesday, Roly will put a contract in front of him. If that happens and Jason signs it, we won't have the funds to buy him because Marine will want ten grand." The caller was Phil Neal.' Neal, Liverpool's most-decorated player, was Bolton's first-team manager.

As predicted, McAteer was invited into Marine's boardroom.

'Marine's chairman, Tom Culshaw, was standing behind Roly.

The pair were as thick as thieves. Roly is such an intimidating character. There were no negotiations on his part. He slapped a contract on the table and ordered, "Sign that." It was for £100 a week, which was quite a lot of money.'

McAteer agreed to the deal in principal but said he'd only sign after he'd discussed it with his family. The commitment was a ruse.

'As soon as I got home, I called Nealy and told him what had happened. Unfortunately, Bolton couldn't get something in place by Thursday, so as soon as I arrived at training Roly was straight on to me again: "Sign it . . . do this . . . or nothing will ever happen for you." He put me under pressure. I stayed strong. He wasn't happy at all.

'Whenever I went back to Marine years later, Roly was that same person. Maybe it was because he took a bit of criticism. If Marine had had the foresight, they would have put a sell-on clause in the deal with Bolton. They didn't and a few years later I moved on for £4.5 million. Maybe Marine would have been a different club today with that money. Instead, they got £500 and a bag of balls.'

By Monday morning, McAteer was being picked up outside the Adelphi Hotel in Liverpool's city centre by Sammy Lee and driven to Burnden Park. Lee had played 295 games for Liverpool before moving to Queens Park Rangers, Osasuna and, indeed, Bolton.

'I did enough in the three or four days to earn a contract until the end of the season. But then Nealy was sacked. It made me nervous, because I was the youngest lad there and the fella that had taken a punt on me was gone. I was praying the new manager would like me. I was having these dark thoughts that involved returning to Marine with my tail between my legs.'

Bruce Rioch, a former midfielder with Everton, had captained Scotland at the 1978 World Cup in Argentina. Yet he too was late reaching the elite as a player. He was twenty-six before he appeared in the old First Division and twenty-seven before the call came to represent his national team. 'Some people begin at the top,' Rioch said. 'With others, like me, it's different. But you're not in this game that long without talent and ability.' Like Neal, Rioch – the next Bolton manager – saw enough, and perhaps a bit of himself, in McAteer and gave him a chance.

McAteer says Rioch was just what he needed: a manager who relished working with young players, someone that knew how to instil discipline but be flexible enough to unlock potential.

Rioch's father was a sergeant major in the Scots Guards and an accomplished athlete, throwing the hammer for Great Britain after the Second World War. Rioch was born in Aldershot and had a typical army childhood, which took him to a different location every few years.

At Middlesbrough, where Rioch went after managing Torquay, he turned a young team round almost too quickly, taking them from the old Third Division up to the First in successive seasons. When they went straight back down again, he fell victim to expectations and was sacked. At Millwall, it was a similar story: into the 1991 play-offs, then a slump the following season. This time it was Rioch who decided to go, and in May 1992 he took charge at Bolton.

McAteer believes, 'I was in the right place at the right time. I could also have gone to Everton that summer but I liked Bruce and figured there would be more opportunities to play in the first team. I'd seen from playing with the Marine reserves how many players had come and gone from Everton. Many of them had ended up at Marine. I didn't want that to happen. Nealy deserves all the credit for taking me from Marine in the first place but probably the best thing that ever happened to me was him getting the sack.

'Bruce came in and told us all that he did not care about reputations or what we'd done in the past. It was all about now. Initially, he pushed all the kids into the reserves and stuck with the players that had been there for a while. But, true to his word, he then integrated the kids.

'It was a dressing room made up of Scousers: David Reeves; Tony Philliskirk, a centre-forward that everyone called *Iceman*;

and Tony Kelly. We'd travel to Bolton and back together every day in the car. We'd meet in Halewood, Speke or Huyton.'

McAteer was a winger until Rioch switched him into the centre of midfield alongside Kelly.

'Tony would sit and play, and I would run off. He was the brain, I was the legs. It was the perfect balance. He had the experience to stop me straying too far. The responsibility gave me a lot of confidence, because centre-midfield is a position where the best players play. A few years before, Roly wouldn't trust me to run up and down Marine's touchline. Suddenly, I was in the old Second Division, scoring goals, winning games and performing to a high standard.'

While the hypnotically skilled Kelly, nicknamed 'Prince' by Bolton supporters, 'loved a night out', McAteer barely drank in his early years.

'It wasn't really my cup of tea,' he says, without any sense of irony. 'I'd been given this opportunity and I was taking it with two hands. I didn't want to mess it up. I wanted to do everything right. I respected Bruce too much. He took me under his wing and was really strict. But I liked it. I had this bond with him, like father and son. I didn't want to let him down, because he'd invested a lot of time in me. He was honest and loyal – two things I craved throughout the rest of my career but never really got.'

With McAteer were other youngsters who felt similarly about Rioch. Darren Oliver had been at Everton. Alan Stubbs, born in 1971 – the same year as McAteer – had also trained at Bellefield as a teenager before being told he wasn't quite what Everton wanted. Mark Seagraves, Andy Roscoe and Stuart Whittaker had been at Liverpool. 'They were all the same: Scousers and determined.'

Rioch introduced a Scottish core. John McGinlay and Andy Walker made up an experienced forward line and became an important focal point for the team.

'There were good players but the spirit between the players and the bond with the fans took us furthest. In the cup runs, tickets would go on sale and the fans would be queuing up for miles down the road. After training, Bruce would tell us to go to the ground and hand out hot cups of tea to all the people waiting. It was an amazing spell. Bolton had a rich history of cult heroes, players like Frank Worthington, Peter Reid and Sam Allardyce. It felt like we'd returned to a truer time.'

Rioch's Bolton were on an upward trajectory. There was a succession of giant-killing cup upsets. In the FA Cup of 1993, Bolton knocked out holders Liverpool in a third-round replay at Anfield. Robbie Fowler, selected as a substitute for the first time that night, remembers dreading the call from Graeme Souness to get stripped and ready for action, such was the desperation of Liverpool's performance. 'I was running up and down the touchline, partly to remind the manager that I was there if he needed a goal, and partly to get away from him, just in case he was thinking about actually throwing me on,' Fowler recalled.

McAteer, then on the fringes of the Bolton team, recalls journeymen like Phil Brown, the future Hull City manager, commenting how easy it had been in the dressing room afterwards. 'We had tougher games against Cambridge United that season,' McAteer insists.

Within twelve months, Bolton had reached the Premier League in a season where they also defeated top-flight opposition in the form of Everton and Arsenal.

'It put us into the shop window. We were making headlines. Before games, me and Stubbsy would go into the ticket office at Burnden Park and ask the girls on the desk who was on the complimentary list. It was a who's who of Premier League scouts and managers. There was Ron Yeats, Alex Ferguson, Howard Kendall, Mike Walker. Without being big-headed, we knew they were looking at me, Stubbsy and Alan Thompson.

'It gave me a lot of confidence. I was naive in a good way. Three years before, I'd been unemployed and in the reserves of a semi-professional club. Suddenly, I was on the crest of a wave. I did not have time to consider the magnitude of the rise. Everything seemed possible.'

McAteer had verbally agreed to join Blackburn Rovers, the reigning Premier League champions, when Liverpool made their move to sign him.

'I met Kenny [Dalglish] and Ray Harford at the Thistle Hotel in Haydock. Blackburn's bid was £9 million for me and Stubbsy.' This was a time before mobile phones. A porter appeared, telling McAteer's agent about an important call at reception. 'So he went out and left me in the room by myself with Kenny and Ray. I was shitting myself. I mean, for fuck sake, Kenny was my hero. I wanted to ask him for an autograph and a photo.'

Dalglish was unimpressed, however, when McAteer's agent explained that Liverpool had registered a £4.5 million bid. 'Kenny just went, "No, you're not speaking to them." He told me that if I left the room, the deal with Blackburn was off. I remember saying that I only wanted the opportunity that was once given to him. He didn't really have a response to that.'

What McAteer saw on his introduction to this Liverpool squad was a group of players 'just as determined as anyone else to be successful' and one that 'knew how to party at the right times'.

'We did not fall short because of anything that went on off the pitch,' he insists. 'The way I see it is this: the United boys socialized in similar circles as us and won the league. We fell just short, so copped all the flak. It's as simple as that. We just weren't quite good enough.'

McAteer can laugh now at some of the rumours that went around about him. There was one about him being in a relationship with Phil Babb. 'Because we were best mates.' And another that claimed he was dating Dido, the pop star. 'I think that one started because we were in the same room once.' The reality was that McAteer ended up in a short relationship with Mel C, a Spice Girl.

'Again, David Beckham was doing the same with Victoria but because United got the results, it didn't matter. Mel and I lived separate lives, so it wasn't something that was sustainable. I was off playing football and she was touring around the world. We barely saw each other. Then it ended.'

What McAteer did do was a shampoo advert for Wash & Go. 'It was my way of having a bit of a laugh at myself. The advert was only supposed to be used in Ireland. The lads slaughtered me after they saw it on TV. It must have put everyone else in the squad off, because nobody followed me down that route.'

Commercial opportunities led to greater wealth. Critics would call it greed. But McAteer claims he was cautious with money.

'The first contract I signed was £100 a week. Bruce [Rioch] promised me the more games I played in the first team, the more money I'd earn. Gradually, I went to £250, then £500 and eventually £2,000 at Bolton. I felt like a proper footballer by then. I'd gotten over the fact that I had been semi-pro not so long before. I was becoming more accustomed to having money and started investing it properly. My mum got involved and she made me get two bank accounts. One was a current account and the other was a savings account. I agreed with her that I should pay myself a wage of £200 a week. The rest would build up nicely.'

McAteer claims the only genuine indulgence he and his teammates shared was clothes. 'We didn't spend our money on drink, drugs, smoking or women, so there had to be something we blew some of our wages on.'

He realizes that fashion sense (or the lack of it) – probably more than any other factor – led to the wrong general impression being formed. When Liverpool's players turned up to the 1996 FA Cup final wearing an all-white ensemble, they looked like they'd been kicked out of East 17.

'People go on and on about the white suits but they didn't make us play any better or any worse,' McAteer says. 'In truth, we couldn't wait to get them off. It wouldn't have made any difference if the suit was black, red or green. When you're at a cup final, all you want to do is get into the changing rooms and put your kit on. We put the suits on in the hotel and took them off when we got to the ground. In total, we probably had them on for forty-five minutes. Man United didn't go into the dressing rooms and take encouragement from it. It wasn't as if they went, "These look like a bunch of cunts, we're going to beat them today." Our focus was to win. It was just something the media got hold of and used to explain why we lost.

'It was the worst game of the season. Nothing happened. Rushy could have scored for us just as easily as Cantona did for them. Admittedly, Jamo [David James] made a clanger there, dropping David Beckham's cross. Maybe the critics would have had a point if we'd lost 4–0 but it could quite easily have been us lifting the trophy.

'Loads of people give us stick and see us as the opposite of United. The reality was we pushed United until the final few games and fell just short in the league, then met them again in the cup final and the same thing happened. We were quite similar teams with similar approaches and similar characters. I look back and it devastates me it never happened, because we were so good.'

Liverpool *were* good. With McAteer raiding up and down the touchline as a right wing-back, this side had gone fifteen games unbeaten in the league to move to within five points of the Premier League summit. Manchester United, Arsenal and reigning champions Blackburn were all defeated at Anfield. Yet the weekend before beating Aston Villa in the FA Cup semi-final, that run came to a shuddering halt with a 1–0 defeat at Nottingham Forest. Within the next fortnight, Liverpool had re-established themselves as potential champions by winning 4–3 against Newcastle in what many observers still believe is the greatest game of the Premier League era before falling again three days later with a 1–0 loss at Coventry City. I suggest to McAteer that maybe Liverpool believed they were, indeed, too good.

'We just didn't deal with the shitty side of the game,' he says. 'We looked too far forward, not at what we needed to handle there and then. It was always the future: the harder game, the more glamorous game. It happened too many times for it to be a coincidence. Coventry, for example. We had Everton ten days later and everyone was thinking about that. We figured our ability alone would be enough to see us through against Coventry.

In our heads, the game against Coventry was already won and Everton was the focus, because if we didn't win that one, our rivals would take confidence from seeing us struggle and open up the gap. There was nobody really saying, "Yeah, but we've got to deal with the immediate task in front of us."'

Surely someone should be held accountable for this: Roy Evans, or the most experienced players, who were allowed to self-govern by the manager, just as they had throughout Liverpool's glory years?

'Again, it wasn't about us getting carried away off the pitch. It was about what happened during the game. The simple answer is we needed players that were more streetwise, particularly at the back, where there were too many mistakes, individual errors. No team wins a league gifting goals. Jamo made a lot of mistakes and there was inconsistency in the selection in defence between Scales, Babb, Ruddock, Wright, Harkness and Matteo. If we had had two stalwarts there every week, maybe it would have been different: a Hansen, a Lawrenson or a Gillespie. We needed a few players that would put the brakes on and stop us from tearing up the pitch and trying to score, to stop us from going gung-ho and scoring two and three when we were already winning 1–0; ones that would say, "Sit in here and grind it out for twenty minutes and go home 1–0 winners." United did that regularly.'

By the 1995–96 season, Liverpool had only two players that had won the league before. McAteer says Barnes particularly was laden with too much responsibility.

'The media was saying that Barnesy was finished. But he was picking up injuries at a time when his game was in transition. He'd gone from being a winger to being an attacking midfielder to being a sitting midfielder. He had the pressure of carrying this young team. He was Roy's eyes and ears. He had a say in tactics and training patterns while leading as captain. He was left with too much to do.

'That stemmed from the fact we did not have enough players that knew what it took and were still capable of winning the league. The first one is always the most difficult because of the psychological battle that goes with it. I found it wasn't the games or the opponents that we were facing, because we feared nobody. It was the mental challenge of all the possibilities, what it would all mean. Everything that went before was fine but in the last few weeks we fell short. We could not handle the psychological battle of the final ten games of the season. We couldn't handle that pressure.'

Conversation now moves on to the individuals that could have made a difference for Liverpool. It has long been argued that Evans needed to sign a midfield enforcer in the mould of Paul Ince, not Paul Ince himself. Roy Keane – McAteer's teammate with Ireland – had chosen to move to Old Trafford instead of Anfield in 1993. So I ask McAteer whether Keane's notoriously corrosive personality would have dovetailed with the characters inside Liverpool's dressing room.

'You've seen Roy as a pundit and he hasn't changed,' McAteer answers. 'A lot of pundits say something out there just to be controversial when they don't believe it. I think people like Roy because what he says is very believable. I don't necessarily agree with everything he says and where Roy lets himself down is when he forgets that his is just another opinion at the end of the day. He's got to be open to the fact that he might be wrong. That's what Roy has struggled with for a long time.

'Roy only developed that reputation when he got to Man United – that winning mentality. At Forest before, he never gave up and that's why United bought him. But just because a certain attitude was good for United and worked for United doesn't mean it was nailed on for success elsewhere.'

McAteer refers to the incident in 2002 when Keane walked away from the World Cup in Japan and South Korea following a furious argument with manager Mick McCarthy. Keane believed that the standards with Ireland, such as training grounds and travel arrangements, were not as they should have been.

'In relative terms, Ireland achieved great things,' McAteer explains. 'Being such a small nation and reaching World Cups was phenomenal success. We did that not by following what went on at Man United but by Jack Charlton's method of building a spirit and sticking together.

'OK, we did not have fantastic facilities – as Roy argued. We used to train next to the airport [in Dublin] and Jack [Charlton] or Mick would be doing their team talk while the ten o'clock from Liverpool would be flying in. They'd have to stop because of the noise. They'd start, then the half-ten would be overhead. It was laughable.

'There was shit everywhere, muddy pitches. But look at England and all the money they had, achieving nothing. We were Ireland, that's what happened. The kit turned up three days late but nobody cared because we had something else: a bond. That'd see us through.

'To walk out in 2002 was the worst possible thing he [Keane] could have done. There wasn't one particular reason why he decided to go home. It was a number of events happening shortly one after the other and he'd had enough. I saw them as little problems.

'I was gutted, but not personally, because we all make choices in life. You have to do what you believe in. I was gutted because, one: at the time, Roy was one of the best players in the world. Two: the team needed him, despite all his faults. He was a loner, Roy. We never mixed, really. Socially, he never added anything. But on the pitch he was phenomenal.'

It does not surprise McAteer that it ended as it did for Keane at United, with him being released on a free transfer and falling out with Alex Ferguson, despite more than a decade of service and unparalleled success.

'Loyalty and honesty – that's Roy. He's like me in that sense. I feel really let down if I don't get that back from people I respect: family, friends, teammates. I struggle to get over it, though I usually do in the end. I'm not sure whether Roy ever does. If he doesn't get the loyalty he expects, then you're dismissed, never back in the circle.

'Not so long ago, I spent the day with Mike Phelan [Ferguson's former assistant]. It was really interesting. He must have been sick of me at the end because I was asking him so many questions. He told me that with Fergie, if he watched a game and a player lost the ball and then found it really difficult to get back into position, Fergie would turn round and go, "He's finished, lost his engine." He'd then try to get the player out of the club. With Roy, Roy was forever telling him it was a one-off – he'd had a bad night's sleep and he was tired for that game. Fergie gave Roy more chances than other players. But once the seed was planted, Fergie would never change his mind.

'You've got to be honest with yourself. Roy was such a brilliant player in such a crucial position, any slip in standard would have felt like an avalanche. What he offered was of such a high standard that when he was on his way down it became easier to spot. But I don't think Fergie knew how to handle a Roy Keane in decline. Roy is a difficult person to deal with. You never know what he's thinking.'

It is impossible to think of Keane tolerating the supposed behaviour of the Spice Boys – a term that makes McAteer want to 'hide behind the couch' when I mention it.

'The reputation of our team was exaggerated. So much has been said and written, it is difficult to know what is true and what is myth. People prefer to believe the sexier stories. It's a case of someone saying something often enough for it to become an accepted truth.

'I have heard all the tales. It pisses me off. Wild parties, drinking, modelling, doing adverts, nights out in London, the celebrity circuit. There were occasions when some of this was true but it certainly doesn't reflect what actually happened day to day. It is easier for people to see it as part of a trail when really they were separate incidents that occurred over a long period of time. We didn't lead a jet-set lifestyle. Occasionally, we let our hair down and it was used as an explanation for all the things that went wrong on the pitch. That was bollocks.'

McAteer admits to frequenting the trendy London nightclub Browns.

'Maybe in the course of a season, when the time was right,

a group of us would get the train down on a Saturday after the match had finished. It was usually when there was an international break. If I wasn't going away with Ireland, I'd travel with a few of the boys that weren't internationals, lads like Razor, John Scales and Jamo. They were all Londoners and knew the scene, so they liked to go where they were comfortable. I didn't see the harm.

'Maybe Roy should have just put a stop to it. But it was never the Liverpool way to stop players from socializing. The club's success had been built on it. I'd grown up on stories about Terry McDermott being out on the sauce but still being the fittest player around. Management had long seen it as a positive. Perhaps they weren't wise enough to the changes around football: the media intrusion, the added expectations because of the wages we were earning.'

While McAteer had a short relationship with Mel C, Stan Collymore was photographed separately with models like Dani Behr.

'Having a celebrity girlfriend is not unusual. OK, you saw the odd page-three girl linked to lads like Phil [Babb] and Scalesy as well as myself, but that kind of thing had gone on for generations behind closed doors without anybody finding out about it. The media were just a lot more aggressive with footballers in the nineties because of the money in the game and the coverage it got on TV. We were expected to be pillars of the community because we were earning a lot more money. But it was new money, a new society with new expectations. Were we meant to become prayer boys overnight? At the beginning, I enjoyed the whole celebrity thing. Who wouldn't? A few years earlier, I'd been broke. Suddenly, Robbie Williams was out with us. Seeing people off the telly – musicians, actors, supermodels and all that – it was fucking ace. Then, after a while, you realize it's actually quite shit.'

The impact of the players' allegedly louche behaviour was felt when Gérard Houllier became Liverpool manager independent of Roy Evans after five months in the role together. The

Evans–Houllier axis was a marriage made in purgatory, one where the pair might as well have petitioned for divorce on the wedding day.

'It was a very confusing period,' McAteer recalls. 'The players did not know who to go to. I'd been dropped from the team along with Robbie [Fowler]. The usual procedure would be to go to the manager's office and speak to him. But whose office did we go to now? Roy told me that he and Houllier had agreed to speak together whenever they dropped a player. But when it came to that time, Houllier always seemed to go missing.'

In Houllier, it felt like Liverpool had appointed the French version of Howard Wilkinson. With no professional career to boast of, in the 1970s Houllier had taught French at Alsop High School, less than two miles away from Anfield. He was an avid student of football, someone who by the late 1990s could lecture on the subject with authority. This he had done on occasion at the behest of Wilkinson, who occupied in England the post of technical director, which used to be Houllier's job in France. Houllier was articulate in the dialogue of football but he failed to qualify for the World Cup finals at his only time of asking with France, whose FA kept him on as spokesman for their national think tank. But as many a theorist has discovered, there is a Grand Canyon between talking a good game in the office and winning major honours.

Houllier brought a small team, Noeux-Les-Mines, to the upper reaches of the French second division. His progress continued at Lens, then, when the biggest club in Paris took note, he won them the French league title. But that solitary trophy was in 1985–86, when Paris Saint-Germain had all the best players in a weak championship. When he failed to consolidate, he retreated into the womb of his national federation.

Houllier was Liverpool's first foreign manager. After forty years, the door to the old Boot Room was closed. He was a coach of schoolmastery rather than old-school persuasion. McAteer believes Liverpool had appointed an academic instead of the charismatic motivator that was needed: someone capable of guiding a young group of British players that had finished third in the Premier League table the season before.

McAteer became concerned about Houllier's suitability when Liverpool travelled to Valencia for the second leg of a second-round UEFA Cup tie at the start of November 1998. McAteer watched proceedings from the substitutes' bench.

'A lot of the lads lost respect for Houllier that night,' he says. 'We'd played badly in the first leg at Anfield and everybody expected us to go to Spain and get trounced. We conceded a goal late in the first half and went in 1–0 down at half-time. In the dressing room, Houllier just stood there open-mouthed like a stunned goldfish. He did not know what to say. He was lost for words. It was really embarrassing. Roy could sense what was going on, so took control and calmed everything down. He got the belief back in us. In the end, we went through on away goals despite being down to nine men at the final whistle after a couple of skirmishes with their players. We weren't happy with the referee's performance. Most of us were a bit hyped up because we thought all the decisions had gone against us.

'We were in a celebratory mood but in the corner of the room Houllier was there rinsing through the kits. Roy asked him what he was doing and Houllier told him that he wanted to give a set of shirts to the French officials. Roy went crazy and told him to fuck off because they'd nearly cost us progression. Houllier then changed his mind and announced they were for the French players in the Valencia team. Roy didn't change his stance and again told him to do one. Moments later, Houllier chucked the kit down and stormed off in a huff.'

Nine days later, it was Evans walking away, announcing his resignation as joint Liverpool manager following a 3–1 home defeat to Tottenham Hotspur in the League Cup. Liverpool were eighth in the table at the time. They finished the season in seventh place.

'I respect Roy a lot for taking himself out of the situation. He only did it because of his love for Liverpool. He could see the team. The players and the results were suffering because the joint managerial role wasn't suiting anyone. It was clear Houllier was going to stay, because he'd just been brought in by the board. So there was only one option. There was no other solution. Roy could have carried on and taken another job at the club probably, but he did the big thing with a clean break.'

Evans made an emotional farewell. After telling the squad at Melwood, his departure was announced at an Anfield press conference. The following day, a picture of Evans wiping a tear away as he left the ground for the last time in an official capacity was published in the *Liverpool Echo*. Different players have spoken of the reaction to Evans' departure. There were suggestions some laughed as Evans left the room.

'Amongst the lads that had been with Roy for a number of years, that's simply not true,' McAteer says. 'We were all gutted for Roy. We wanted him to stay. Nobody wanted Houllier in the first place. The chairman should have been stronger and given Roy another year, because we weren't that far away.'

McAteer was dismayed at the Frenchman's approach as he quickly set about dismantling the team. McAteer was the first player Houllier sold, leaving for Blackburn at the end of January. Cameroonian Rigobert Song was brought in as his replacement in the same week.

'The way Houllier was speaking, it was as if we were on the verge of relegation. It was as if we were a gang of lads on the Club 18–30 circuit. But the season before, we'd gone as close to the title as any Liverpool team had since 1990. He had an exciting group of young players at his disposal, with talent that just needed harnessing a little. But Houllier came out with loads of comments about us being technically inferior. He made out we were crap. Then he spoke of a five-year rebuilding job to make us "contenders" again. We were fucking "contenders" five months earlier. He was getting his excuses in, buying himself time. A lot of the foreign managers do that now.

'Houllier was wrong. A huge rebuilding job wasn't necessary. There was no need to go and spend nearly £100 million on foreign players and get rid of the young internationals Liverpool had on their books. Roy had helped the development of six players that went on to become full England caps. Under Houllier, the promotion from within all but stopped. He was the worst kind of survival manager who tried to solve all problems with a chequebook.'

McAteer believes Liverpool fell into the trap of appointing a foreign manager just because it was the 'cool' thing to do.

'Wenger had come into Arsenal and revolutionized the place. He changed the style of the team very quickly. There were players like Tony Adams, the leader of the team but someone who'd suffered with off-field problems [Adams had been to rehab for alcoholism], and suddenly under Wenger he'd become a new man. It was like he rediscovered himself.

'Houllier came in and didn't analyse anything. He already had the idea that we were a bunch of party animals who were out all the time. It was so far from the truth.

'Maybe the game was evolving too quickly, not just for Roy but for Liverpool. Football changed so quickly. The money, the media, the TV, fitness, diet – everything. Whether Roy was up to speed with all that, I'm not sure. But he had a young team who never questioned him on anything. In the dressing room, the voices were John Barnes, Mark Wright and Rushy. Never ever did one of the young lads pipe up. Otherwise Ronnie Moran would be in your face. Roy built some team. When he left, it was reaching its peak. Houllier didn't know what he had.'

After leaving Liverpool, McAteer's spell at Ewood Park ended abruptly after he clashed with Graeme Souness. He moved to Sunderland and finished his career at Tranmere, where he was eventually appointed as assistant to John Barnes in 2009. Three wins in fourteen games left Tranmere in the relegation zone. Even in the hard times, McAteer can see the funny side. There is room for one last story.

'I sensed that the sack was imminent for me and John. I went to the training ground and John, as always, was in early. He'd just done his pre-match press conference with the media for the Saturday. The chairman [Peter Johnson] called John into his office and I had a feeling it was going to be bad news. I went to put my training kit on. When I got to John's office, John looked me up and down and said, "Put your jeans back on. We've been sacked."

'I asked him whether he wanted to go for a coffee to chat about everything. John used to ride a bike into work to keep fit. He said, "That's fine, I'm going to ride out of here." I told him he couldn't do that. He'd just done the press conference. They were all over the place. If they saw him riding out the training ground, there's the headline already: "ON YOUR BIKE". I could see it.

'So I suggested he put the bike in the car. He agreed it was a good idea. So we go to the car park and lift the bike up but it won't go in. It was like the fucking *Krypton Factor*. John was on the phone as he always was. I had it in this way, I had it in that way . . .'

McAteer's mobile phone began to vibrate.

'It was my mate. He goes, "Macca, turn the wheel the other way – the bike will go in . . ."

'I was like, "What?"

'"Turn the wheel the other way, it'll go in."

'I look around the car park and say, "Where are you?"

'He says, "I'm at home, you're live on Sky now – turn the wheel and it'll go in!"

'I went, "Cheers, mate." So I put the phone in my pocket, turned the wheel the other way and we drove off.

'So there we were, live on Sky, being sacked. Brilliant.'

With that, McAteer's attention tails off and the sound on the Dictaphone fades to laughter.

CHAPTER SIX

cultzeros.co.uk

JAMES BOND,
John Scales, 1994–96

OUTSIDE A CAFE ON WIMBLEDON HIGH STREET, JOHN SCALES reaches into the right pocket of his hoodie and casually pulls out a half-empty packet of cigarettes. 'You don't mind if I have the odd smoke, do you?' he asks considerately, waiting for permission to spark up while he flips a lighter low on fuel between his fingers. 'It's a bad habit of mine.'

It is a curious sight, seeing a professional footballer chugging away, whether or not he is currently playing. It is not quite midday but the wave of surprise is not suppressed by the fact he prefers to drink espressos instead of lager, although the espressos are doubles and he shoots three of them down like chasers. Each one includes a hunk of Demerara sugar.

'I've done things the wrong way round,' Scales says ruefully, offering a faint smile. 'In my playing career, I drank a lot – too much at times. As for the smoking, I've managed to cut that down to a reasonable level. I'm more of a social smoker than an addict.'

Scales admits he has a rebellious streak, something he believes resulted from his earliest experiences as a footballer as he attempted to fit into the 'brutality' of dressing rooms at Leeds United then Wimbledon. At Liverpool, he concedes the players went out too much and acknowledges that, aged twenty-eight, he should have been confident enough to put a stop to it.

When Liverpool unveiled their new strip before the 1996–97 season, Kathy Lloyd – frequently seen topless in lads' magazines such as *Maxim*, *Loaded* and *FHM* – was involved in the photo shoot wearing a full goalkeeper's kit, her arms wrapped around Scales's shoulders, Scales looking slightly uneasy. 'I went with the flow for far too long and eventually it caught up with me,' he says.

In his defence, however, Scales reasons that expectations of Liverpool's footballers were contradictory at the time and remain unrealistic.

'Until the mid to late nineties, the lad culture ruled inside all clubs,' he explains. 'It was no different to any building site across the country. You had to be tough, sharp with your tongue and prepared to stand up for yourself. But now the papers began pouncing whenever you tried to be one of the lads in public. All I wanted to be around other players was myself, but this was a time when being honest seemed almost rebellious. I did not want to be a typical footballer. But it was something I probably ended up becoming; otherwise, I wouldn't have gotten along.

'As more money was ploughed into the game, players ceased to be players and clubs became international businesses. Image ruled. Clubs have come to regulate the way players act. They are given media training and, because most of them don't give anything away to the papers, any sign of someone having a bit of personality is seized on and exaggerated. It has led to an unhappy situation, a different type of falseness.'

This is Scales as he wants to be: smoking and enjoying brunch as morning leisurely breaks into afternoon. He will spend the rest of his day with his two young daughters who are on half-term. As he eases into a steel seat, stretching out his long and powerful limbs, he insists he's happier in his forties than he was twenty years ago.

'The trouble with the football dressing room then was that it was defined by the lowest common denominator, which, with all due respect, is the majority of people involved,' he continues. 'Anyone who wanted to be different stood out a mile – as in society generally, I suppose. Football is often a reflection of society. But because there is so much money involved and, sadly, a lot of jealousy, society does not want to admit it.'

Scales is a tall, blond, well-spoken and clean-cut-looking man and, even though he is not, he appears every inch a public school boy. It is hard to imagine how he fitted in, particularly at Wimbledon, proponents of the sabre-rattling welt down the middle, football's imitation of the 2nd Panzergruppe.

I suggest to Scales that he possesses the appearance of the intelligent kid at school who ends up mixing with the wrong crowd.

'On the face of it, that's how it seems,' he admits. 'But I had to find a way to fit in, otherwise my career wouldn't have followed the relatively successful path that it did.'

Scales talks about the bubble of football and describes a prohibitive environment where he was not alone in acting insincerely. As the only singleton at Wimbledon, in an attempt to impress his teammates, as well as convince them that he wasn't gay despite the sniggers inside the dressing room, Scales courted a 'trophy girlfriend' and took her to the 1988 FA Cup post-final dinner. Scales went further and tried to be 'one of the lads again' by heckling the Lord Mayor of London during a speech that celebrated Wimbledon's remarkable achievement in beating one of the greatest Liverpool teams that has ever been. 'I sat there shouting, "Boooring ... boooring." It wasn't in my character to make a fool of myself, but mix footballers with copious amounts of alcohol and the one-upmanship is unbearable.

'In football, everyone plays a role. When I finished my career, it was a relief because every day I'd drive through the gates of the training ground and become a different person. You need to act in a certain way to earn acceptance in a dressing room. I'm not proud to say I did that. You should have the strength of character to say, "This is who I am and you should accept me." But I was affected by the environment. A big part of that was drinking a lot and going out – being one of the lads. I hid behind bravado. I'd train, go to the pub, stay out late and sweat it off the following morning, then repeat the process. It was an intense routine that takes it out of you.'

Jason McAteer was an example of this at Liverpool. Despite being perfectly sensible when he wanted to be, he was considered a bit of a clown. At Tottenham Hotspur, Scales later met Ramon Vega, a Swiss defender of Spanish parentage, who was exactly the same.

'Ramon was the butt of all the jokes. He'd love being the centre of attention, playing the fool. Yet he's one of the brightest guys I know. He now works as an investment banker. There are a lot of people like that in football. It's often a mechanism to deal with an insecurity or vulnerability.'

It disappoints Scales that taboos still exist in football and he believes it is holding the game back.

'You can't show insecurity in football. If you show any vulnerability, you get slaughtered – maybe by your peers, maybe by the press. It's as simple as that. That's why no active footballer has come out as gay. Players think they've got nothing to gain and all to lose. If you can't be true to yourself, your performance – no matter your field of work – is not going to be at its maximum. It is to the detriment of the sport we all love.'

Scales's career began at Leeds United, a club he joined late at seventeen mainly because his school in Harrogate only had representative teams for rugby union, cricket and athletics. Any volume on Harrogate's football success, indeed, would make for a short read.

'I was the high-jump champion and sprint champion of

North Yorkshire,' he says proudly. 'I dreamt of emulating Daley Thompson. I would have preferred to be a decathlete rather than a footballer.'

His path to Leeds began when Rossett School received a letter from the county's football association asking the head of PE to nominate players for trials.

'At the same time, I was doing maths, physics and graphic design at A level. I flunked my mocks and didn't know what I was going to do. Fortunately, my dad's best mate lived next door to Eddie Gray, who was a Leeds legend and had taken over as manager. He leant over the fence one day and asked Eddie to do him a favour by sending down a scout to watch me play for the county.'

Scales was offered non-contract terms by Leeds.

'I was too old to be given apprentice forms and too young to become a professional. The uncertainty didn't bother me, though, because I loved sport. Going and playing for Leeds wasn't a case for me of thinking, "Oh my god, I'm going to play for Leeds." It was a case of realizing that I was going to be outside every day in the fresh air playing sport. What better thing is there to do?'

Scales was wise enough to realize that merely being recruited did not mean he was set for life. The wages also reflected that.

'A mate of mine opened a tennis and squash clothes and equipment shop in Leeds city centre and I went into partnership with him. It was called No Sweat. The business eventually made enough to open a couple of other branches and we had three in total. In those early days, I'd train in the morning then go to the shop in the afternoon and work my balls off.'

Leeds were First Division champions in 1974 and then reached the European Cup final only to lose to Bayern Munich in 1975. The intervening years had been stormy and by the time Scales joined, Leeds had been relegated to the old Second Division.

'The system was different to what it is now, where seventeen year olds are integrated into youth systems. For me, it was straight into the first-team squad with legends like Peter Lorimer and Frank Gray. You trained together, showered together and drank together. Younger boys like Neil Aspin, Scott Sellars and

Denis Irwin were there but Leeds continued to struggle. The club was in the doldrums and there didn't seem to be any way out.'

Scales did not play a first-team game in the fifteen months he was there and found the integration into a squad of forceful personalities testing.

'It made me wonder whether football was right for me. I considered switching back to athletics. When you aren't used to being in the environment of a football club and a group of lads who are driven – compared to the laid-back way I was – it's very hard. Although I was born in Harrogate, I moved at a young age to Norfolk. Then suddenly, when I was ten, my mum and dad split up and I went back to Harrogate with my mum and two sisters. I grew up with three women and wasn't used to the macho culture that existed in football. I was very shy, almost introverted.'

Although Scales's mother remarried, the relationship ended within a year. Scales found living in Harrogate oppressive.

'It was a traumatic period. Tourists to Harrogate see Bettys Tea Rooms, the spas and the general wealth. But there's also an undercurrent of social problems. I found growing up there suffocating because everyone knows everyone else's business. It's not very healthy.'

None of this prepared him for what he describes as 'the brutality of a dressing room'.

'I struggled to embrace the banter. The Sheridan brothers, John and Darren, were Manchester lads and had come from a tough inner-city background. Everyone thought I was a posh kid because I spoke with a pronounced accent, and they let me know about it. I'd never been subjected to this before, so I couldn't relate to it. The reality was, my upbringing had been fairly normal. There had been hardships. I'd regularly speak to my dad and tell him that I wasn't enjoying it. I liked the games but everything else was a bit shit to be honest.'

Scales was let go by Leeds and considered abandoning a career in football before it had really started.

'The moment they called me into the office to say I was being released hurt terribly because it was a rejection. It wasn't about my dream of football being shattered. It was that feeling of not being good enough and having to make decisions about my future before I expected to. I didn't have a clue what I was going to do.'

A chance meeting on a ferry to Denmark between two of his former Leeds coaches and Bobby Gould, the manager of Bristol Rovers, led to an unexpected opportunity.

'Bobby wanted to sign Dave Mehew, who'd been with me at Leeds, straight away. Dave's nickname was Boris because he had bright-red hair like Boris Becker. Bobby asked about the other players Leeds were getting rid of and my name cropped up. I'd only played as a winger and a centre-forward before joining Leeds but in the last few months before being released I'd moved to full-back, excelling there. Bobby was interested but in my first pre-season trial Tony Cottee, who was one of the best young strikers around, tore me a new hole. West Ham were battering us and it was embarrassing, so Bobby dragged me off at half-time. I could tell he wasn't sure about me but thankfully he offered me another chance and a few months later I signed a professional contract. The club put me in digs with Larry Lloyd's mum – he was a Liverpool defender in the Bill Shankly era. It was chaos. Larry's got a huge family in Bristol. There were always people around.'

As a goalkeeper-clattering centre-forward, Gould played for nine clubs across the Football League, from Arsenal to Hereford United. When Dave Bassett left Wimbledon to replace Graham Taylor as Watford's manager in the summer of 1987, Gould was appointed as his replacement and took Scales with him for a modest fee of £70,000. In turn, Scales left Nick Tanner behind, his teammate at Rovers and a player he describes as 'all right, not bad, not brilliant'. Only thirteen months separated the pair in age, yet Scales would take five years longer than Tanner to reach Liverpool and by then Tanner was close to retirement. 'I wasn't the player in 1989 that I was in 1994,' Scales insists. 'Then again, I'm not really sure what sort of a player Nick was in '89, because he used up so much energy charging about.'

In signing for Wimbledon, Scales was stepping into a unique

ecosystem of a club that had only been in the Football League for ten years, a place where Darwin's survival-of-the-fittest theory was applied to football.

'I had a really torrid time being alone in London as a twenty year old from Yorkshire. It felt like being at Leeds all over again. You had people like Wally Downes, the first-team coach, waiting to cut you down at any opportunity. But there was something in me that helped me get through it. My mum is a really steely character. She's very much a person who gets on with things and makes the best of what she's got. I stuck at it and wouldn't give up. Wimbledon may have been the best thing for my career, because it brought me out of my shell, made me streetwise and developed me as a player. Most importantly, it made me realize what was needed to flourish within football.'

Scales was intimidated by the substantial personalities within Wimbledon's dressing room. Scales was six months older than Dennis Wise and Andy Thorn but felt years behind in terms of social development. 'They were sharp, quick and ruthless – a totally different breed to me.'

Scales speaks about the merciless way he was initially singled out.

'In one of my first pre-season games, I remember the ball being pushed towards me at full-back and rolling under my right foot and out for a throw-in. Wally screamed at me from the touchline. Afterwards, I could hear him in the showers, "Fucking Scalesy, why have we signed that sack of shit. Seventy grand for that? He's fucking useless." I was one of several new players that Bobby had brought in with him. There was also Eric Young, Terry Phelan and Clive Goodyear. "What's Gouldy done? These new faces aren't up to much," Wally continued. He was shouting and knew I could hear. I just sat there on the bench, my head in my hands. I should have stepped in and confronted him. It was something I'd only learn with time.'

It was only when Thorn left for Newcastle and Scales was moved into the centre of Wimbledon's defence that he was able to deal properly with his issues of self-worth.

'I found a real confidence on the football pitch. We played Newcastle away in 1989 and I had a great game. I remember feeling instantly comfortable. I'd found my position in the team. Suddenly, I started adapting to life in London and the culture that existed within the Crazy Gang. Previously, I felt like an outsider peering in. It took me five and a half years to get to this point when you include the time spent at Leeds and Bristol Rovers. If I was playing now, I'd have no chance. This is an era where we demand that the players have all the answers at the age of eighteen and nineteen. It's fucking ridiculous to be honest. A lot of it is down to money. Because players are rewarded too quickly, we expect them to be instantly brilliant. Most of them have no experience of life, so it's an impossible ask.'

Scales recognizes that nobody was perfect at Wimbledon. It was the imperfections, in fact, that drove the team further than anyone on the outside expected.

'What Wimbledon did really well was pick up players with a point to prove. Most of them were from lower leagues and had suffered rejections at some point earlier in their career. These were players that had developed personalities but still had a bit of insecurity, which meant they were not in their comfort zone at any time. It meant they had to push themselves in order to flourish. This led to a mutual respect, I guess. We were in it together and needed each other for our own purpose. Maybe at other clubs there was exceptional talent and arrogance in individuals, resulting in the collective suffering. Wimbledon was all about a strong group. If one wasn't doing it, everything came tumbling down, and if you couldn't hack the abuse that followed, you were out.'

Wimbledon were owned and run by Lebanese businessman Sam Hammam.

'People saw Wimbledon as a chaotic club but really it was run with a lot of consideration. Sam and the chairman, a lovely old bloke called Stanley Reed, appreciated what needed to happen in order for it not just to survive but progress as well. They appointed the right managers: Dave Bassett, Bobby Gould then

Joe Kinnear. When they got one of the appointments wrong – as they did with Peter Withe – they were ruthless in getting rid.'

Hammam would accompany the players on nights out and spotted that Withe was struggling within a few weeks of his arrival early in 1991.

'Sam was the ringmaster. We went to Tenerife on a bonding session and Sam was the last one standing at 6 a.m., still singing on the karaoke. Withey was overwhelmed by the culture of Wimbledon. He probably underestimated how wild it was. We were playing five-a-side on the beach one morning, sweating all the alcohol off, and one of the players clattered into him, splitting his eye open. He was walking round afterwards with an expression on his face that said, "This place is unique." He didn't last very long. We partied hard, trained hard and knew when to turn it on and turn it off.'

On the pitch, Wimbledon were led by Vinnie Jones and John Fashanu. When a visiting team lined up in the tunnel at Wimbledon's Plough Lane ground, the pair would infamously walk up and down the line, sizing each opponent up while making derogatory comments. When other teams tried similar tricks, the reaction was severe.

'We went to Spurs, who cut the power in the dressing room and stopped the ghetto blaster from firing out the music that got us all really pumped up. The sockets were all taped up and the people at Spurs seemed quite happy with themselves. Rather than moan about it, Vinnie legged it round to the nearest corner shop and bought a packet of batteries. We placed the ghetto blaster against the door and put it on full volume just to piss Spurs off. It resulted in a fight in the tunnel. We ended up winning the game.'

Scales believes that although their backgrounds and life experiences were different to his, both Jones and Fashanu were also acting out roles in order to succeed within the framework of the dressing room. Jones, for example, was from a reasonably wealthy corner of Hertfordshire even though he managed to peddle the character of a classic London east-end tough man.

'Vinnie's sort of got a split personality,' Scales says. 'He can be the nicest, most engaging and brilliant company you could wish for when you're one on one. If you wanted someone to have your back on the pitch, it would be him. On the flip side, when he's in a different type of group, and with people he wants to impress – and I'd include Fash in that group – he plays the rogue or the thug. If he had too much to drink, he'd be a nightmare. He had an aggressive streak and that could be intimidating. One minute he'd be charming then suddenly he'd be flying off the handle. Occasionally, it was scary.'

Before the 1988 Cup final, Scales met a reporter from *The Sun* in the Dog and Fox pub, over the road from where we are now.

'He wanted to know how I fitted into it all at Wimbledon. He switched the tape off and we shared a beer. He asked me about Vinnie – what he was really like. "Vinnie's a nutter, a lunatic, isn't he?" I fell straight into the trap and agreed, thinking it was off the record. The following morning, Gouldy called me up, warning me that I better not show for training because Vinnie was patrolling the car park waiting for me with a baseball bat. The reporter had fucked me over. I managed to avoid Vinnie for two whole days until he calmed down. Even then he managed to grab me by the throat. All I could do was apologize. I rarely spoke to the papers after that experience. Certainly never *The Sun*.'

Scales understands why players are so reluctant to show any personality in the papers now.

'The clubs don't allow the players to express themselves, and when they do the media often exaggerate it. The players get their fingers burnt and decide from then on to be neutral. That's why Wimbledon was so great and unique. Wimbledon did not even have a sponsor. It did not care about public image. Sam Hammam and Stanley Reed encouraged people to express their individual personalities. It would cause chaos but there were no skeletons in the closet. Nobody was really surprised by the comments about Vinnie in *The Sun*. It meant there were no great revelations and in turn it fostered the right environment for the club to thrive.'

Fashanu was the son of a nurse from British Guyana and a Nigerian barrister. When his parents separated, he was sent together with his older brother, Justin, to a Barnardo's home. The Fashanu brothers were soon fostered by a white family and brought up in rural Norfolk. Whilst at Wimbledon, Fashanu would present television programmes like *Gladiators* in his spare time.

'More than anyone else in the squad, I had a love–hate relationship with Fash,' Scales says. 'He's got an unbelievable presence. When he walks in the room, everybody stops what they are doing. He's got arrogance, which is his strength. We all knew it was due to insecurity from his childhood. I know he had a tough upbringing. Physically, he was incredible – a very powerful and intimidating figure.'

Yet Fashanu's reputation counted for nothing when it came to pranks.

'Fash was always wanting to impress people. He wasn't just a footballer but a businessman and a man about London. He claimed to know everybody. There were connections supposedly in Africa, the Far East and the US. He tried to elevate himself above everybody else. He had a chauffeur that drove him around in a Rolls Royce. One day at the training ground, he stepped out of the car with a fur coat and a briefcase. He looked immaculate. He had a pair of Concorde tickets and he made sure everyone saw them, claiming he'd just flown in from New York. Before training, he'd always wander off for a massage. Roger Joseph was one of his best mates and he told everyone that rather than being in New York Fash had been out in Maida Vale with a couple of mates in a restaurant. "It's a complete lie," Roger told us. At that point, Wally Downes got Fash's expensive pair of shoes and nailed them to the floor with a hammer. Fash's fancy Ralph Lauren tie got cut up as well. We rubbed Deep Heat into his boxer shorts and Vaseline inside his coat. After training, we made sure that everyone was present when he returned to the dressing room. Fash emerged from the shower, dried off then tried to pick up his shoes. He went ape shit. Boy, he had a temper. It was like a tornado.'

Scales was on the receiving end of a Fashanu reprisal after a 'loose' comment about another player's sexuality made in an attempt to escape the digs about his own.

'Little did we know at the time but Fash's brother Justin, God rest his soul, was gay. I could sense that Fash wasn't happy that I'd broached the subject of homosexuality. It touched a nerve and ten minutes later he reacted by forearm-smashing me in training, knocking me straight out. I couldn't breathe. Fash stood over me, glaring, not saying anything. It was clear why he'd done it.'

Wimbledon's image was based on confrontation.

'Immediately after a game, each player would chip in with comments. We'd challenge each other. You had to be strong to listen to the truth. If you were good, you'd get praise but if not they'd dig a grave and throw you in. Every Monday morning, we'd get called into a video meeting by Gouldy or Joe Kinnear when he became manager. Everyone dreaded this. We'd huddle in the manager's office and, once again, you'd get picked out. "That's not good enough, you've let your teammates down here . . ."

'On more than one occasion, Gouldy reached into the wardrobe in his office and pulled out a pair of boxing gloves. He offered to fight people who dared to contradict him. Dennis Wise went too far once, so we all piled outside and they had a fight while we stood around in a circle. They knocked shit out of each other and Wisey ended up breaking Gouldy's rib. Nobody called for an ambulance. Gouldy had to take himself to the nearest Accident and Emergency.'

This was the way Wimbledon solved problems. The next day, Gould and Wise had moved on. Resentment was rarely harboured for long.

'It was all about getting negative feelings out of the system. It was medieval. *Got a problem? OK, let's fight.* I wouldn't say there were no grudges, because Sanch [Lawrie Sanchez] and Fash had a simmering feud for years. Somehow, on a pitch we'd come together on a Saturday and look after one another. It was a dysfunctional family that worked.'

Wimbledon's dressing room was governed in a similar way to

Liverpool in the 1980s. Self-regulation ruled. Tactically, however, Wimbledon were considered as opposite to Liverpool. No other team was routinely attacked with anything like the vehemence reserved for Jones, Fashanu and the boys. The England striker Gary Lineker once commented dismissively, 'The best way to watch Wimbledon is on Ceefax.'

'We were long ball but weren't kick and rush,' Scales insists. 'That's an insult to the organization that existed at the club. It was a direct style of football built on the percentages of creating chances. To make that successful, you needed a technical execution. We didn't lump the ball forward just for the sake of it. We were much more cultured, sophisticated and technically good than people give us credit for.

'In defence, for example, I knew that Fash would be running in the channel in between the centre-half and full-back. I knew that Fash had the technical capabilities to receive a long pass on the chest and bring other players into the equation. There were times when you wouldn't hit the target man but it was nevertheless part of a plan. The midfield would know the importance of winning the first phase after the knockdown. We worked at it, trained at it, day in, day out.

'There was the right blend between coaching and strong man-management at Wimbledon. Gouldy and Joe Kinnear were the motivators. There was a method behind everything we did. Everybody accepted their limitations and the emphasis was on getting more out of what we were good at. It was sophisticated. Dennis Wise, for example, was one of the best crossers of the ball I've seen from set pieces. On the training ground, we spent hours practising runs from Wisey's deliveries, getting across the defender.

'In the early days, we were coached by Don Howe, who was a visionary and one of the best at his job in the country. Then there was Ray Harford, who later joined Kenny [Dalglish] as his assistant at Blackburn. When Liverpool came in for me, Blackburn did at the same time and it was really tempting to go there because I knew how good a coach Ray was and, obviously, there was the legend of Kenny.

'Football is not as complicated as people make it out to be. If your strengths are playing the Liverpool way, which is pass and move, that's what you should do. In the 1980s, Liverpool's players passed the ball and made an angle better than any other group of players around. But it was still about understanding the sum of all the parts and making it work. Ours was a direct style of football but we did it better than anyone else, had more success with it and therefore got more criticism.'

The long-ball tag did not bother Wimbledon's players.

'We loved it, we really loved it,' Scales smiles mischievously. 'It was the old process of creating a siege mentality. Everybody hated us but we treated that as a positive. Man United did the same. Nobody liked them apart from their own supporters. That only magnified their arrogance. It made them more cohesive as a group. We felt we could beat anybody. We never played with fear or were intimidated. We relished going to the big clubs. As the upstarts, we were desperate to go to places like Anfield and Highbury and start a riot on the pitch. It was all about wrecking the establishment and upsetting the status quo.'

Scales did not play on the occasion in the early nineties when Vinnie Jones scrawled 'Bothered' underneath the 'This is Anfield' sign that informs teams they are about to walk out on to the pitch at Liverpool, a moment that made Liverpool's manager Graeme Souness realize his players were not up for the fight because of their meek reaction towards the desecration. 'They just laughed it off,' Souness said.

Scales believes Wimbledon ended Liverpool's aura of invincibility by beating them in the FA Cup final of 1988. Scales was on the bench that day.

'We appreciated we were up against one of the great, great sides. But we took everything to another level. In the dressing room, the music was a lot louder. In the tunnel, Vinnie was screaming crazy stuff like, "We're going to rip all of your heads off," although I'm not really sure it bothered the Liverpool players. It was as if we were going to war. It concerned me that everyone was so wound up we'd forget our responsibilities. But when we got on the pitch, the intensity continued. We only worried about ourselves and tried to stamp our personality on the game rather than let Liverpool impose theirs. And that's exactly what happened.'

In terms of league positions, Wimbledon were catching up with Liverpool and in the 1992–93 season finished just five points behind Souness's team in the table. A year later, Liverpool were toppled by the same margin, Wimbledon securing an all-time high of sixth with Liverpool at an all-time Premier League low of eighth.

It was in this period that Scales decided to move on. Wimbledon had played at their original ground from 1912 until May 1991 before moving to Selhurst Park in a share agreement with Crystal Palace after the Taylor Report reduced Plough Lane's capacity to just nine hundred. Despite the team's rise up the table, Scales believes Wimbledon's soul was lost in that moment and things would never be the same again. By 2004, the club had moved away not just from the borough of Merton but outside London altogether, relocating to Milton Keynes and being renamed MK Dons.

'Souness made a bid for me in 1993 but Sam Hammam didn't tell me about it,' Scales says. 'I really wanted to go. It was a massive compliment because no player before had moved from Wimbledon to Liverpool. Even though Wimbledon were direct, I was a ball-playing centre-half. I was an athlete and incredibly fast. I was also aggressive, because I had to be at Wimbledon. I knew how to organize a back four and Don Howe had helped me with being assertive and more communicative with the other defenders. I felt mentally strong enough to play for Liverpool. So I put a transfer request in and missed Wimbledon's pre-season trip to Hong Kong with a mysterious flu bug, which in reality had everything to do with my frustrations. Sam and I had a verbal agreement that if a big club came in for me he wouldn't stand in my way, but he sent me a message that read: "No way, Jose." He put a silly smiley face as his signature. That really irritated me. Liverpool ran out of patience, so I had to stay at Wimbledon.'

Scales believed that his only way out was to play well the

following season and encourage a bid that Hammam could not afford to reject.

'I got my head down and won player of the year. When Graeme left in the winter and was replaced by Roy Evans, I figured I'd probably end up elsewhere. But I found out that Roy was behind the original offer and he came back in with a better package. This time, Wimbledon accepted. Sam owed me a loyalty bonus of around £15,000, which was a significant amount of money but not huge in the grand scheme of things. I was really angry with the way Sam had handled the situation a year earlier and we hadn't spoken much since, so I ended up taking the matter to a tribunal at Lancaster Gate. I sat opposite Sam and Joe Kinnear, and Sam told me I was ripping his family apart. "You're my son, look what I've done for you." I love Sam to this day and we're fine now but it was bullshit and more bullshit. Sam's argument was based on the fact I'd put a transfer request in. But he'd turned that down. I produced the note that he'd sent me and when the panel saw this they burst out laughing and sided with me. Jim Smith, Derby's manager, was chairing the case. Begrudgingly, Sam paid me the money in hundreds of bags of coins. It was typical of him.'

Scales joined Liverpool twenty-four hours after Roy Evans broke the British transfer record for a defender by signing Phil Babb. Together, the pair cost £7.1 million. Financially, Liverpool were moving into a new stratosphere of spending. Scales says his wages increased tenfold.

'The price didn't bother me. The pressure came from within: always wanting to succeed; never taking anything for granted; mixing with a group of players who were incredibly talented and had huge reputations. John Barnes, Ian Rush and Jan Mølby were there – great players from the previous generation. Could I meet their expectations? Then there was Robbie Fowler, Steve McManaman, Jamie Redknapp – youngsters with immense ability. Would I fit in?'

As he admits, Scales 'went with the flow'. Having struggled initially upon moving from Leeds to Bristol Rovers to Wimbledon, he did not want to jeopardize his future by taking a lot of time to settle. At Liverpool, he appreciated any new player was not afforded such a luxury.

'I jumped in the deep end,' Scales says. 'The lads were out and enjoying themselves. We'd go out in Manchester and bump into the United boys all the time. Roy Keane was there, celebrating United's victories. He was always play-fighting with Jason McAteer and Babbsy, because the three of them knew each other from Ireland. There was this weird, macho, passive-aggressive thing going on.'

Scales's closest friends soon became McAteer, Babb and Jamie Redknapp.

'We had great fun, although it wasn't particularly vulgar or reckless behaviour. We ate together a lot at Est Est Est on the Albert Dock, our favourite restaurant. We played golf, went shopping, went out in London, went out in Liverpool to Cream, Nation or even the Paradox [in Aintree]. We tried to keep things as normal as possible. We were like any other group of lads. We did some daft things. But there were lots of half-truths. Maybe we did spend money on a car. But it was never as much as people said. Maybe we did go out in Soho. But we never stayed out quite as late as it was made out.'

Scales moved next door to Babb in Woolton Village. Howard Kendall was in between jobs having left his post as Everton manager in 1993 and he owned property on the same exclusive estate.

'Babbsy and I took turns driving to Melwood and most mornings Howard would collar us before leaving. "Make sure the two of you pop round this afternoon," he'd tell us. Howard always had champagne in his fridge and he'd let us raid it. We had some hilarious conversations. We'd sit there for hours, trading stories. As he's a big Blue, you'd think Howard would be giving us plenty of stick, but he just loved being around footballers. Howard was a great character, I loved him.'

Living in Liverpool posed new challenges for Scales.

'You can lose yourself in London. There are so many football clubs and so many wealthy and high-profile people – not just footballers; you can slide into the background. That's not the case in Liverpool. Because it's a very close community, everyone knows everyone else's business. The scrutiny and the attention is way more intense. Other boys were in Wirral, Southport or Cheshire. In Stan Collymore's case, he was all the way away in Cannock. That wasn't beneficial to himself or the team.'

Scales had an impression of Liverpool FC that he thought was unshakable. The reality was different. His assessment of the club at his point of arrival to the point of exit has the effect of a truncheon cracking an antique into a thousand pieces.

'Wimbledon were a rag-tag group of lads playing football at a high level. To me, Liverpool were a sophisticated club with an incredible organization that was underachieving but could get back to where it wanted to be. What I quickly discovered was that Liverpool was not sophisticated and the club was stuck in the 1960s. Ronnie Moran's training had not changed since that time. The wooden target boards were still used and they were rotting away. There was no tactical or technical analysis. Diet did not come into any discussion. For away games, we'd turn up in jeans, just as all the players had done in the seventies. There were so many bad habits. Mentally, the team was underprepared at a time when football clubs were figuring out like the rest of the world that good mental health improves physical performance.'

In terms of talent, Liverpool were way in advance of Wimbledon. Robbie Fowler was the most naturally gifted footballer Scales played with or against. By the time Fowler was twenty-one, he'd already broken the thirty-goal barrier in three different seasons.

'Robbie was lazy in training. But that's the way strikers are. Ian Rush was the same – Liverpool's all-time leading goalscorer. Ronnie Moran would scream at Robbie and Steve McManaman, telling them to keep up. They were as thick as thieves, those two. I saw them in Istanbul and nothing had changed. Macca didn't need to run, because he was the fittest lad there and didn't have an ounce of body fat. Maybe Robbie did [need to run] but he was bursting on to the scene and phenomenally gifted. The work he got through on the pitch, the closing down and chasing lost causes, making things happen – it compensated for the training, of course. His finishing ability was the greatest I've seen. Inside the box, outside, headers, the bravery. He had everything, Robbie.'

Then there was David James, a goalkeeper with international-standard attributes but also a few flaws. By 1997, he was commonly known as Calamity James after the comic character from *The Beano*.

'It didn't help Jamo that he was Bruce Grobbelaar's successor and Bruce had made a fair few mistakes in his time only for the quality of the team to take the edge off the negative press he got.

'Jamo was incredibly imposing and a brilliant shot-stopper. He was phenomenal in his build and stature but had not yet developed the communication skills needed to organize a back five where everyone else was older than him. Coming for crosses, his handling wasn't as good as it became later.

'Jamo was a tortured creative genius. He was hyperactive and maybe that affected his decision making. When I first signed for Liverpool, nobody would room with him because he had a reputation for sleepwalking. They persuaded Stig Bjørnebye and on one away trip Stig woke up in the middle of the night to find Jamo trashing the room. Stig proceeded to run down the corridor screaming, "Jamo's trying to kill me!"'

Scales is adamant that the talent at Liverpool was as considerable as it was at Manchester United. Yet this potential was not harnessed in the right way.

'United had Alex Ferguson in charge, who instilled the discipline and focus that was needed to be successful. In Roy Evans, we did not have that. In any walk of life, if you give people an inch they'll walk a mile, especially young lads. Above Roy, it wasn't there either. The chairman David Moores could have been more forceful on a lot of issues. If a club does not have structure, then it's not going to function on the pitch in the long term. The whole approach at United was more professional from top to bottom. Old Trafford was set up for the twenty-first century and was forward thinking. Liverpool looked to the past for all the answers but did not apply those principles to what was happening in the present. Liverpool was caught in a time warp. Melwood was undeveloped. The only official merchandising at Anfield was sold from a little shop in the corner of the car park. Whenever the team bus rolled into Old Trafford, there was a megastore and thousands of fans queuing up to buy shirts.

'The fact that the United boys were doing the same socializing, meeting in the same places, proves that to be successful you've got to have all the pieces of the jigsaw in place. You've got to have the right set of players. You need the right manager and coaches. You need the right owners, commercial and marketing teams pushing things forward financially. United had all of this. Liverpool did not, although we weren't far off. It wasn't as if United were finishing twenty-five points ahead of us and we were mid table, struggling.'

Scales believes what was once one of Liverpool's greatest strengths had become its weakness before he'd even moved there.

'Money changed the game and it's no surprise really that a club with socialist principles was the first to fall by the wayside. Liverpool were the first victims of football's revolution. At Liverpool, the collective ruled. Suddenly, the players realized the wages they were on would not be able to sustain their lives after football, so they tried to claw as much money from the game as possible. The atmosphere changes. Graeme [Souness] tells them to stick or twist; many of them twist. It unravelled quite quickly.'

Under Souness, a fissure had opened up in Liverpool's squad, and spirit had drooped to the point where only five players turned up to the end-of-season trip to Tenerife after winning the FA Cup in 1992. Evans attempted to address the issue by allowing the players to go out when they wanted, drink what they wanted, and generally liberated them. Liverpool's players seemed to genu-inely enjoy spending time together once again – just like before – and Evans must have considered this a positive, something that would be reflected by good results on the pitch – just like before. The rediscovered unity was illustrated when Liverpool's squad invested a couple of grand each in a flat racehorse.

'We were in Est Est Est over lunch trying to come up with names. It was classic Scouse humour. Robbie said, "Imagine if the commentator says, 'And there's Some Horse coming up on the outside.'" We all laughed and went with it. It won its first three races at Haydock. Unfortunately, I'm the worst gambler in the world and only bet on the fourth race when it didn't even finish.

'The camaraderie was absolutely brilliant at Liverpool,' Scales continues. 'It was the best I've seen anywhere. We went out win or lose. But we went out when we lost because it was the mechanism young lads at that time would use to switch off from the disappointment. The training was intense and we'd play two games a week. The decision to go out wasn't a show of disrespect or an abuse of our status. It was just a way of unwinding and releasing the pressure of playing with a group of mates – your teammates – who were going through the same emotions. Of course, we'd never sit there talking about the pressure. We'd have a drink and talk about something else to escape it further. Nobody on the outside seemed to mind whenever we won, because people wanted to be associated with success, even though – again – we were going out to relieve the tension that had been generated to secure a good win earlier that afternoon.'

Liverpool's players had shared strong working relationships with members of the press in the 1970s and eighties. By the nineties, however, the attitude towards football coverage in the media was shifting.

'In the previous era, the players relied as much on the journalists as the journalists did on the players,' Scales claims. 'The journalists would go on tour with the players and accompany them on nights out, then show up at the Christmas parties and get involved in all the fun. There was a respect, an equilibrium. That quickly changed when the red-top newspapers in London started hunting for more gossip to fill their columns. Football changed too, with footballers becoming the new rock stars in the eyes of the media. A lot of people think of the football press as one living and breathing organism, but it's not. There are muckrakers and there are journalists. Unfortunately, the football press wasn't in charge of its output any more. Unfortunately for us, anyway. Liverpool were the most popular and successful club in the land and were falling just short of the standards that were previously set, at a time when media intrusion was intensifying to a level nobody had seen before. We were always going to be targeted.'

Scales believes Liverpool's players were almost too familiar with one another. It was rare that cruel words were exchanged. Evans' attempt to draw them together had gone too far.

'Collectively, we should have been more like Wimbledon, where there was an understanding that if things were going wrong, we had a responsibility to do something about it. At Wimbledon, the self-governance came from the senior players, who appreciated the sacrifices that needed to be made to make Wimbledon successful. At Liverpool, what had been successful for the senior players previously was not going to be successful for our team due to the acceleration of professionalism. Because the manager believed it was the senior players that should dictate the way things were run – as it always had been under Shankly, Paisley and Dalglish – Liverpool lost their way. At United, Ferguson was orchestrating everything.'

Scales can't recall a meeting being arranged where the players' responsibilities were outlined forcefully.

'If it did happen, it had gone too far for Roy to get the right response. It would have fallen on deaf ears. It is sad because Roy is the nicest fella you'll ever meet. But unfortunately, in my opinion, he didn't have the respect or gravitas that he needed to meet the expectations of the club just when football was changing. I think it frustrated Ronnie Moran, who was the opposite of Roy in terms of temperament. It must have frustrated Sammy Lee and it probably frustrated Roy inwardly too. I regret it. We missed a great opportunity to be something special. I honestly feel that group of players could have defined the era and reclaimed the glory of the eighties.'

Scales considers it unfortunate that there have been worse Liverpool players since – certainly with less talent – that have been a part of a squad that has won more and therefore are remembered with more reverence.

'We're the Spice Boys and it's something we have to accept now because it will never change. It frustrates me. It's very easy to forget the incredible highs. I only need to talk about the 4–3 win against Newcastle when Stan Collymore scored the winner in front of the Kop in injury time for the hairs to stand up on the back of my neck. At the end, the crowd rose and the sound of "You'll Never Walk Alone" was deafening. I'd lost my voice and had a ringing sound in my ears by the end of that night. The emotion was incomparable to anything I've ever experienced in my life.'

Three days later, Liverpool lost at Coventry City, a result that more or less conceded the title to United.

'It was a shambolic display: one extreme to the exact opposite. It was terrible. I was terrible. Roy can't take the blame for that. Individually, we all made errors. There were times when we all got too excited and lost our focus. Certain things just shouldn't have happened. Robbie Williams was on the coach, maybe more than once. *Why?* Robbie was a great lad and we had some laughs. But he was going through his exit from Take That. His drink and drug problems were well known. How can you have someone in that situation on the coach going to games? Why the hell was that allowed to happen? It fuelled the whole Spice Boy thing. We all hated the tag but the truth always hurts, doesn't it? I know I could have done more to avoid it. All the boys could have.'

The Liverpool squad's reputation as a group of flamboyant hell-raisers was intensified by the way the team played. Evans demonstrated his commitment to the Liverpool way by selling Julian Dicks and Don Hutchison immediately following his appointment, as well as by freezing out Paul Stewart, Mark Walters and, initially, Mark Wright. In midfield, Liverpool re-established their credentials as the best passing team in England, keeping possession better than any other side. In Scales's first season on Merseyside, 1994–95, Liverpool conceded thirty-seven league goals, better than champions Blackburn Rovers and worse only than Manchester United. But despite the statistics, even the dogs on the streets around Anfield knew of Liverpool's defensive crisis.

'It was the crucial times we conceded goals that formed this impression,' Scales says. 'Roy chopped and changed it a lot. I played in a back three alongside Neil Ruddock, Phil Babb, Mark Wright, Dominic Matteo and Steve Harkness. Then on the flanks there was Stig Bjørnebye, Jason McAteer and Rob Jones. Every week, it was a different combination. I felt that we were never allowed to settle. It's no wonder there was an inconsistency, especially at set pieces, when your responsibilities change depending on who you are playing with. You look at the stats and it worked pretty well. But not well enough.'

In the 1995–96 season, only once did Liverpool concede three goals in a match and that was during the famous victory over Newcastle United that Scales has already referred to. It came at a late stage when both teams were chasing the title.

'I'll always remember Razor putting his hand up for offside while I was following the man, not realizing Razor had made the call. There was no pressure on the ball either. [Faustino] Asprilla ran through and scored. We were all over the place even in victory. The defending might have been dubious but it was football at its most expressive.'

There were other occasions at Anfield when Liverpool were losing and the pressure inside the stadium was unbearable.

'You could hear a pin drop,' Scales says. 'I remember giving the ball away or not quite winning a tackle. The groan that followed – there's nothing worse. The pressure was massive. I hear other footballers say that whenever they play, it's their space and all their issues off the pitch are forgotten in ninety minutes. You couldn't at Liverpool. You were stepping into a cauldron, representing the hopes and dreams of everyone watching. I knew the supporters would give their last breath to try to force a win. Dealing with that knowledge isn't easy. Liverpool supporters are not like other supporters because the majority of them have played football themselves. They're very educated. They understand the emotions of the game. If there's tension on the pitch, the crowd feel it too. They just *get* it. The connection between the supporters and the players is closer at Liverpool than I've experienced at any other club or seen anywhere else. There is an emotional intelligence, a bond that is unrivalled.'

Liverpool's progression under Evans was marked at the end of Scales's first full season with a 2–1 victory in the League Cup final over Bolton Wanderers at Wembley. 'You win a final and you feel proud. But it was our ambition to win leagues and FA Cups. No way did we feel it was an achievement that put us back to where we wanted to be at. It was satisfying but it wasn't enough.'

Twelve months later, an FA Cup final against Manchester United presented the opportunity of fulfilling an ambition.

'Everything was different: the build-up, the enormity of playing United. It was a moment where we knew we really blew it, losing 1–0. It showed up our inadequacies as a team and it was the lowest point in my career. Stepping off the pitch, I was angry. If you look at the photographs taken that day, you'll see it. There was so much right about our team and so much wrong. It encapsulated everything: coming so close to being successful but feeling a million miles away.'

Scales reacted by rowing with Sammy Lee and Doug Livermore on the coach.

'Somebody's wife was invited on; I won't say whose. I lost it. We'd just lost what was probably the most important game in a lot of our careers. But once again, the organization was random and chaotic. We were wearing our white suits. I'd had enough of it. I told them that things had to change. The structure and discipline wasn't right. *What are we doing? Where are we going?* I think it contributed towards me leaving Liverpool, because I challenged the coaching staff openly. This isn't me trying to sound clever after the event. I was exasperated by that point. I think the players wanted the discipline. By that, I don't mean someone grabbing you by the throat for being naughty. Just the basics being right: arriving on time, being quiet when the manager speaks. Not having a big party in central London after you've just lost an FA Cup final . . .'

Scales expected to be included in Terry Venables' England squad for Euro 96 that summer but was surprisingly omitted. He was also scheduled to get married to Ruth and had already been on the stag do with his Liverpool teammates in Dublin when the wedding was called off. 'I got really down. I returned to pre-season training in July three days late with laryngitis because of the stress. I was all over the place. It was the beginning of the end.'

Scales played ninety-four games for Liverpool and was usually selected when fit. At thirty, he started suffering from more injuries.

'It was just as I began to really *get* football. But the injuries were self-inflicted. I would train too hard at times, pushing my body harder when I'd had a drink. But of course my body was tired, maybe run-down. I'd have been better off resting.

'When I first signed for Liverpool, I stayed at the Haydock Thistle and every morning after a night out I'd go running round the racetrack to try to sweat some of the badness out. I thought I was doing myself some good. Because the complex is huge, I got locked in on one occasion and had to do a massive run back to the hotel. On Friday at training I felt fine but by Saturday my legs had locked up. I was in bits. I had a nightmare of a game that day. I could carry on with this type of behaviour when I was twenty-one or twenty-two but as I got older I wasn't listening to myself. It caught up with me.'

In late November 1996, Scales received a telephone call from Roy Evans.

'He said that Leeds had made a good offer for me. I'd been in talks with Liverpool about a contract extension but things had gone quiet. I reminded him of that. "All I can say is, we've accepted the bid," Roy kept telling me. But then he said that if I wanted to sit on my contract, I was entitled to. Spurs also made an offer. I wanted to stay at Liverpool, so I rang Roy twice that weekend hoping to hear something positive from him – that he really wanted me to stay. His final words were, "It's your decision." It probably sums up his management style. He wanted the players to have the right answers.'

The problems with structure that Scales witnessed at Liverpool also existed at Tottenham. 'Again, the jigsaw wasn't complete. We had Jürgen Klinsmann, Teddy Sheringham, Darren Anderton, Sol Campbell, David Ginola and Les Ferdinand. But we were miles away.'

Scales retired from football in 2001 after a brief spell at Ipswich Town. He is still involved in the game, working as a commentator for foreign television stations, and also works in commercial licensing at clubs as prestigious as Inter Milan and Juventus. 'It is one step removed, where the glare isn't on you,' he says. 'It's given me an incredible opportunity to explore and be the person I really am without trying too hard.'

With that, Scales stubs out a final cigarette and, after a polite farewell, disappears into the sprawl of south London.

cultzeros.co.uk

PADDY, THE EVEN BETTER-LOOKING ONE,
Patrik Berger, 1996–2003

PATRIK BERGER IS THE KIND OF MAN THAT WOMEN STALK. THERE HE is, striding purposefully through the hotel foyer: tall, olive-skinned, cropped dark hair – generally very handsome.

'He could wear a bin bag and still scrub up,' my mother once told me. That was before she moved predictably and somewhat disappointingly on to José Mourinho. Today, Berger is sporting a pair of stonewashed jeans, a plain white T-shirt, sandals and a set of multicoloured beads around his left wrist. His warm eyes exude kindness and an understated strength. He has manful gritty stubble dotted across a chiselled jaw. Beneath there are the shoulders of a Titan. It is exhausting just watching him.

Not much has changed. Aged forty, Berger remains the drop-dead gorgeous pin-up boy from the wall poster. The female bar staff gravitate in his direction from all sides, like he is a planet with its own orbit. Even though he is initially accompanied by his extraordinarily attractive blonde wife, Jaroslava, it does not stop them gazing.

I decide to tell Berger the information about my mother immediately. In the manner of Roger Moore, his right eye begins an involuntary angular rise as I splutter out the slightly embarrassing tale. His sigh reflects that of a gentleman who has heard this story many times. His response is perfectly indifferent. His fluency in English also makes my ineptitude in foreign languages feel quite shameful. 'Well,' he begins, with the flick of a hand, 'if a lot of women liked me, what can I say? Power is an aphrodisiac. If you play for Liverpool and you are young, you will get the attention, especially if you go to town for a few drinks, for shopping or to dinner. And I do not think there is anything wrong with that. If you are young, free and single – so what?'

Berger's arrival at Liverpool in late summer 1996 acted as confirmation that a footballer with a head shorn like a billiard ball was yesterday's news. There had been Jamie Redknapp and Jason McAteer before him but Berger was distinctive. Who was this talented and mysterious Eastern European with a tawny complexion that belied his heritage? Months before, Berger had scored a goal against Germany at Wembley in the final of Euro 96 only to later finish on the losing side. He was twenty-two years old; a Bundesliga winner with Borussia Dortmund; a person for whom career possibilities seemed endless. Over the next seven seasons in almost two hundred games he would score thirty-five goals for Liverpool, the majority arriving via his cannon of a left boot. After scoring twice in his second game for Liverpool, Leicester City's goalkeeper Kasey Keller said he'd never seen a ball move so fast in his life. Steven Gerrard later claimed Berger's shooting was some of the most ferocious he'd ever seen.

Yet Berger owed his emergence to something that was completely beyond his control. He was sixteen years old when, in 1989, Communism collapsed in the old Czechoslovakia. He considers it fortunate that he was afforded opportunities that were not there for previous generations.

'The world opened up,' he explains, with a brooding gaze that surely could melt flesh. 'The future was exciting. I knew I was living in a free country, a place where I was able to make choices. I was part of the first wave able to have fun. Perhaps that made me seem more rebellious. But surely it's a natural reaction for a person used to being told what to do.'

Berger was born in 1973 and raised in District 8 of the Czechoslovakian capital, Prague. It was a standardized existence. He lived in a featureless apartment block. Most people had similar furniture, clothes and aspirations. Like other families, the Bergers were consigned to a waiting list for a Trabant car. There was limited access to music and goods from abroad. In school, Berger was taught that the Soviets had saved his country from the tyranny of the West. Housing, jobs and healthcare were provided. But only if you accepted the system.

Throughout the 1970s and 1980s, the government's emphasis on obedience, conformity and the preservation of the status quo was often challenged by individuals and organized groups seeking greater autonomy. Although only a few of their activities would have been deemed political by Western standards, the state viewed any independent action, no matter how innocuous, as defiance of the party's control over all aspects of Czechoslovak life. Those who did not comply were not only intimidated and put under surveillance but also subject to house searches, during which the Secret Police invaded citizens' privacy while searching for illegal literature. Bribes abounded; the presence of listening devices in homes prevented open speech; there were long lines at the shops; people were imprisoned for filing complaints or signing petitions. If a citizen defected, the family left behind was severely punished. Any person that met with a dissident was interrogated.

Despite the harsh realities, Berger does not look back on his childhood as a struggle.

'When you are young, you do not understand what it really means to live in a Communist state, because you are not really conscious of anything different,' he says. 'My parents tried to protect me so I didn't see the bad stuff. I had friends, we played out on the street. I had everything I needed. I remember only a happy time. My parents gave me the very best they could give. We had holidays but only in Czechoslovakia. Some families went to Bulgaria or Poland – states that other Europeans did not want to visit. We did not have much choice. But we still had holidays. I did not know of a different way. Maybe that was comforting.'

Berger wondered why he was not able to travel extensively, why he was not able to learn any foreign language other than Russian and, indeed, why he was only able to hear whispers about the achievements of football teams from other countries but never watch them on state television. At the time, though, this all seemed normal. His father would return home each day from his nine-to-five shift as a lorry driver for the local brewery, Prazan, while his mother worked hard teaching infants at a nearby primary school.

'When people ask me what it was like growing up behind the Iron Curtain, most expect to hear stories about bread queues and the police raiding homes. They are usually disappointed when I explain the mundane daily routine.'

Berger appreciates that older members of his family would speak less positively about the era than he does, having dealt with the privations for much longer.

'The thing was, pretty much everybody had the same. There was not really a gap between rich people and poor people. The families were equal. I was happy. We were not poor; we were not rich. We had food on the table every day. It was ordinary. I cannot complain. I also appreciate that my parents might think differently because they had lived under tough conditions for their entire adult life.'

His mother and father were children when, in the 1950s, Joseph Stalin directed the Czechoslovak Communists to carry out purges and the nation held the largest show trials in Eastern Europe. Over a five-year period, from 1949 to 1954, the victims included military leaders, Catholics, Jews, democratic politicians, those with wartime connections with the West, as well as high-ranking Communists. It spawned a society based on paranoia. Five years before Berger's birth, an uprising had led to a brief period when the government of Czechoslovakia, led by Alexander Dubček, wanted to democratize and lessen the stranglehold Moscow had on the nation's affairs. The Prague Spring ended with a Soviet invasion, the removal of Dubček as party leader and an end to reform within Czechoslovakia. It would be another twenty years before the Czechs had their independence.

Berger remembers the euphoria of the Velvet Revolution. He remembers the masses of protesters huddled in Wenceslas Square, demanding change before being brutally dispersed. Hundreds were arrested. Thousands came back. Within four days, eight hundred thousand people were gathered in Prague's city centre. Remarkably, an anti-government rally was screened on state television. Six months later, free elections took place for the first time since 1948. It all happened in a period when Berger's football career was accelerating. He recognizes that history could not have unfolded more conveniently.

'I grew up thinking that life began and ended in Czechoslovakia. Footballers were not allowed to play abroad unless they were thirty-three years old and had more than fifty international caps. For that achievement you were granted the privilege of movement. Yet few top European teams wanted to sign Czech players when their careers were almost over. They'd end up in countries like Switzerland or Austria, or the German second division. But because there was limited information about football in Germany or England, I did not think of any other place. I was not brought up on the legends of Beckenbauer or Dalglish, so my dream was to play in the Czech First League. That was it.'

His ambitions broadened after travelling with Czechoslovakia's under-16 side to the European Championships in the summer of 1990. Berger scored in the final: a 3–2 victory over Yugoslavia. The experience was an 'awakening'.

'The tournament was held in East Germany and, although the

way of life there was very similar to home, it opened my eyes. For the first time, I was playing against teams from other countries: West Germany, France, Scotland and Portugal. The voices, the style of football was sometimes faster, sometimes slower. It was exciting.'

Berger's uncle Jan had followed a similar path: winning gold at the 1980 Moscow Olympics before being named Czechoslovak footballer of the year in 1984. In a different life, his performances in the centre of Sparta Prague's midfield would probably have been enough to attract attention from more significant European clubs. Instead, aged thirty-one, he signed for FC Zürich.

'Although he enjoyed his career, his story taught me to seize opportunities,' Berger says. It goes some way to explaining why upon returning to Prague and finding his exploits would not automatically result in a promotion to the first team of his club Sparta, whose youth sides he'd represented since the age of six, drastic action was taken.

'There were no contracts in Czechoslovakia under Communist rule,' he explains. 'When it collapsed, everything was changing and suddenly the clubs had to offer players professional deals under the new capitalist system. People were free to sign for whoever they wanted.

'I was training with the first team but only being selected for the B team. It was very frustrating, so I did not sign the contract. My father went to the manager and asked him what his plans were for me. He saw me as a squad player amongst twenty-two others. There was no immediate commitment. I was desperate to play.'

Slavia Prague were aware of his situation.

'The manager, Vlastimil Petržela, came to my father and told him that he'd give me a chance straight away. He thought I was good enough. That gave me a lot of confidence, so I decided to go there. It was a big deal in the Czech Republic, because the Berger name carried a lot of weight and it was associated with Sparta through my uncle. He was a big star. Everybody expected me to succeed him in midfield. I grew up supporting Sparta and all

I wanted to do was play for them. But I got the impression they weren't quite so keen. That made my decision.'

Sparta had dominated the Czechoslovakian First League in the 1980s, winning six titles. Slavia had not recorded that feat since 1947. Although the league's second most decorated club, even the city's two other clubs, Dukla and Bohemians, had achieved greater domestic success in the years before Berger's move.

'I spent four years there and the run continued,' he says ruefully. 'We did not win a thing. Sparta were always ahead of us. But I don't look on that as bad. Personally, I could have stayed at Sparta during that time and been a part of it all, celebrating in the background. I wanted to be playing. That's all that mattered to me.'

Petržela pushed a group of young players to the foreground. Berger, Vladimír Šmicer, Radek Bejbl and Pavel Kuka would all feature for the independent Czech Republic national team that reached the final of the 1996 European Championships.

By then, Berger had done enough at Slavia to be spotted by the scouts of Borussia Dortmund and he moved to Germany in August 1995 for £500,000.

'Dortmund was an unbelievable side: Matthias Sammer, Jürgen Kohler, Andreas Möller, Júlio César, players that were champions – six World Cup winners. They'd played in Italy, there was experience, know-how, guys that knew all the tricks.'

Previously, Berger had played as an attacking midfielder or centre-forward. In Germany, coach Ottmar Hitzfeld used him as a screen for the defence.

'Hitzfeld saw things very differently. He was a genius in terms of man-management. This was a squad full of huge egos, players with personalities and big opinions. Everybody thought they knew the right way. There were seven huge stars. But the manager always knew how to handle them so well. Ultimately, that was why we achieved success.

'Players like Möller and Sammer, they would speak to the manager all the time. *Do this, do that. Why do we have three training sessions today?* They were asking questions constantly.

Ottmar was having to listen to everybody. You could see that some of the things the players wanted to change were big and others were small. If they were small, Hitzfeld would bend a little. *OK, if you're tired, you can have a day off, guys.* It made the players feel like they were important, as if they were able to have an influence. Really, though, it was always the manager's call. If the changes were big, the manager would go his own way. He was dictating. He was very clever.

'It made me realize that the best managers guide. At that top end, you are not teaching the players to play, are you? They are stars anyway, people who have won everything already. They know what to do, how it works. Even the training sessions, they were not very special. On the outside you think of a secret. *What is going on in there? There must be something magical.* The reality is, training was always basic, very simple. The most important thing was the man-management, having the dressing room on your side.'

Berger helped Dortmund to the Bundesliga title, playing twenty-five games. Then his focus switched to the European Championships.

'It was funny. I remember the last training session. I was running and Jürgen Kohler was alongside me. We were talking. "Hey, Patrik, what are you doing this summer – a holiday?" I told him that I was going to Euro 96. "What? You're going to watch some games? How did you get tickets?"

'"No, Jürgen," I told him. "We've qualified and we're in the same group as you." I'm still not sure whether he was teasing me or whether it reflected what outsiders we were. Nobody expected us to do anything.'

Berger was introduced as a half-time substitute when the Czechs met Germany in their opening match. By then, Germany had already opened up an unassailable two-goal lead. Few would have foreseen the same teams performing in the final a few weeks later.

'We were huge underdogs. In the groups, we also had to play Italy and then Russia – a match of significance for bigger, more political reasons. Most of our players were still very young and playing in the domestic Czech Republic league. We were unknown. It was the last tournament before the Internet age. You couldn't just go online and find out about us. You had to watch and learn. That helped us a lot. We had nothing to lose.'

The success of the Czech team led to many of their players moving abroad. In the months after the tournament's conclusion, Slavia Prague lost Jan Suchopárek to Strasbourg, Bejbl to Atlético Madrid, Šmicer to Lens and Pavel Nedvěd to Lazio. Karel Poborský might have joined Berger at Liverpool but elected instead to join Manchester United.

'For us to reach the final was like winning the tournament,' Berger insists. 'The Czech Republic had only achieved independence from Slovakia in 1993. We were a new country with a smaller pool. It meant that the manager had to look to youth, and players like me were given opportunities that might not have been there as a united Czechoslovakia. That was a strength because it generated camaraderie. We understood each other. We were very naive but had no fear. I remember playing against Belarus in the final qualifying game and we had to win. There were no nerves. I scored. We won.'

Berger was told about Liverpool's attempt to sign him by his agent before the Czechs' last training session ahead of the final. After just one season with Dortmund, he appreciated it would be difficult to agree a release from his contract.

'Dortmund had been great to me and it was not a pretty way to leave. As a footballer you sign a contract and if you are lucky there is a lot of money involved. But life is short and sometimes you might only have one opportunity. The clubs can be as ruthless as players. Sure, Dortmund wanted me then, but what about in a year's time? Managers, owners, chairmen, they all change. Attitudes change. My childhood taught me that if you wanted something and were in the position to take it, you must do everything to make it happen. As a human being with the freedom to make choices, you owe it to yourself to exercise that privilege.'

Berger was on the verge of going on strike to force the move through. In the end, he arrived at Anfield on the first day of August 1996 for £3.25 million. He was surprised by the 'very basic' nature of the club's Melwood training facility.

'It was behind in terms of the places I'd seen at other European clubs,' he says. 'I was a little bit shocked Liverpool should have it like this. Everything was old. The only thing that was up to date was the grass, which they cut every day.'

Berger accepted that this was the way it had always been at Liverpool.

'The club had achieved so much success, why change it? I spoke to the other players and that was clearly the idea that had been indoctrinated. I was young, new and had not mastered the language, so I thought it best not to ask any questions.'

The spirit in the dressing room also surprised Berger.

'It was a lot louder than in Dortmund, more joking, laughing,' he continues. 'A lot of us were the same age with similar attitudes. Stan [Collymore] was on his own, because I think the key players had figured out he wasn't really interested in being with us. He did not want to make himself available to the group. I soon realized people on the outside saw young players with a lot of confidence and sharing an identity as a bad thing because we did not win trophies.'

Berger admits that sometimes behaviour was stretched a little too far. He too fell into the trap. Berger was already married by the time he arrived in Liverpool. His wife was also expecting their first child. 'The boys would go out but they respected the fact I wanted to be with my family most of the time. I trained hard and I went home to Southport, where I was very happy.' But then he recalls the Christmas party of 1996, an event that led to Liverpool's players appearing on the front pages of the tabloids after police were called to the Moat House Hotel on Paradise Street, a favourite haunt of the squad since the late 1970s when Bob Paisley introduced a nap to the pre-match routine. On this occasion, strippers were ordered and the drinks flowed. It did not help that Merseyside Police headquarters was based just around the corner at Canning Place.

'It was my intention just to have a few beers and go home. I remember telling Robbie Fowler that at the start of the night as he walked past. He just laughed.'

Fowler tells a story about seeing Berger towards the end of the evening. 'I was leaving the club and saw Paddy with a large brandy in one hand and a cigar in the other, with him going, "I love your Ingleeesh parteees!"'

Berger smiles at this suggestion. 'If Robbie says that happened, it probably did. That was a rare night out for me. People might remember it.'

Berger backs Fowler's suggestion that only the stragglers remained by the time the police stormed through the doors. 'It was harmless fun,' he says. 'All the players had departed by then, at 4 a.m. I am told there were some problems at the bar, so the hotel security called 999. Unfortunately, BBC Radio Merseyside was situated over the road and they figured out that something was going on, so the news spread quickly.'

The following morning, the players emerged from their rooms blurry-eyed, hungover and still in their fancy dress. The press were waiting.

'Even though none of us had anything to do with the problems, it confirmed everyone else's belief that we were just a group of party animals, not serious about the football.'

Berger believes he was 'thrown' into that group purely because of his appearance. He marked his Liverpool debut by scoring two goals a few months earlier at Leicester City. During that game, he sported an Alice band. 'Every decade has its seminal moment of football fashion,' *The Independent* wrote:

The first time George Best wore his shirt outside his shorts, when Nobby Stiles took to the pitch without his teeth in, when Kevin Keegan walked into his barber's and said, 'I can't do a thing with it – can we try a perm?' Ever since the first Saturday afternoon that Eric Cantona pulled on his jersey in a hurry, Sunday footballers all over the land have been cavorting around with their collars up in homage. But now there is a new contender for the fashion detail that takes football into the new millennium.

The report mentioned Berger's stunning footwork:

> But had anyone glanced upwards they would have noticed the little black item with which the Super Czech kept his flowing locks in place . . . Is Berger mad? Is he brave? Or is he at the cutting edge of soccer style in a sport in which in ten years' time, Nike twinsets and Diadora pearls will be commonplace? By then, of course, they will have changed the name from Alice band to something more in keeping with the culture that will have so slavishly adopted it.

'Because I did not speak English and could not read English, I did not know what was being said or written about me,' Berger says. 'My understanding was very poor but people like Jamie [Redknapp], Jason [McAteer] and Robbie [Fowler] liked to keep me up to date with affairs in the media.

'I was playing and my hair kept on getting in the way. I'd just moved from Germany and did not know or trust any hairdresser. So my wife suggested I try the band. After scoring in the first game, I decided to keep it. When you are playing well, nobody seems to care. But when you or the team plays badly, it becomes an issue.

'The Spice Boys consisted of six or seven players and the press changed the names of those individuals to fit the story they wanted to print. I wasn't a drinker at all but because I looked a certain way and happened to be at certain events I was viewed as part of the group even though I was living exactly the same life as I did when I was in Germany. There is a saying here: "guilty by association". I had my wife. I had my first baby. When the training session was over, some players would leave Melwood and go for a pint. Some might go to the golf course or for a coffee. All I wanted to do was go home. That's what I did. I did not lead an exceptional life.'

Berger had been in Germany when Dortmund's closest rivals Bayern Munich first earned the dubious nickname FC Hollywood. Spawned during Giovanni Trapattoni's tumultuous first spell as manager, which ended in 1995, it was a reaction to the infighting and the club's ability to drive soap-opera storylines, not always entirely related to the football. This was a club so concerned by the off-field antics of star midfielder Mario Basler that it hired a private detective to monitor his movements. Later, the wife of Thomas Strunz left him for teammate Stefan Effenberg, the same Effenberg who was once asked about his €5 million salary. 'Five and a half million,' he interjected, by way of correction. Effenberg loathed Lothar Matthäus, the Bayern midfielder, and Matthäus loathed him – their public battle was a feature of the 1990s.

From afar, Berger quickly became wary of what he says basically was 'too much socializing'.

'I hear people in this country [England] say that you should always look after number one. Now, I am not sure whether that is the right thing to do because eventually you always need someone else's help. It's a selfish outlook. But in a working environment, sometimes I think it is a good thing to keep a distance. It is very important that you generate a spirit for the benefit of the team. But sometimes it goes too far. You have to find the balance between professionalism, comradeship with your teammates and family time.

'When you compare Liverpool's supposed problems to those that existed at FC Bayern, you realize maybe our team was not so bad. Again, that Bayern became front-page news was a reflection of the changing time in football. Both Bayern and Liverpool were the biggest teams in their country. Yet in the nineties you see both Bayern and Liverpool getting beaten by the likes of Norwich in important games [Liverpool in the final game in front of the free-standing Kop and Bayern in the UEFA Cup]. Both clubs aren't doing as well as in the past. The media is more powerful, more aggressive. There must be a reason for this. The team's players not being quite as good as before is just not sexy enough. It has to be for another reason. So they hunt for stories. They find players doing things they have always done. But they do not understand the routines of a footballer. Conclusions are made. So this must be the reason for the failure.'

In his first months, Berger's bravura performances inspired Liverpool. After the two goals against Leicester, he scored another two in a 5–1 victory over Chelsea the following weekend – his full home debut. The Anfield crowd fell for this tall, elegant, skilful and powerful attacker whose shots were released like missiles. Berger says the power generated was due to the hours spent on the road in front of his apartment block as a child, blasting the ball against a wall. 'I'd do it again, again and again. There was no teaching. Just repetition. I had strong legs.'

At the end of September, Berger was named the Premier League's player of the month. 'I felt really good. It couldn't have started any better. I was flying. The team was flying.'

Typically, this Liverpool team soon crash-landed. After a defeat at Old Trafford, the Reds were overwhelmed at Blackburn Rovers, losing 3–0. Suddenly, Berger was on the substitutes' bench. From November onwards, only two more goals were scored. His manager Roy Evans seemed to lose faith very quickly. After such a blistering start, Berger's fall was puzzling.

'I really don't know why,' he answers unconvincingly on the issue of his non-selection. 'Probably he [Evans] was not happy about the way I was playing.' Berger then mentions the presence of Collymore. 'It always felt like there was a straight choice: me or him. Stan was his record buy. I was not.'

I asked Evans why he signed Berger, 'a natural talent and a left-footer', and, indeed, why he decided so quickly to stop playing him. Again, Collymore came up.

'Patrik may have thought it was a straight pick between himself and Stan but really I wanted an alternative to Steve McManaman. That was something levelled at us for a while: what happens when Stevie doesn't play? Patrik was the solution. Initially, we pushed him up as a centre-forward alongside Stan, because Stevie was performing well. Then Robbie came back. The team lost a few games. I had to put Robbie in.'

By the end of the following season, Berger was 'bored' of waiting for a sustained run.

'Under Roy, I was not happy, because I wanted to play,' he says. 'I tried to force a move away and Benfica were very interested. So were AS Roma. I spoke to their president on the phone, who told me about big plans for the club. Fabio Capello was going to be the manager. There were going to be other signings like Gabriel Batistuta. But when it was all set to happen, Peter Robinson said no. He explained to me that changes were happening at Liverpool too. They planned to replace Roy with a new manager, a manager that wanted me to stay.'

I suggest to Berger that his situation was a classic case of being the right player at the wrong time. After Evans' departure in 1998, Gérard Houllier initially appeared to be his saviour but in the long term Berger never really fitted with his functional, more direct style of football. Berger could have been brilliant for Liverpool. Despite nearly a double century of games, a feeling remains that he suffered from mismanagement.

Berger, though, speaks highly of Houllier, a person, he says, who 'understood the ethics of Liverpool'.

'My impression was that the club accepted Roy's time was over but did not really know how to deal with it. The solution was to recruit Gérard as a joint manager. He had time to evaluate the strength of the squad and plan for the future before Roy's inevitable departure. Football history teaches you that when new managers are appointed, players come and players go. I considered it fortunate that I was one of those Gérard wanted to keep.'

Berger retired as a professional in 2010 after returning to play for Sparta Prague following spells at Portsmouth, Aston Villa and Stoke City. He now lives in his home city and at the time of writing played amateur football for Dolní Chabry, a team in the sixth tier of Czech football, one that is based a ten-minute drive away from the area he grew up in, District 8. The club is owned by his long-time friend Vladmir Šmicer, someone who remains a teammate despite his administrative position.

'We usually get seventy people watching us. On a good day, we might get a hundred. There are a lot of young boys playing and they do all of our running. The standard is high.'

I wonder what the incentives are for a forty year old with forty-two international caps to play at a low level.

'Winning, of course,' he smiles. 'When that happens, Vladi serves us beer and plates of sausages as a reward.'

CHAPTER EIGHT

cultzeros.co.uk

MIGHTY ATOM,
David Thompson, 1993–2000

'I HAD TO SMACK HIM IN THE FACE. IF I DIDN'T, I'D LOOK LIKE A TIT,' David Thompson reasons, as he recalls the incident where he punched David Hopkin, the Leeds United midfielder, during a reserve game in front of 917 people at Knowsley Road, St Helens' old rugby league ground. It was the moment that led to his relationship with Gérard Houllier crumbling.

'Hopkin had red hair like yours, only shorter,' Thompson continues, lifting his substantial right bicep and jabbing it in my direction. 'He was a Scottish midfielder with no front teeth, giving the impression that he was tough. But he'd made a coward's challenge.'

Thompson says he'd been 'bang-on his game' that night, setting up Liverpool's goal scored by Richie Partridge during a 1–1 draw.

'Then Hopkin – a seasoned pro – absolutely annihilated me off the ball. I was angry because I thought he was trying to deny me an opportunity to impress Houllier.

'It was freezing cold and I spun up in the air, landing face first with a mouthful of grass. Immediately, I felt embarrassed. Then suddenly I felt lucky, because he could have broken my leg. I was never going to let him get away with it. I could see him running away, looking back with a smirk on his face.'

This was not an occasion for 'handbags', as Thompson puts it.

'I chased him across the pitch. Rather than just a bit of pushing and shoving, I smacked him. Then I went again. He didn't like it, so we started brawling.'

The referee sent the pair off.

'I could see Houllier's expression in the stand as I walked down the tunnel. He was sitting there with his arms folded initially, then started waving them all over the place. He was open-mouthed, looked like an angry fish.'

Having already been red-carded in two reserve matches earlier in the 1999–2000 season, as well as once for the first team, this incident led to a four-game ban for Thompson, with the suspension landing during a period when Liverpool were attempting to qualify for the Champions League. Thompson was banished to train with the youth-team players at the club's academy in Kirkby and Liverpool's manager issued a warning in the press that, at twenty-one, Thompson risked jeopardizing his career unless he learnt to govern his temper.

'David let himself down and the team down. It is awful, really,' Houllier said. 'If a tennis player argues with the referee or whatever, then he is the only one to suffer. But football is a team game and it is the club and his teammates who are suffering from his silly behaviour.

'I think players can confuse commitment with a selfish attitude sometimes and if he wants to make it at the top he has got to control himself. When you don't control yourself, you cannot be tactically aware or team-minded.'

As I read this quote to Thompson fourteen years later, his wince turns into a smile.

'Typical of Houllier, that,' he says. 'I needed someone to have confidence and to trust me. I had the ability. I could create. I could spot a pass. I could keep the ball. I could tackle. I could do it all. I just wanted the chance to express myself. Don't ask me to conform too rigidly, because it bores me. You're blunting me. Houllier blunted me.'

Thompson tells another story about a game for Liverpool's reserves at St Andrew's in Birmingham twelve months earlier.

'We won 3–0 and I was the best player on the pitch. Dave Sexton was heavily involved with England's under-21s and he was waiting on the touchline. He shook my hand and said, "You know what, you were absolutely sensational there. You dominated the match for ninety minutes from start to finish with your passing and skill." It was an occasion where I'd been allowed to express myself. Within a few months, Houllier was appointed full-time and a lot changed at Liverpool.

'Houllier ostracized me after the incident with Hopkin. It was the wrong thing to do. It put a wedge between me and him. He obviously didn't understand me. Rather than trying to channel that desire and energy into something positive, he punished it. I was never going to allow someone like Hopkin to bully me. That was the way I reacted.'

Thompson was in the middle of what would appear to be his best season for Liverpool's first team. Yet beneath the surface, he was not happy. He was not happy out of position on the right side of Liverpool's midfield, unable to play his natural game. He was not happy with the defensive style of football. He was not happy being substituted regularly. Even though Thompson had appeared in thirty-one games, Houllier had substituted him on fourteen of those occasions and in seven Thompson's number was up first, leaving him unable to contain his frustration. It contributed towards an outpouring of juvenile angst and anger.

'I'd been brought up by managers that had preached the "Liverpool way". Houllier was different. Steve Heighway had always taught us to prepare properly and drill our own game

197

plan: let the opposition worry about us. Suddenly, this manager comes in and he's worried about the opposition. I was thinking, "We've got fantastic players here, I'm not used to not going forward"; instead, we were camping out and parking the bus.

'I could see the impact it was having on my game. I felt like my legs had been cut off. Sammy Lee used to use that term a lot when Houllier sent him to reason with me. "We're not cutting your legs off, lad . . ." I felt they were. I felt like my creativity had been stifled. We were being asked to nullify the opposition. In the past, I'd nullified the opposition using my strengths. To me, this new way was shithouse tactics.'

Thompson believed he was being singled out when it went wrong for the team. In the 1999–2000 campaign, Liverpool finished fourth, having failed to score in thirteen of their thirty-eight league games. With a place in the Champions League possible for the first time since it ceased to be the European Cup and after UEFA decided to extend the number of entrants, Liverpool did not register a single goal in the final five fixtures and missed out on qualification to Leeds United, with a 1–0 defeat at relegation-threatened Bradford City on the final day proving crucial. By then, Thompson had been left out of the squad altogether, along with Robbie Fowler – another player Houllier did not really get along with.

'I'd never go all guns blazing to him with an issue in front of other players,' Thompson says. 'But If Houllier made a comment to me at half-time and I did not agree with it, I'd answer back. If I felt he was out of order, I'd fight my corner. I wouldn't just sit there and bite my lip. Others did and went further.

'He shoved me out on the right of midfield on what me, Danny Murphy or Stevie [Gerrard] would call the graveyard shift. None of us wanted to play there because it meant you were getting hauled off after an hour. It pissed me off. The other lads were able to hide their emotion but I wore my heart on my sleeve. If I was ever upset, it showed. So when I was walking off, I'd shake my head. It was impulsive. I couldn't hide it.

'I'm not a charlatan. You always know what's going on with

me. What you see is what you get. Houllier didn't like that. He saw it as disobedience. He'd call me into his office like a head teacher does at school. Then I'd tell him straight that I didn't feel I was being given the right platform to perform to the best of my ability. I wasn't reaching my maximum potential. I was being honest. He didn't understand where I was coming from.'

Thompson lives in Knutsford, the prosperous Cheshire town, where we meet in an Italian restaurant. He insists he is now a wiser version of the shaven-haired scallywag who, despite the relatively short period of time he spent playing for Liverpool, managed to harness the passion and spirit from the Anfield terraces with displays of enthusiasm, cleverness and atomic aggression. Our encounter is an intense experience. He regularly engages with the waiting staff and other customers. His phone rings constantly. Many of the calls are from his bikini-model girlfriend, Nina. He is well mannered, explaining that he likes it this way – being busy and, significantly, in demand.

'I appreciate that some of the stuff I'm going to tell you here might make it sound like I was a spoilt brat,' Thompson begins. 'What you have to remember is, Houllier was a grown man who should have had the ability to see beyond my bluster. I wasn't a bad kid. He just came in with the idea that all young British foot-ballers were tearaways. That couldn't have been further from the truth with me. I wanted it so badly that when it didn't happen, I reacted impulsively.'

To understand Thompson, you do indeed need to understand where he came from. It becomes obvious that Thompson's career was influenced by his childhood as one of the smallest kids on the Ford Estate in Birkenhead, Wirral. To avoid confrontation would be to betray everything he had known.

Thompson was eight years old when, in 1985, Howard Parker, then a reader in social-work studies at Liverpool University, wrote a book called *Living With Heroin: The Impact of a Drugs Epidemic on an English Community*. Many of the case studies came from Ford, a concrete settlement of avenues, maisonettes and council flats. There was a small shopping precinct, a school and a notorious pub called the Buccaneer, a centre for beer swilling and fights. Parker claimed that Ford in the eighties was one of the toughest estates in the country. 'We monitored the Multiple Deprivation Index done by Wirral Council, and Ford was right at the top,' he said. 'Unemployment was high, there was a lot of crime, vandalism. There were gangs, tough men. I think that there was quite a lot of dumping of problem families on to Ford. Certainly it got into a mess for a while.' Other writers spoke of a 'lost generation', where 'there was no purpose for those kids, no point'.

Though Thompson speaks endearingly about his upbringing, with admiration for his parents 'who made all the sacrifices' to make him a footballer, he admits that Ford was the hardest of environments.

'It was a working-class area,' he says. 'It was rough and there wasn't much opportunity. As a kid, you needed to have your wits about you. My dad was unemployed for a long time during the recession. He lost his job working for British Steel. He wasn't alone on that front. A lot of people were in similar positions. It was a struggle. He eventually became a driver for Wirral Council, working with local libraries transporting books around. Me mam was a cleaner.'

Thompson says he had two options: to get into trouble or to play football.

'There was nothing to do,' he continues. 'There was plenty of open grass where they'd planned to build extra houses but it never happened. So we'd run about on there causing mischief. We'd throw stones at windows and kick balls around. I was obsessed with the ball. When you find a wall and kick a ball against it constantly, you get to know where it's going to bounce, the spins with the kerbs and the bumps. It refines your anticipation and judgement. I think it's a great exercise for kids now: just kicking a ball against a wall. It used to happen at Melwood too. They had a big wooden structure with numbers. You could practise passing, volleys, headers – everything – while improving your control at the same time.'

At school, Thompson was taught by a Mr Boyle.

'He was very competitive. He loved football. There was a sports centre that was a two-minute walk, so he used to arrange five-a-sides most days. He'd pull me out of lessons for a game. He'd go on one side and put me on the other because there was nobody other than me that was capable of levelling the teams out.

'I remember being really good from a young age [at football]. I don't know where that came from. If I saw something I liked from a live match on the TV, I'd go and copy it on the street straight away. I'd spend hours until I got it right. I had two older brothers, so I was knocking around with them and playing with bigger lads. That helped me too. I had to learn to handle myself. I had to adapt. I couldn't let anyone who was bigger get the better of me. You learn to swim. If you don't, you sink.

'Other teachers at school would say I was cheeky bordering on naughty and a bit easily led. If a practical joke was going down, I'd make sure that I became a part of it. Obviously, I wasn't very academic. If I put my mind to it now, I think I'd do OK with exams. But I never had the patience. My focus was only on football. I liked football because it never stood still. It's a dynamic sport. I'm exactly the same now: my life bores me if it's not dynamic. With football, every day was different, no two games were the same.'

Even though they did not have the money to pay for luxuries, Thompson's parents found a way to help him. During the school holidays, a course was taking place at the IM Marsh sports grounds affiliated to the University of Liverpool in Aigburth, across the Mersey river. Scouts from Liverpool Football Club were said to be in attendance.

'It cost £80 for a week and me mam and dad scraped the money together from somewhere. They begged and borrowed to make sure I was there. And, fair enough, some of the sessions were laid on by Hughie McAuley and Dave Shannon – two of the main men at Liverpool. Frank Skelly was a scout and he was observing everything on the touchline. Jamie Carragher was there too. We played against each other and flew into a few tackles. Carra was tough. But I always thought I was tougher.'

Thompson learnt to execute the Maradona and Cruyff turns.

'We practised them every day. It seemed to be the way at soccer schools. At the end of the week, we played a game. I did the Cruyff turn then went into the Maradona immediately. I'd taken the coaching on board and I could hear Dave [Shannon] telling someone else on the touchline, "That kid's got something." After that session, I was asked over to Liverpool.'

Carragher was invited along too and the pair soon became close.

'Carra was the same type of person as me, although I wasn't quite as loud as him. His dad was as hungry as my dad. You could hear their voices above the other parents during games. They'd push you. They were very driven. Carra had been the best in his age group for Bootle Boys and I was the best for Wirral. We'd played against each other a couple of times and I could tell he was a top player. It's easy to forget he was a centre-forward who scored a ton of goals. You couldn't stop him. He was power-ful, very fast and technically brilliant. You know when someone is extra special, though, because they always want possession of the ball. They have desire. They hate losing. They hate being beaten in a tackle. You can tell how much it upsets them. Carra has always been like that.'

Like Carragher, Thompson had grown up as an Evertonian.

'All the family were Blues. I'd go to Goodison as much as possible. I grew up hating Liverpool. They were the team I wanted Everton to beat the most. But at the start of the nine-ties, Liverpool's youth system was better. Tranmere had shown a bit of interest in me but I really wanted to go to a place where I knew I'd have the best chance of developing. The people made it. People like Steve Heighway and Hughie McAuley made me feel wanted and loved.'

Being an Evertonian eased any nervousness.

'Maybe it takes the edge of the pressure off a little bit because you're not in awe as much as the lads that support Liverpool. You go in there and think, "Fuck it, I'm stamping my own identity on this place." Me and Carra would arrive at Melwood wearing our Everton shirts. I used to do it for attention. I was as staunch as they come. But you quickly change. You're being given an opportunity to display your talent and take on a career in a sport you love. When you start playing for Liverpool against Everton, you realize how much it means to the players, the coaching staff and the parents. For those ninety minutes, there's hatred everywhere you look. You're desperate to beat them. You can't afford to wish you were playing for the other team. Otherwise you'll play badly and lose the game.'

Thompson was aware then that the journey to Vernon Sangster – the playing fields that used to be just over the road from Anfield where Liverpool's youth teams trained – was a burden on his parents.

'Initially, it was twice a week. We didn't have a car, so they had to pay out again for public transport. I was too young to travel by myself, so I needed one of them to come with me and it cost double. We had to get the bus from the Ford to Hamilton Square in Birkenhead town centre before getting the train over the river to Lime Street, then another bus. It was an hour and twenty minutes each way. I fell asleep on the way home most of the time.'

After progressing from a schoolboy to the YTS, the journey to Melwood, even further away in West Derby, needed to be made each day.

'Again, it was bus – train – bus, with full-time training in between. After sessions, we had numerous jobs to do: collecting bibs, cleaning balls, cleaning boots, cleaning kit, sweeping the dressing-room floor, wiping down the toilets. It was dark by the time you went home. I enjoyed it because it really gave me a sense of purpose. But I also remember feeling absolutely fucked. It started to tell on my performances. I'd gone from being one of the leading schoolboys on the books, tipped to become a first-team player, to being so lacklustre it was a joke.'

Thompson's struggles were noticed by Steve Heighway, who

ran Liverpool's centre of excellence. He had played nearly 475 games for the club after being spotted as a winger at non-league Skelmersdale United while completing a degree in economics and politics at the University of Warwick.

'Steve came knocking at the door one evening. He thought I was on recreational drugs, because they certainly weren't performance enhancing, I was playing that badly. Steve was asking whether I was going out partying or whether I had a new girlfriend distracting me. None of that was true. I couldn't cope with the transition from part-time to full-time. It was a burden on me physically. It felt like I had glandular fever.'

It transpired that Thompson's biggest problem was his diet.

'The next question from Steve was about food. It had remained the same from the age of six to sixteen. It was chips with everything: beans, egg – always fried. Me mam seemed affronted: "His diet's fantastic, great! He has fried rice on a Tuesday, curry on a Wednesday." You could see Steve's face drop. Inwardly, he must have been saying, "What the fuck?" So he gave me mam a telling-off and me a telling-off. I hadn't adjusted to professionalism at all.'

Heighway's role in helping Liverpool's young players grow was significant.

'I was slow to develop both physically and mentally. I was immature. I remember Steve telling me when I was fourteen that I probably wouldn't mature until I was about twenty-one or twenty-two. What he meant by that was that I wouldn't be ready for professional first-team football at Liverpool until that age – maybe a little bit later than everyone else. Although he was right, that comment hurt me at the time and it stuck with me. I was determined to prove him wrong.

'I didn't reach maturity until I was twenty-five. Steve had that eye for knowing how kids were going to develop. He understood the psychology of football and was great at assessing people. He was one hell of a coach. But he was outstanding at helping players not just become good footballers but good people as well, teaching lads how to become men.'

Thompson was eighteen when, under Heighway's leadership, Liverpool won the FA Youth Cup, beating West Ham 4–1 on aggregate after winning both at Upton Park and Anfield in May 1996. Goals from Jon Newby and Davy Larmour secured a 2–0 victory in London before Michael Owen and Stuart Quinn helped wrap up the tie on Merseyside. Thompson says this team was different to that of Manchester United, which four years earlier had won the same competition with a group of players that would become the cornerstone of the club over the next decade: Giggs, Scholes, Beckham, Butt and the Nevilles.

'That United side had more natural ability than ours,' Thompson concedes. 'We were a team filled with passion and rage. Aside from Gareth Roberts, who was from Wrexham, and Michael [Owen – brought up in Hawarden near Chester], every lad was from Liverpool or Wirral. There were a few Irish boys on the fringes and they contributed massively too. We spent loads of time together both professionally and socially. There was a team spirit. We all got on really well. On that pitch, every time we stepped over the line something twigged. There was a chance another side might beat us by a piece of individualism or skill. But they'd never out-fight us. We weren't dirty but we'd always be in their faces. We'd go to the end and we wouldn't give up.'

The approach was epitomized by Thompson agitating in the centre of Liverpool's midfield.

'Hughie McAuley was another coach whose influence was as great on the lads as Steve Heighway's. Hughie drilled it into me that ability only takes a footballer so far. It's mentality that takes you furthest. If you didn't have the bollocks, you're screwed. That stuck with me too. If I got tackled, it upset me. If I made a bad pass, it would make me feel bad. If someone dribbled past me, I'd get angry. At the age of nine or ten, I'd be aggressive if things didn't go my way. By the time I reached the first team, it'd be even worse because the expectation was on me to do better. I was meant to be on a level playing field with these players, so to have someone out-do me would feel embarrassing. Because I was smaller and not as quick as others, coupled with the self-doubt, I'd compensate for it by being an angry head.'

Thompson says two players made the difference for Liverpool. One went all the way in their career and the other did not. Their names were Michael Owen and Jamie Cassidy.

'Michael was a few years younger than the rest of the group but even as a teenager he was a world-class player. I'd heard there was a special kid on the books at Liverpool but the first time I saw him play was on the TV for England at Wembley. He scored an incredible goal. It looked like nothing fazed him. In the Youth Cup run to the final, some of his performances were incredible. He was so, so quick. In many ways, he changed the way the game was played in this country because suddenly every club was looking for someone with the same pace. But there was only one Michael Owen. He was a phenomenon.'

Cassidy was a left-winger who would play eight times for Cambridge United before dropping into non-league football with Burscough.

'Cass was very elegant but forceful with it. He knew the game. He could hug the touchline but join the play in central areas too. He was a very modern footballer. Then he did his cruciate and broke his leg in separate injuries in quick succession. He probably lost his pace a little bit at a crucial time. Otherwise he would have been a first-team player. I always looked up to him. He was held in higher esteem by Steve Heighway than me and Carra at one stage.'

It frustrated Thompson that West Ham were rated so highly and expected to beat Liverpool.

'At Liverpool, you weren't brought up to blow your own trumpet. It was nice to receive credit. But if you achieved something, you weren't supposed to talk about yourself. It was all about letting your football do the talking. As a group and as individuals, we were very humble off the pitch. If you see our interviews and compare it to the London players, they used to big themselves up and we did not. It used to annoy me, that. Rio [Ferdinand] and Lamps [Frank Lampard] were the worst ones for it. Every time I turned on Sky Sports, Rio and Frank were there talking about how great this West Ham team was. Nobody was talking about Liverpool. It really motivated us.'

Their cup triumph earned the group extra respect from younger members inside Liverpool's youth system. In his autobiography, Steven Gerrard recalls how shy he was around Carragher, Thompson and Cassidy, a trio of sharp tongues.

'Steve Heighway used to highlight all the good players in the higher age groups. That would keep you reaching and striving to reach their standards,' Thompson says. 'For me, it was Iain Brunskill, Andy Harris, Phil Charnock and Dom Matteo. Steve would always say to me, "Watch them, follow them . . ." But I also know Steve was telling younger age groups the same things about me, Carra and Cass. He was very fond of us. It was clever because it meant there was a hierarchy and you never got too far ahead of yourself at a young age.'

Thompson says, 'I remember speaking to Stevie [Gerrard] and you could tell he had admiration for us at that time. But his acceleration into the first team was rapid, so it didn't last too long. Stevie had something. He was very small and very slight as a teenager but he used to dominate games with his passion. He was slamming people, getting stuck in. His running and movement marked him out. You could tell he had the potential to be special. But you didn't know how tall he was going to be or whether he was going to fill out. Then suddenly he grew these legs and shoulders. He had growing pains because he grew so quickly. He arrived at training one day and it was as if he became a man overnight.'

In August 1996, Thompson was selected on the first-team bench for the opening game of the season at Middlesbrough. With the team wearing an ecru-coloured kit, the game came to represent the best and worst of Roy Evans' Liverpool in ninety minutes: breathtakingly rapid in attack, often hapless in defence. Fabrizio Ravanelli scored a hat-trick for the hosts to secure a 3–3 draw. Two nights later, Thompson was introduced as an eighty-sixth-minute substitute for Robbie Fowler when Arsenal were beaten 2–0 at Anfield.

'The pace of the game was astonishing,' Thompson remembers. 'Everyone else on the pitch was a real man. I was a boy. I wasn't even shaving. I was ten stone wet through. Fellas like Steve Bould were trying to tackle you. I was more of a technical player than pacey. So I had to figure out ways to get past him. I was thinking to myself, "Fucking hell, is this what it's going to be like every week? Am I ready for this?" You're always doubting yourself at that age. Bould was a proper bruiser.'

Thompson had always believed that he was destined for first-team football at Liverpool until he started to train with John Barnes and Jan Mølby.

'They were the two that made you realize how far you had to go. I used to dribble a lot and take too many touches because I didn't trust anyone else on the ball. I put too much effort in. Barnesy would point out that I was eventually going to make a simple pass, so there was no point making all kinds of twists and turns. He told me it was important to conserve energy. He told me that just because someone else is five yards away it does not mean that it's not a great pass. I was always looking for the Hollywood ball. Just by changing the angle, the game opens up. Football was a game of angles. It was so simple, it was genius. Playing in that position in the centre of the park latterly in his career, I never saw Barnesy surrender possession.

'Jan was on the same level. He'd come through the Dutch system of playing and some of the knowledge he passed on to me was crucial to my development. I wish he'd stayed a little bit longer but instead he went off to Swansea to become their player-manager.'

Ronnie Moran's backroom presence was also important. Moran was entering the final phase of his long career as a Liverpool player, reserve-team manager, first-team coach and temporary boss by the time Thompson first encountered him. Moran was the disciplinarian on the staff.

'Ronnie could cut you down with one comment,' Thompson says. 'He was black or white. That's what was good about him. You knew what was going to upset him and you knew what was going to make him happy. He was very passionate. He was tough and never allowed you to get ahead of yourself.'

Thompson felt Moran's wrath on a number of occasions.

'I'd just got into the first team and it was winter. All the senior players were wearing jumpers because it was cold. I hadn't been issued with one because I was still considered a reserve. So I had to go out and train in my shorts and T-shirt. Before the session started, I went to put a jumper on and straight away Ronnie was on to it. "Oi, take that off, you're not a big 'ead yet, lad." I stood there embarrassed, thinking to myself, "Fucking hell, Bugsy, the Communist period's over now . . ."

'Later, I'd signed a one-year extension to my pro contract and I was sitting in the foyer at Melwood with a big cheesy smile on my face. I couldn't wait to tell everyone because it was recognition for my efforts and a clear indication the club fancied me. Financially, it was also a big improvement. My first pro deal was worth £750 a week and this took me up to around £4,000. Carra was in there at the same time and the only thing we haggled over was the number of tickets we were entitled to for games, because we had big families and all of our mates wanted to go.

'Ronnie walks past and goes, "What are you two dickheads doing 'ere?"

'"I've just signed a new contract, Ronnie," I told him proudly.

'"What – they've given *you* a new contract? *You've* only been doing well for two minutes. *You're* nowhere near good enough yet." Then he jumped on the bus and left me there. I felt like I'd been buried in the ground.'

Undeterred, Thompson enjoyed the trappings that came with being tagged as one of Liverpool's most promising young players.

'I used to love going out and getting recognized. It gave me a sense of achievement. It spurred me on. It was nice to feel that you're appreciated, because it gives you that little bit of confidence. Ultimately, that's what football's about: having confidence and using it as a tool to do better. It can either push you on or undermine you. You need to have an ego to stand on a football pitch and perform in front of forty-five thousand people.

'I wasn't the best-looking kid on the block but being a Liverpool player enabled me to have my fair share of women. It was a great time around the city. You had a line of clubs on Slater Street. Then there was Quadrant Park in Bootle and the Paradox in Aintree. They'd opened off the back of the rave scene, which really thrived in Liverpool. It wasn't as if we were out all the time, though. I wasn't part of *the* scene. Week to week, day to day, it was just football. When I look back now, I ask myself whether I was too focused and too driven and too wound up.'

While other players speak of the problems they had with 'the bubble' of Merseyside, in relation to dealing with the expectations of the fans, Thompson saw it as an advantage.

'I always knew as a local lad that you can have a bad game but the fans would forgive you as long as you fought and were aggressive, although you'd never get away with doing that consistently. Eventually, they'll start calling on you. I never felt extra pressure. But if we were playing Man U or Everton, there was an extra level of importance for the local boys to do well. You did not want to make a mistake that cost the game. That comes from understanding the situation a little bit more, the importance for the community.

'The desire to push on and do well comes from within. It didn't mean any more or less whichever club I played for, whether it was Coventry or Blackburn, I just wanted to prove myself to myself. Nothing beats stepping out at Anfield, though. Especially when the Kop's singing your name. You emerge from that tunnel and you can see the fear in the other team's eyes. You know they're scared. The roar, that noise when it's in full swing – it's electric. The hairs on the back of your neck stand up. A couple of times I looked at Carra and we were both thinking the same thing: "How the fuck did we get here?" Two little scallies playing for Liverpool. It was mad.'

Following a productive loan spell at Swindon Town, where he learnt 'the true value of three points: you could see it on the faces of the dinner ladies on a Monday morning', Thompson started a Liverpool game for the first time in February 1998 – a 2–1 defeat at Aston Villa. The previous summer, Stan Collymore had been sold to the club he supported as a boy and he promptly scored both of Villa's goals. It was one of those results that undermined Roy Evans' management.

'Something wasn't quite firing and maybe Roy felt like he needed to mix it up. He dropped Paddy Berger for me and I know Paddy was very upset about that. He spoke publicly about it and disrespected me, saying I was just a kid from the reserves and it was the lowest moment in his career. But I'd been around the first team for around two years by then. I'd played very well in training and in reserve matches for months. I deserved that chance. Unfortunately, I didn't take it, because against Villa I performed poorly. I felt isolated and underprepared. Perhaps the moment had come too soon. I assisted in our goal but I gave the ball away too much. I was too nervous. The pace of the game was unbelievable and the pitch at Villa Park was massive. The crowd were bang up for it. It was a bad way to start.'

Like most of the squad, Thompson found the short period afterwards where Evans and Houllier shared managerial responsibilities confusing. 'You don't know who to approach, who to talk to. Naturally, I'd go to Roy but I feared that might piss the other fella off. The players could see it was a marriage of convenience rather than something both Roy and Houllier really wanted. It wasn't a healthy environment.'

Soon 'Houllier' – as Thompson calls him throughout this interview – was in sole charge.

'The discipline tightened quickly. There was a fine system. If you were late, bang – you got done. If you turned up in the wrong flip-flops, bang – you got done. I didn't like being told what to do, especially in Houllier's regimented fashion. What difference does it really make if we all wear exactly the same tracksuit top for an away trip on the coach? Houllier was hot on that. But he couldn't make me do it. Wearing certain clothes wasn't going to make me play better. It was draconian: rules for rules' sake. Maybe it was what Liverpool needed to a degree but he took it too far. He wanted a group of squares: players without personality. He was particularly tough on the young ones like me. After a while, I got fed up with it, so I didn't conform. I was anti-establishment.'

Thompson says his frustrations were purely professional.

'I'd been tipped to go all the way as a centre-midfielder and I was aware that I was very, very good. I was dominating the play: getting it, giving it, leading with assists, and getting forward having shots at goal. So I never understood why I ended up on the right under Houllier. I always seemed to be a seven or eight out of ten every game. Although I could be a nine, suddenly I was a six quite a lot. I didn't enjoy it. Maybe it was Houllier think-ing I wasn't tall enough or quick enough. That pissed me off because I got pigeonholed. I was happy doing a job for the team but when things went wrong, I was the one getting singled out. It was unfair and bad management.'

Despite featuring regularly in Houllier's first full season, Thompson felt inwardly that Liverpool's manager was consider-ing replacing him.

'You have to accept that at Liverpool the manager is always trying to find a way to improve. It is a club with a global following and they're always on the hunt for the best players. I don't think anyone can feel secure. It didn't bother me if Houllier was said to be interested in signing foreign players, because you'd assume he'd know what he was doing on that front. His knowledge of foreign players was supposed to be good, particularly the French. But when I saw us being linked with young British lads it used to piss me off. Lee Bowyer was one. From 1998 onwards, it was suggested he'd move to Liverpool. It used to get on my nerves. I was thinking, "Why the fuck are we going for him? We've got me and Carra here. We've got Stevie and Danny Murphy. You've got a midfield right there." Carra could play in midfield and scored on his debut there, of course.'

As the 1999–2000 season reached its conclusion, it was rumoured that Nick Barmby was on the verge of leaving Everton for Liverpool.

'That *really* irritated me,' Thompson says. 'Not only had Houllier pushed me out from my natural position but he was also planning to spend £6 million on someone who would perform exactly the same role. Barmby was another player who'd played in the centre before being shoved out wide. He was no better than me. It drove me crazy because I knew I was better than Barmby. I felt like I'd already done my stint on the bench and getting pulled off after sixty minutes was doing my head in.

'I went to speak to Houllier with my agent and asked him straight whether he was planning to sign Barmby. I told him that I could have understood if he was trying to get hold of a winger with a proven track record, someone who was clearly a better player than me, because that's how you improve as a team. When you sign players, they have to be better than the ones you already have. Barmby was not.'

Although Thompson was offered a new contract, he was not convinced he would play.

'I didn't trust Houllier. Carra got a new deal on the same day and his terms were far better than mine. It revealed how much I was valued. Because Houllier was prepared to spend £6 million or £7 million on Barmby – a player from our nearest rivals – he'd be under pressure to justify that fee, so he'd end up playing him over me, a kid. Houllier was one of those stubborn managers who didn't want to give anyone a stick to beat him with, so it was clear I'd be the one missing out.

'I went outside to the car park at Melwood to clear my head. I flipped a coin. Heads and I'd stay at Liverpool; tails, I'd go. It fell on tails. So I went back in and told Houllier that I wanted to leave. Had he fought hard to keep me, I'd probably have stayed but he didn't. At the end of the day, if the manager doesn't fancy you, you've got to go somewhere else.'

Within twenty-four hours, Coventry City had faxed a bid of almost £2.5 million.

'Houllier said I could go down and speak to Gordon Strachan. I wasn't really taken with the idea, because Coventry had struggled for a few years. I'd played really well at Highfield Road a few months before and we battered them 3–0. But when I met Gordon, I felt loved and appreciated straight away. It was quite astounding. Leeds, Everton and Villa all spoke to my agent but I was blown away by Gordon's warmth and ambitions. He wanted me to become the main man in the centre of the park. The money was there and the money was right – the club made me their highest-paid player. So I agreed to sign for him there and then.'

Thompson believes his career might have mirrored that of Jamie Carragher's with a different manager leading the team at a crucial time for his own development. He thinks of a world where he'd remained at Liverpool. He thinks of a world with Roy Evans in charge or Steve Heighway, someone he believes could have become an 'outstanding' manager for Liverpool had the club offered him a promotion from the youth section.

'I'll be straight with you,' he says. 'I never rated Houllier. I could see through him. OK, later he won five trophies and that's a fantastic achievement. He signed some good players. But he signed some terrible players. That list is endless. What he did was a short-term job. I didn't like the way his team played. Teams can play that way and get success short term but never long term. It's not an enjoyable way to play.

'Yeah, Gérard had had his problems with me in terms of discipline – getting into fights – but I was filled with hunger and the desire to do well. It could have been channelled in a better way. If it wasn't for him, I don't think I'd have left Liverpool. He misunderstood me. I probably misunderstood him. There could have been a middle ground. I was sure I could play at the highest level, sure I could play at centre-midfield. But I didn't feel he was being fair with me. If he had handled the situation better and been a bit more open-minded – as he claimed to be – he could have got more out of me, as other managers did.

'Had a British manager been in charge – someone from a similar background – it wouldn't have panned out like it did. From day one, I thought there was a language barrier and a cultural barrier between us and I don't think he was willing to get over it. With a bit more time, I'd have matured like Steve Heighway said years before. But Houllier never considered that. And he didn't listen as closely as he should have to Steve.'

In appointing Houllier, Thompson says, the traditional Liverpool way of operating was abandoned.

'When Steve [Heighway] released that group of us into the first team, Ronnie Moran took care of us, along with Roy [Evans] and Sammy [Lee]. The four of them talked a lot. There was a transparency about what they were trying to achieve. But when Houllier came in, Steve's importance was dismissed. Houllier tried to take credit for Steven Gerrard coming through. Hang on a minute – Steve Heighway's been guiding him for the last ten years but Houllier was bleating about his role in the last four months. It was unfair. Houllier wanted to score points with the fans all the time and protect his own interests rather than those of the club.

'The danger with a foreign manager like Houllier is that they come in and the communication between the first team and the youth team breaks down. The youth-team manager remains the same and he's already been through the process of high-lighting the individuals that he believes can really be successful. The club tailors a programme to make sure they've done everything they possibly can to make that happen. Roy Evans had been watching us for five or six years. He knew us and had confidence that we could handle situations. Suddenly, the club changed the manager and, with that, the whole philosophy at youth level changed. It happens at a lot of clubs, it has to be said. New managers usually want to implement a new style of play. It feels like a lot of good work goes to waste because the kids have to learn a new style of play too. There's no legacy from genera-tion to generation or from manager to manager.

'Liverpool fucked up with that and have done so a number of times. They went from a French manager to a Spaniard to an Englishman. Each one of them had different ideas. When you keep changing managers, cultures and nationalities, it confuses what goes on in the youth system because the coaches aren't sure what they're meant to be looking for in the long term. The Liverpool way was lost. It meant that the club couldn't move forward. It's remarkable that this was allowed to happen, because the foundations of Liverpool had been built on that philosophy of gradual evolution. Not a revolution every couple of years just because of a few lean results.

'People ask why Man United had a lot of success over the years. They still brought in a lot of players. But the core was always there. The blueprint was always there. OK, a manager can come in like Houllier and get results as he did in the short term. But what are the results at the under-18 and under-16 levels – are these teams winning, playing good football? Do the players understand the requirements of the first team? The answer at Liverpool was no. The answer at United was yes.

'I knew what the Liverpool way was. So did Carra. So did Michael. So did Stevie. You could have had a core of local players there representing the club for more than a decade, leading the team forward. Instead, Houllier didn't like me or Robbie and [Rafa] Benítez wanted to get rid of Michael Owen and Danny Murphy. The education we had was priceless. But that education process stopped in 1998. It was bad for my career, while it was great for Carra's career because he accepted the change. Maybe it worked out well for him because Houllier wanted to go defensive and by then he'd become a defensive player. For me, I had to change my game to fit in. I was being told to sit back on the right-hand side and help the right-back out, rather than thinking about bombing forward and being creative. It was depressing, this rigid team block. I wasn't accustomed to it. I wasn't alone. I couldn't believe the club would bring someone like Houllier in because he didn't want us to play football like Liverpool. The way we played under him was boring. It was one-dimensional. There was no pass and move. It was never going to rebuild the empire.'

Thompson accidentally commuted to Melwood rather than Coventry on at least two occasions in the weeks after agreeing a move to the Midlands. He believes it was a subconscious reaction, as he didn't want to leave. He admits, however, that being away helped him 'grow into a man' more quickly than he would have done had he remained at Liverpool. 'You have to do the shopping, cook and clean for yourself rather than let your mum do it, as well as socializing and making new friends.' Yet when he returned to Anfield for the first time in a Coventry shirt, the sight of Houllier made the old demons return.

'I still had that familiarity with the club and it felt really weird. I ended up scoring a goal from twenty-five yards at the Anfield Road end. It was surreal. I didn't know what to do. In the end, I shouted "Fuck off" to Houllier. The crowd heard it and the cameras picked it up. I felt embarrassed when I saw it on TV later that night. It was a moment where all of my anger and frustration bubbled up. Yeah, I had a good career and I'm very happy with how it went but it could have been better as a centre-midfielder. I know it could have been, because I'd always been the best player in my team when playing in that position. That's where the anger came from. That's why I told Houllier to fuck off, because my life changed when that man changed my position.'

Thompson admits that it still upsets him, missing out on Liverpool's 2000–01 campaign when, under Houllier, the Reds lifted the League, FA and UEFA cups, while qualifying for the Champions League. Despite Coventry's struggles and a season that concluded in relegation, he was nominated the club's best player, even though he was stationed, once again, on the right side of midfield.

'I was being selected every week, getting ninety minutes and influencing the outcome of matches. Gordon knew how to get the best out of me. I wasn't in the centre but he said to me that my crossing was as good as Beckham's. I knew he was only saying it to convince me that playing wide was a good idea. Whereas I only got criticism from Houllier, Gordon made me feel as if I could be a success in another area of the pitch. I felt loved again, as I had at Liverpool before Roy left. I didn't need love to perform well but I needed love to perform brilliantly. I reacted well to positivity. Not someone blowing smoke up my arse, telling me I was great; just someone telling me I was valued. I'd always been like that. If I didn't feel appreciated, I wouldn't hang around. At Coventry, I did.'

Another player of the year award in the Championship resulted in a move to Blackburn Rovers, where his manager was Graeme Souness.

'Souey was someone I had a lot of respect for. He'd won three European Cups as a player when I was growing up as an Everton supporter, so the image of him holding that big trophy aloft was something imprinted on my mind. I resented him but admired him too. He was a man's man. He appreciated me for who I was. He didn't try to mould me into something I wasn't. He encouraged me to be me. So I thrived under him. For twelve months, I was on fire and ended up in the England squad.'

Thompson says Souness's best trait was allowing players to be individuals within the framework of a team structure.

'He trusted you. He commanded a certain level of performance and if you didn't achieve it, he'd go mad. He lost it a few times. The formation was there. But he'd never complicate it, allowing you to play to your own strengths and express yourself. If you made a mistake, he'd trust you to learn from it and develop. When we lost the ball, he'd want us to regain our shape quickly and go again. With the ball, there was a lot of freedom. We repeated that day after day in training. The younger boys really flourished under him, lads like Damien Duff.'

Having already led the club to promotion back into the Premier League before securing the League Cup with a surprise 2–1 victory over Tottenham Hotspur, Souness guided Blackburn to a top-six finish during Thompson's first season at Ewood Park, one he believes was his career best.

'We were playing Fulham on one of those winter days where the weather was cold and the stadium was flat. Craig Short tried to control the ball on the halfway line and pass it with his instep when he should have just headed it away. So from one side of the pitch, I screamed, "Just fucking get rid!" As I shouted it, the whole ground fell silent. Everyone heard it.

'I thought nothing of the moment. I've gone in at half-time and I'm undoing my boots. Suddenly I felt this crack on my head. It was a big water bottle and it was Shorty. "Don't you ever fucking talk to me like that again," he said. He threw the water in my face. So I've jumped up and we've started smacking each other. We were rolling round for fifteen minutes. It was murder. The whole of the half-time was lost.

'We were 2–1 down and went back out and caught fire, managing to get a draw. The following Monday it was 1 April and me and Shorty were in the gym, having made up. The canteen was in the next room, so I went and picked up a load of ketchup sachets. I squirted them all over my mouth and told Shorty to get one of the lads to run in and tell the physio he'd just knocked me out. So I sat there with my tongue hanging out and ketchup pouring from my mouth, nose and ears. Shorty's standing there shouting, "You deserved that, you little cunt", and the physio comes running in and puts me in the recovery position. He's shouting, "Get the defibrillator! Get the doc!" Then I jumped up. "April Fools!"'

Thompson believes what happened next illustrated the difference between Houllier and Souness.

'Souey's called me into the office and I'm thinking, "I'm on for a fine here", particularly for the Fulham incident – definitely on for two weeks' wages. Souey goes, "See what happened on Saturday, at half-time . . ." I've gone, "Yeah, about that, gaffer, I'm really sorry . . ." But he stops me. "No, Tommo. I love all that. I want that in my dressing room. It got the team going, didn't it? We were brilliant in the second half. Well done." Then he's given me a bottle of red wine that cost about £400. I'm used to drinking Jacob's Creek. "It's a nice one, that," he told me.

'I knew when I did well after that for Souey because he'd call me in on the Monday and go, "Hey, here's one I rooted out of the cellar." He was brilliant.'

Thompson's form earned international recognition and he was soon called up to represent England in games against Slovakia and Macedonia by Sven-Göran Eriksson. In his first training session, he fell, holding his knee. It was the start of a run of injuries connected to the same part of the body. He could play. Then he'd be struck down again. Operations followed, two of which were conducted by the renowned Bayern Munich doctor Hans-Wilhelm Müller-Wohlfahrt and Richard Steadman, the specialist knee surgeon from Colorado. Aged twenty-six, Thompson knew his best days were behind him.

'Louis Saha was in the next bed and Dr Steadman told both of us that we had to think about the quality of our lives when we were old. I retired. Louis did not. He played for another six years, including one great season at Everton. He carved out a great living for himself. It's probably something I could have done too. But I just felt I was being a bit of a fraud. I wasn't myself as a footballer. The play was going through me but I wasn't dynamic. I was getting picked for Premier League teams like Wigan, Portsmouth and Bolton. I wasn't letting anyone down. I was still nicking a few assists and a few goals. But in my mind I knew I could be better and my body wasn't allowing it, and it frustrated me. Before games, I was having fluid taken out of me with a syringe. It felt like I had a serious disability. My performance levels dropped to a five or six out of ten. That devastated me.

'I've got friends like Jamie Cassidy who got struck down at the start of their career. Then I've got friends who got struck down at the end of their career, so they're thankful for the time they had. So I shouldn't really moan about it. But it leaves a really bitter taste in my mouth because I'll never know how far I could have taken it. It happened to me just as I was beginning to find myself.

'I know, of course, inwardly how far I think I could have gone but I can't prove it. The way I viewed myself is that I didn't see Frank Lampard as being better than me. At the time I was called up for England, he had no more than ten international caps. I'd grown up playing against him and I never had any problems. I felt I was better than him. So, although I don't feel jealous, it's hard to see someone like Frank go on to have a great, great career when I think to myself that it could have been me. In those months before being called up for England, I was confident of being the best player on the pitch every week, regardless of who we were playing. I knew I was going to get an assist, a goal or a killer pass. I was having an impact in games whether they were against big opponents or teams we were expecting to beat. Everything was coming together and I felt another season playing at that level would earn me the recognition I really wanted. Suddenly, the chances of that happening were swept away.'

Thompson believes he'd have played professionally at a high level until he was thirty-six had his body allowed him.

'I loved everything about football: being paid to kick a ball for a living; getting out of bed every day knowing I was going to be out on that field. Psychologically, it still distresses me because I wanted to prove that I was a top player.'

Since retiring in 2007, dealing with the time and space has not been easy.

'I think I've had some sort of crisis or breakdown. It changes you as a person. Me in the football world and me in the real world are two different animals. It's strange. It's weird. I don't mean that I've only just discovered how to wipe my arse. It's in terms of having confidence and decisiveness. You lose what you had before. When you play football, it masks a multitude of problems in life. You get up every day, you've got that drive and happiness, a routine. It's fulfilling and it can be very settling. You swipe that away and you're left with frustration. You're left with a lot of unused energy because your body is used to blood running through it. It can be very destructive. It feels like you're floating or drifting along with no purpose.

'I can't understand these players that say they don't miss it. I want to bang their heads on the floor. How can you not miss it – running around, getting a sweat on, filling your lungs with air, kicking a ball on grass into nets with all your mates behind you, ready for the battle? If you don't miss it, there's something wrong with you.

'I'm still trying to channel it. I've realized that I'm a very dynamic person. I like to have a lot of things going on at any one time. I've got four businesses. I couldn't just have one, because that's not dynamic enough. I'm better when I'm on the edge, when there's competition and adrenalin.

'My body still knows when it's Saturday. It's pre-programmed. Although it's fading, it's still there. In the first few years after

I retired, I'd wake up every Saturday and my heart would be beating against my chest. I'd have that butterfly feeling in my stomach. There was a breathlessness. It took me a while to figure out that my body was preparing itself as it always had.

'Then your missus tells you you're going to Sainsbury's. It was Saturday. It was meant to be the best fucking day of the week.'

CHAPTER NINE

cultzeros.co.uk

MAD ERIK,
Erik Meijer, 1999–2000

'I AM NOT TWO-FOOTED. I AM NOT SMALL AND QUICK. I AM THE opposite. I am the big guy in front who lets the ball drop in the space so someone else scores a goal. I am the one who made others play better. I helped offensively and defensively. Tactically, when the manager told me to do something, I fulfilled his instructions. I was somebody who liked to involve the audience, the referee, the opponent and my own teammates. I played with rage.'

Erik Meijer tells me this without blinking once. It is his response to the opening question of an interview where a guided walking tour of his hometown of Maastricht is incorporated into four entertaining hours. Pauses are brief and his sentences are well structured, delivered with the sort of bewildering intensity with which he once played football. He has a beautifully Dutch way of explaining feelings, using idioms I have never heard before. He has piercing pale-blue eyes and his focus is consistent. I instantly believe him to be scrupulously honest.

During eighteen months at Liverpool, Meijer played twenty-seven games, scoring just twice. Both goals came during a 5–1 win at Hull City's old Boothferry Park ground in the Worthington Cup. He was not so successful in the league, though it was a competition where Liverpool never lost on the seven occasions he was selected by Gérard Houllier in the starting eleven.

His doggedness, however, was embraced. Liverpudlians appreciate a trier. In a survey that took place six years after his departure, Meijer was voted ninety-ninth in a list of one hundred players that shook the Kop. Amongst other members of the squad, he was well liked. When Meijer was on the receiving end of a rough tackle in training, he responded not by lashing out at the teenage perpetrator but by kicking a dressing-room door instead in frustration.

Few Liverpool strikers in the club's history could match Meijer for passion – a commodity that can lift a footballer to improbable heights or bury him in reckless pursuit of the impossible. At Anfield, Meijer was christened 'Mad Erik'. Many of his appearances came from the substitutes' bench, his physical presence and heading ability proving useful when Liverpool were chasing a result or protecting a lead. It soon became a familiar sight: the game halted for a throw-in or a corner kick and Meijer entering the pitch, sprinting to the near post and demanding the ball. He'd gesticulate wildly and bellow instructions to random team-mates before hunting opponents like an irate father in pursuit of a hoodlum, crashing into a tackle as a king-size mattress does into a skip.

As Meijer says, he 'involved' the crowd. Every match was treated the same: as if it were a European Cup final. He would lead the attack in reserve games at Knowsley Road in St Helens, with Danny Murphy often playing behind him. When Derby County were the visitors and there were no more than fifty spectators in attendance, Meijer hunted a right-back who played the ball to his teenage goalkeeper. Meijer continued on his quest only for possession to be switched to the left-back on the other side of the pitch. Undeterred, Meijer eventually managed to block an attempted clearance, conceding a throw. He responded to that by immediately leaping to his feet, pumping his fists in the air, yelling, 'Come on!!! Come on!!!' to the handful of diehards freezing on the touchline.

Meijer remembers the moment clearly. 'This is me, extreme,' he grins. 'It is in my genes. I cannot help it. My reaction to a challenge is to put all of my weight behind the response. Even if I might not be successful, I go all-out.'

He emphasizes that he is not merely a one-man war, though away from the game his outlook is just as enthusiastic.

'I work hard, I party hard,' he continues. 'I like to live. I like good food. I like a good glass of wine. When I go out with the boys, I like more than one beer. I like to have people around me, enjoying life. But I am concentrated and focused when I play football. I never used to drink during the week. As soon as the game was finished, the first thing I took was an ice-cold beer. If the physio told me it was not good, fuck it. Football was like a balloon. You could not always have it under pressure. Sometimes you have to let a bit of air out.'

Meeting Meijer felt secretive. I had arrived in Maastricht in the early hours of a Wednesday morning. Landing in Charleroi near Belgium's French border, I crossed country by hire car before entering the southernmost part of Holland, an area that hangs down from the rest of the country like an appendix, hemmed in by Belgium and Germany. It was this precarious position that saved the town from war damage in 1939. The Dutch government didn't bother mounting a defence. Yet German forces still chose to blow up the bridges that stood over the curving Meuse river.

Today in late autumn, there is a feeling that something is about to happen, although in reality it probably never will. I awake to a concerto of police sirens. There are the bells of a Catholic church and every hour the town-hall clock sounds a chime. It seems that every road has a cycle path and most people in Maastricht are slim. Winter is coming and those milling about in Vrijthof, a huge cobblestoned square, wear heavy coats, scarves and mittens, protecting themselves from blustery winds. There are elegantly dressed men and women taking breakfast in cafes, and plenty of students, the majority of them in jeans. More than a fifth of Maastricht's one hundred and twenty thousand population attend its university, which specializes in international business, meaning English is the dominant language spoken on the streets.

Meijer suggested we convene at Maastricht's oldest pub, In Den Ouden Vogelstruys. I am told by the waiter in a bow tie that the building has been here since 1730 and was originally a staging post for traders. Inside, the room is dark, with dimmed lighting. There are candles, mahogany panels, muskets on the ceiling, drawings of the inn's regular customers and photographs of bygone days. Frothy cherry-coloured Trappist seasonal beer is served.

As the clock strikes twelve, Meijer, chin nuzzled into his breast in an effort to escape the chill outside, slips through the wooden doors, bringing with him the scent of sweet and savoury breads being baked in a nearby French patisserie.

Meijer is a strong, lean, tough-looking man. His walk is upright and confident. His lips are fleshy. His nose has surely suffered many knocks. His hands are thickset and seem as though they could crush another human being. 'You being English, I am surprised you are not already drunk,' he announces, laughing loudly before engaging the other customers, who had previously been enjoying a quiet one. To the untrained eye, it would appear as if Meijer is the licensee of this establishment, greeting his public with robust handshakes and slaps on the back. He is charismatic. 'You have come all this way. I am very surprised and very pleased someone from Liverpool still wants to speak to me,' he adds modestly.

Meijer removes his purple quilted jacket and rolls up the sleeves of his light–blue-coloured Ralph Lauren shirt as if he means business. He begins by telling me why he thinks he will always live in Maastricht, a place he insists is 'the centre of the continent'. In 1992, a treaty signed here led to the formation of the European Union.

'In fifteen minutes, you can be somewhere different, where everybody speaks Flemish, where everybody speaks French or where everybody speaks German,' he says. 'Within one hour, you can be in Cologne, Dusseldorf, Brussels or Eindhoven. On a fast train in two hours, you are in Paris. Maastricht is a beautiful place: family, friends, Michelin restaurants. There are more hills in Limburg than anywhere else in the Netherlands. They say we live like people in Burgundy in France. You can walk and escape. Why should I be anywhere else?'

The night before, Meijer had travelled an hour and a half from Amsterdam, where he works as a pundit for Fox Sport, covering football. In two days' time, he will fly to Munich to appear on German Sky Television. Meijer is forthright and typically Dutch in his appraisal of the nationalities he is surrounded by and encounters on a weekly basis.

'I think the word "arrogant" is a French word. That says something about the French. They do things their own way. They don't want to change. Belgians are a little bit relaxed during discussions. They don't like to get involved if there are problems. They stay out of it. Then you have the Germans: focused, hard-working, always on time. The Germans have strict rules. It is also why Germany is economically the most successful. And the Dutch? Big mouths. Always have an opinion and they say it. If the trainer says we go to the right and the Dutchman sees space on the left, that's the way he will go.'

Meijer was the Premier League striker who had it not been for the 'intervention' of football would have been a butcher like the rest of his family. His father never allowed him to kill livestock, although he can remember the sound of squelching blood in his shoes during his trips to the abattoir as a child. You could imagine Meijer running a slaughterhouse.

'My grandfather was a butcher. My father and mother were butchers. I should have been the next one,' he tells me. 'We had a shop in Meerssen, just outside Maastricht. I ate a lot. My father would have steak fillet for breakfast and I liked black pudding. In the evenings we'd have *gehaktballen* [meatballs] with potatoes and cabbage. It was unhealthy but it was all we knew. It helped me grow tall and strong.

'My father was very strict. There were certain rules. If you didn't live by those rules, he'd give you a smack. It was normal in those times. It helped me understand the difference between right and wrong. If you are wrong, you should be punished.

'Before I had a professional football contract, I'd work with my father. Every morning, I'd be at the butcher shop at 6 a.m. I'd work hard, hard, hard. Then I'd get my sports bag, step on my bike and cycle to training in Maastricht. For other kids, training was all they'd do all day. I'd already done twelve hours' work. It was a learning experience that gave me an edge over the other boys. I earned €300 a month. If I didn't become a footballer, I knew what was going to happen. It made me more determined. It also made me appreciate the money that football could bring, although it was not my priority. My priority was happiness. And money does not always deliver that.'

Meijer's father was a decent amateur footballer.

'He was pushing me, always. Pushing, pushing, pushing. We were a very sporty family. My mother played volleyball and my sisters, basketball. The washing machine was always running. My father said, "OK, boy, you need to make a decision: football or the butchery store." He gave me two years to see if I could make it as a footballer. If not, he would welcome me back into the family business. At the end of my career, when he realized I wasn't coming back, he sold the store and retired.

'I was a lively kid. Football helped me burn energy. But the two things I loved most about football were the team effort and the feeling of victory. Winning meant everything to me. I wanted to be the best. There were times when I realized that I wasn't as good as other players. So I exercised more, training harder. I did the extra miles. The other players were lazy in comparison. While I was outside kicking the ball around the field, they were in the shower. The biggest bonus that I had was character and belief. It was the basis to play for eighteen years as a professional.'

Meijer was incorporated into the youth system of his local club, SV Meerssen, by future Dutch national-team coach Bert van Marwijk.

'Bert was a legend with MVV [the professional club in Maastricht] and had finished his career. In the 1980s, a lot of ex-players went into youth training because they did not know anything else. Bert was one of these guys. Maybe he would have run a pub like the ex-players in England if that did not work out. But Bert, he was a clever coach. He started really low with Meerssen. He was really calm, a big supporter of mine. He cared about the players and advised me to go out of town and sign for a club where I could train with better kids and progress on to a higher level.'

Meijer spent a year with MVV before moving to Fortuna Sittard, a thirty-minute drive away in northern Limburg. Mark van Bommel, who became Netherlands captain, was there at the same time.

'Sittard had the best youth academy in this region. I was four years above van Bommel but everyone knew about him. He was small and skinny but he acted like a warrior in midfield. The key players in the senior team would tell me, "Look at that kid, van Bommel. He will be big some time." And he was.'

While Meijer was at Sittard, the Netherlands won a major competition for the first time: the European Championships of 1988, held in West Germany. Meijer was influenced by what he saw.

'They were successful because they were a team,' he says, emphasizing the word 'team' by raising his voice a few decibels. 'The Netherlands had some big players, big names: van Basten, Gullit. Van Basten was the example of how a striker should be. He was also long – like me. He was very skinny – like me. But technically he came from Mars. He was a goalscorer – good heading, good shooting. For me, he was the perfect striker. But even more important, the Netherlands had players that knew exactly what to do. Berry van Aerle was the right [sided] defender.

229

He knew that he had to make his runs to allow Gullit to be a better player. In a team, it is always about the balance. There is also the influence of the coach, Rinus Michels, who was in the autumn of his career but in the position at the right time; like a good red wine, you have to drink it at the correct moment.'

I suggest to Meijer that considering its relatively small population of seventeen million people, the Netherlands' success in developing brilliant footballers is remarkable.

'I think we started earlier than any other country with the youth academies,' he responds. 'It's in our genes and way of thinking. We like to encourage the kids. We like to see young football players thrive. We are taught to play in more than one position. We understand that all the positions are linked. If you are a left-back, you should also learn to play as a left-forward. When you return to left-back, you feel what the left-forward feels.'

Aged fourteen, Meijer played half a season as a centre-back.

'It was curious. I learnt a lot because it's the mirror for a striker. I almost always had a big guy against me. I learnt how to deal with myself. When I returned as a striker, I understood how a defender thinks, what he is trying to do. You see the situation from the opposite point of view. This gives you an advantage.'

The experience saw Meijer fast-tracked from Sittard's under-15 age group to the under-18s. He recognized the jump in class.

'The basic technique must be good. You must have a normal speed – if you have more, OK, it's a bonus. But you must be able to choose the right pass and have an awareness of where you are on the pitch, where the solution is. The idea in the Netherlands is to produce players who can, if required, play central-midfield – the most demanding position. Here, you need to be able to play with both feet, take a pass from the left and move it to the right. There is no hesitation and the game speeds up. From there, you kill the opponent.'

Meijer moved to Antwerp in Belgium at nineteen but never played a league game in a period where the rules permitted only two foreign players and he was the third and youngest. He soon returned to Holland, joining second-division FC Eindhoven, where five goals in fourteen first-team appearances prompted Sittard to sign him again. He then joined MVV in Maastricht, the team he had watched as a teenager, cycling to games every Saturday afternoon. The most productive spell in goalscoring terms during his entire career followed.

'All the boys were from here, from Maastricht,' Meijer says, pressing his index finger into the wooden table that separates us as if to claim territory. 'In Limburg, we speak a distinct dialect. People from Amsterdam don't understand us. In the dressing room, we were loud. We'd bang on the walls. It would intimidate the teams that came to play us in Maastricht. There was a connection amongst the players and the supporters. I was the butcher's son, then you had the son of the cobbler as a goalkeeper and the baker in defence. We were very, very close. It was like a family. Plus, we had an excellent coach in Sef Vergoossen, who was more like a second father. He gave me his hand, pulled me in and said, "OK, I have done something for you, now you must help me." He helped improve my heading technique. I jumped with my left foot, I jumped with my right foot. My balance became a lot better and so did my timing.'

Thirty-four goals in sixty-six games from Meijer led to MVV finishing an improbable seventh place in the Eredivisie in successive seasons. In the summer of 1993, he could have moved to Ajax, Feyenoord or VfB Stuttgart in Germany but chose PSV Eindhoven because it was closest to his home and he felt the transition would be easier, offering him greater exposure for national team selection.

His partner up front initially was Wim Kieft, who had played in Italy with Pisa and Torino before helping PSV to the European Cup and the Dutch to the European Championships five summers before.

'Wim was so cool, so calculated. I was like a bull charging around using my arms and being aggressive. He told me to slow down, to be smart. I struggled with that.'

PSV were in transition and behind Ajax in terms of domestic success.

'Ajax had the de Boer brothers, Overmars, Reiziger and Finidi George. We had kids like Boudewijn Zenden, Eidur Gudjohnsen and Arthur Numan. Then, after three quarters of a year, Ronaldo came. He was so good.'

Meijer does an impression of the Brazilian, using his teeth and hands as if to mimic an otter.

'Ronaldo came in on a day like today [grey skies and dank]. We were in shorts and a T-shirt because we were familiar with the weather. He was wearing a tracksuit and gloves, looking very, very cold. He did not look like he would survive. At the end of the session, we had a four versus four game. Ronaldo went to take the defender, Mitchell van der Gaag, one way on the outside, then turned quickly on to his inside. The defender fell over, then he chipped the ball over the goalkeeper, Ronald Waterreus. Everybody stood there open-mouthed. In his first year, Ronaldo scored more than thirty goals. He was seventeen years old.'

Meijer believes Ronaldo's success was based on his personality as much as his ability.

'He was clever, a very smart boy. He learnt the language very quickly and Flemish is not the easiest. He used yellow Post-it notes on every object. They were all over his house. The bed. The tables. The refrigerator. The curtains. When he knew the word, the note was not there any more.'

Ronaldo's talent meant that Meijer would not play as much as he would have liked.

'Ronaldo had a good connection with Luc Nilis. I was the third striker. I scored my goals when the opportunities were there. Dick Advocaat was the coach and I told him that I wanted to play more. He told me, "Erik, there is Ronaldo, there is Luc, what can I do?" It was not going to happen at PSV. So I decided to go to KFC Uerdingen in Germany.'

Not for the first or last time, Meijer took one step backwards in the hope it might lead to him springing forward. Despite finishing bottom in the Bundesliga, his eleven goals at Uerdingen earned him another move, this time further into the Ruhr Valley with Bayer Leverkusen.

'Uerdingen was the most important period in my career because it proved I could influence games when the team was not so good. I could have chosen to go to Schalke 04 or Werder Bremen but Leverkusen had a lot of young players and that excited me. I liked German football because it involved more power and more running. The tempo is quicker than in the Netherlands. Physically, you have to be at a very high standard. It suited me.'

With Meijer and Ulf Kirsten providing a classic little and large combination, Leverkusen qualified for the Champions League. 'We had Jens Nowotny in defence then Carsten Ramelow in front with a couple of Brazilians in midfield. There was Emerson and Zé Roberto.'

Leverkusen were coached by Christoph Daum, who would have taken up the same role with the German national team in 2000 had it not been for a scandal that outed him as a cocaine abuser.

'Christoph was a very demanding trainer who liked his wingers to put crosses in the box,' Meijer says. 'I liked him.'

At the end of his third season at Leverkusen, Meijer was offered a new four-year contract. He could have also signed for Borussia Dortmund. Then Liverpool called, offering close to £15,000 a week.

'I could not believe the wages. My wife was screaming in the house.'

Meijer tells me about his first conversation with Gérard Houllier, using a dubious French accent.

'"Hello, Erik, I am Monsieur Houllier. I would like you to join Liverpool FC," he told me. 'The hairs on the back of my neck were rigid.'

Meijer had become fascinated with Liverpool as a teenager.

'I had a feeling for the red shirt. I watched the European Cup finals and remember Graeme Souness in 1984 against Roma. He was leader of the army. I wanted to be that man. I also liked Ian Rush. He was long and quick. He moved like an animal trying to kill prey. He was aggressive too. I liked that.'

Meijer would ask his parents for a Liverpool shirt at birthdays and Christmases.

'Some people think of Barcelona, Real Madrid, or, in the Netherlands, Ajax. Me? I was always Liverpool. England was the place I wanted to play. I liked the rainy weather, the wet pitch and the screaming audience. Seeing spectators shouting, "Come on, come on!!!" was beautiful for me, something special. I liked this period, the kick and rush. I liked seeing the defender and the striker fighting. At the end of the match, the defender would have a bleeding eye and the striker would be missing his teeth. But they shook hands. Football is just a mask.'

His impressions of Houllier were mixed.

'Gérard was very demanding. He was very French, very difficult to figure out. I never knew what he was really thinking. Yet he had strict rules. Hard. Tactically, he was very clever, always looking for the right mixture in the team. He also had his English assistant.'

Meijer is referring to Phil Thompson, Liverpool's former European Cup-winning captain from Kirkby, a disciplinarian who'd been sacked by Graeme Souness at the start of the decade for supposedly being too harsh with reserve-team players. Houllier's first act was to reappoint him.

'Phil – he was not an easy man. I respected him. But he loved to shout and tell people off. Not every player could deal with that. I saw a lot of players who had problems with him, although I did not. We clashed a few times.'

Sammy Lee, the first-team coach, was different.

'I could easily work with Sammy. He was totally on my wavelength. He'd lived abroad [when playing for Osasuna in Spain]. He was good at understanding situations from the other point of view. He could see when I was ready to explode. There were times when I wanted to tell Phil [Thompson] that he had a big nose but Sammy would stop me by just giving a look. I had a very good connection with him. It was the same with Patrice Bergues [Houllier's first-team coach].'

Meijer was one of seven players signed by Houllier in the

summer of 1999. He became close with the two recruits from the Eredivisie, Sander Westerveld and Sami Hyypiä.

'The club looked at what was necessary. Signing so many play-ers at one time was not the way Liverpool had done things before. But look at the success that came. Within two years, Liverpool won the UEFA Cup, the FA Cup, the League Cup, the European Super Cup and the Charity Shield. You cannot say this was not a wise decision by the manager and his board of directors. It was the right investment.'

Out of all the new players, including Westerveld, Hyypiä, Stéphane Henchoz, Titi Camara, Vladimír Šmicer and Dietmar Hamann as well as Meijer, it was Meijer's relationship with the Anfield crowd that blossomed quickest, even though he was in the side the least. Soon, he was known as 'Mad Erik'.

'I was proud. Fans know their team better than anyone else. They understand if they see an idiot. They understand if they see a professor [an intelligent player]. For me, I think they found the right word. I was a little bit crazy, that's true. In my period at Liverpool, I just wanted to show how much I loved this moment. That's why I was aggressive and gave everything. I'd played for other teams where it did not matter as much.

'Respect goes two ways. There have been strikers with better skill and strikers who have scored a lot of goals. But maybe those strikers were not willing to die for the club. They keep a distance. I wanted to please the fans. It is true that without the fans, foot-ball is nothing. I see the slogans. If anyone ever asked me for an autograph, I obliged. I'd played in front of six hundred people for FC Eindhoven in Holland and that was not nice. I appreciated playing in front of a full stadium with screaming fans.'

Meijer recognized the power of the crowd and their potential to alter the outcome of a result. It was a tactic he often used before a corner kick in front of the Kop, waving his hands like an inspirational conductor does to his orchestra, generating a for-midable noise.

'You try to achieve a reaction. If the crowd becomes 4 per cent louder, it might make a difference. I would place my focus on one person and stare into his eyes. Your teammates feed off the crowd. Players think, "Hey, if Erik goes for it and the crowd does too, we will follow."'

Meijer says that the ringtone on his mobile phone is 'You'll Never Walk Alone'. He plays it to me and begins to sing along.

'It is so intense, isn't it?' he asks. 'It's very special to me. I think it should not be played in any other stadium, just at Anfield. It belongs at Anfield. Celtic Park is OK. But it is not the same as Anfield.'

Meijer speaks about football as a 'mental challenge', where he 'goes to the edge of the table without falling off'. At Leverkusen, after being treated for swelling of the ankle, he threw ice cubes at a moving ball upon his return to the game. 'The left-back was confused and he made the wrong decision.' At Liverpool, Meijer would roar at defenders when challenging for headers, trying to put them off. After a fierce clearance hit him in the face against Bradford, he fell to the ground and bounced straight back up, immediately giving chase again. 'Everybody expects you to get some water. But that is weak. Just get your mind set on something different, like revenge.'

To escape the attentions of Leeds United's Michael Duberry, he ran around the back of the goal from a corner kick. 'I did that in Germany too and I scored from it. If you think out of the box, you can have success.' He would talk to opponents and try to make them feel insecure. 'There was the guy at Middlesbrough, [Gianluca] Festa. I said to him straight, "I saw you last week, you did not play very well. You made some very bad passes." He was thinking about me rather than the match.' The approach was not so successful with Gary Pallister, 'who could see through my bullshit'.

Meijer tried his best to make his personal duel 'a fight'.

'Tony Adams, Martin Keown – they were the guys I liked playing against. I could lean in and hang in the air. They would push me and I would push them back. I would do anything I could to take their mind off the game and give me the advantage. I would always say sorry afterwards. The pitch was there.

And now I'm Erik again. I liked to put my face out and risk getting a smack.'

Meijer would also engage referees.

'Oh, yes, I liked the bastards in the black,' he says. 'In England, they are much better than in Germany, where they are militaristic. In England, there was Paul Durkin, who was the best. He understood that football is an emotional game and sometimes you might say something that is a little out of line. Those times it was, "Hey, big guy, I heard what you said . . . I saw your elbow. That won't happen again. Next time, you're in trouble." That was fair. The referees had their own personalities and I think this is good. Players are more accepting of personality. It is bad when they cannot impose their character. They now officiate more to a system and the authorities do not trust their experience enough. Sometimes a match will have a feeling: "Hey, Tony [Adams], I know you are going to kick. I will allow it only once." That builds up a respect between the player and the referee, and the game is better. David Elleray was more like a German referee. He was a schoolmaster in private education, wasn't he?'

Journalists were also targeted. The *Liverpool Echo* reporter at the time, Chris Bascombe, remembers asking Meijer for a quote ahead of a big game with Leeds United at Anfield. Meijer gave him one line. 'I told him to use this as the headline: "THE BIG DUTCHMAN IS READY".'

Meijer was happy to cultivate his own image.

'I embraced this identity. Football is a serious business. But every now and again you need to loosen it up a little bit, give something for the show. If you see the puzzle of Liverpool in 1999 and 2000, that was my role: to be The Big Dutchman.'

On another occasion the following season when Meijer was not in the squad, Bascombe did not mention his name in a report about Houllier's striking options. 'I was not happy about this,' Meijer recalls. 'So I went to the reporter when he was looking for a story at Melwood.' Meijer stands up, pointing into the middle distance, re-enacting the moment. '"Hey, Christopher, I am still here, you know. I will fight until the end."'

In his first months as a Liverpool player, Meijer was used as a substitute. On being introduced, it was as if he were already in tune with the emotions of the game, barking orders at teammates and challenging defenders immediately.

'I knew exactly what to do. I was thirty by then. I trusted my experience. When I sat on the substitutes' bench, I'd watch what was happening in front of me very closely. I did not complain that I was not playing, fiddling with my tracksuit top, playing with chewing gum in my mouth, or wasting time tying the laces of my football boots. I'd see my opponent, his weaknesses. I focused. This was one of my qualities. During the ninety minutes and at the training ground before, I would never stop. I needed the focus in my training to be good at the weekend. There are players who need to be relaxed so they can explode at the weekend. I was not one of those. For me, it did not work. I went all-out in the training sessions, then a little bit calmer the day before a match. All other times it was 100 per cent. War.'

Titi Camara, the Guinean striker signed from Marseille in the same week as Meijer, was his opposite.

'Titi was a lazy cunt during the week,' Meijer smiles. 'He did nothing. Last in all of the sprints, his shooting was off. He would get tackled in five-a-side matches. But as soon as the whistle went on a Saturday, he was good: fast, skilful, quite powerful too. Titi also had a good relationship with the fans. There was a feeling.'

At Hull City, who were eighteenth out of the twenty-four teams in England's bottom professional division when Liverpool travelled across the M62 on a cold Tuesday night in September 1999, Meijer, partnering Michael Owen in attack, was selected for the first time. He scored twice, both goals arriving by his weaker right boot. 'I did my celebration, hands pumping in the air, and the crowd seemed to like it.' At the beginning of October, he was given his full league debut against Aston Villa away.

'We wore an ugly green shirt,' he recalls. 'Steve Staunton got a red card after thirty minutes, so we spent an hour fighting for a 0–0. I went into the dressing room at half-time shattered. I could not move. The pitch was so big at Villa Park and the tempo was so high. With ten men, it was very demanding. My feet were burning. Gérard was talking but I couldn't hear him. I was gone. I knew I had to go for another forty-five minutes.'

Between the end of October and the beginning of February, Meijer was restricted to appearances from the bench. Then an injury crisis offered an opportunity at Anfield with Leeds the visitors.

'An hour before the match, Gérard told me I was the striker. Leeds had a very good team under David O'Leary and could have won the league. I was calm. I shared a few jokes with the other players. I put my tapings on. I went out to warm up and the Kop was half-empty. Then the referee's whistle blew and we had to wait in the tunnel. You can see the "This Is Anfield" sign, which is a piece of history. You step up into the stadium and there is a roar. "You'll Never Walk Alone" is playing. The hair on my arms and neck go up. I am 1 metre 89. But I feel 2 metres 10.'

Meijer did not score during the 3–1 victory but supplied Danny Murphy's third in injury time. He did enough to be selected in the win at Arsenal the following week then again at Old Trafford, with both of his parents in attendance having flown in from the Netherlands.

'Jaap Stam fouled me for a free kick and Patrik Berger scored in front of the Stretford End. That gave me a tremendous buzz. Jaap was probably the best defender in the world: a massive bloke, an ugly guy. He would try anything to stop you. I was right up for it. I knew the supporters really wanted to win this game. Manchester people don't like Liverpool people and vice-versa. I could hear the chanting. This is what happens at football matches between two massive clubs.'

Meijer had experienced the intensity of the rivalry when attending Mike Tyson's fight with Julius Francis at the M.E.N. Arena two months before. Tyson destroyed Francis, registering five knockdowns in four minutes, the final and most significant arriving at the end of the second round. But there was nearly another brawl that took place that evening.

'I was with Sander and Sami. Some United supporters

recognized us. They were shouting. They tried to come over. So I walked and stood in front of them. I was a lot bigger than the main guy, a lot bigger. I looked into the guy's eyes and put my arm around him. I then told him that he had three options. He could fuck off like a scared cat, he could join me in the ring or we could all drink beer. He chose the beer.'

Meijer was given a run of games following a series of committed performances for Liverpool's reserves at Knowsley Road in the Pontins League.

'There were concrete terraces on all four sides. That for me was a real sports atmosphere. Too perfect is not so good. There is real grass but mud somewhere. You get dirty when you make a big tackle. The light is dim – not like Anfield when you feel like an actor on a stage. Here it is like the backroom of a pub. My idea was, if you can play well at St Helens, you can also play well at the beautiful stadiums in the world.'

During the 1999–2000 season, Meijer scored seven goals in fourteen reserve games. Unlike other foreign players, he took these encounters very seriously.

'Titi, he would play for the reserves and not be bothered, but me, I knew it was very important. If I scored a goal, it proved I was capable – it showed others I could do it. When you are there, you have to do it for yourself and your own pride. That way, the manager focuses on you. When the manager makes his next substitution, he will be thinking about Erik Meijer who played well for the reserves, not about David Thompson who did not move his ass on the pitch, for example.'

Meijer was fond of Thompson, the midfielder who could not force himself into Houllier's long-term thinking.

'He was a very technical player and a great lad. I would say to him, "Come on, David, move your ass, you can do better than this." But our situations were different. I felt like I had to show everybody all of the time that I had the quality to play for the first team. With David, his quality was obvious. Maybe he didn't feel the need.'

Jon Newby was often Meijer's partner in attack. Newby was

the reserves' leading goalscorer. He would make four substitute appearances for Liverpool's first team before moving between a host of lower-league north-west clubs. In 2013, he was registered with Warrington Town.

'Jon came from the academy, didn't he? He was a small, skinny and technical guy. He played off me, buzzing around like a wasp. I think to have a good career everything has to fit. You need to have a good body, a good mindset, the character and a little bit of luck. When you have that all together, then things can happen.'

What Meijer really wanted was to score in a league game at Anfield. He did it twice versus Celtic in an end-of-season testimonial for Ronnie Moran. But never in the league.

'There was a header against Middlesbrough,' he says ruefully. 'The score was 0–0. A cross comes in from the left side and I connect with it beautifully. Trickling, trickling, it goes wide. This is the one I think about even though it was fifteen years ago.'

Meijer would have celebrated by jumping in the Kop.

'Even if the goal was at the Anfield Road end, I would have run the length of the pitch and hurled myself beyond the hoardings to celebrate with the fans. If the referee sends me off, who gives a fuck?'

Robbie Fowler and Michael Owen were already ahead of Meijer in the first-team reckoning when Houllier bought Emile Heskey for £11 million from Leicester City, a record fee for the club. Meijer says Heskey was similar in style to him, 'only he was faster, stronger, more technical and scored more goals'. Meijer's future appeared bleak.

'Robbie was the best striker at Liverpool, though he was also lazy in training,' Meijer says. 'As soon as it came to finishing or being cool during five-a-side matches, he was unbelievably good. Robbie was better than Michael Owen. But Robbie was also living his life. Robbie was out with the boys. He enjoyed the booze. But that was part of him. He was a human being and this is a far more important thing. It was the way he'd grown up. Football and the pub belonged together.'

Owen was career-driven.

'Michael was a kid. He had so many cars. Every day, he would turn up to training in a different one. But I didn't want to swap my life with him. Everywhere we went with the team, there was a buzz. The young girls, the teenage footballers, all the cameras were focused in one direction. I remember being at the airport and a bunch of people were looking his way. "Erik, Erik, let me hide behind you . . ." That's the other side of being a very popular sportsperson. It is a different type of pressure both mentally and physically. Michael's game was based on speed, being able to open up his hamstrings. He suffered a lot from muscle problems. Maybe that was a result of the pressure: always being at the press conference, always Michael, Michael, Michael. He was always relaxed when he was at the training ground with the boys. He was such a nice guy, like a younger brother – always drinking Coca Cola and never alcohol on a night out. But for the media, there was a different face. It had to be this way.'

Meijer enjoyed Steve Staunton's company the most. The Irish left-back had returned to Liverpool under Roy Evans and was not in Houllier's plans.

'The Irish and the Dutch always get on well,' Meijer continues. 'We enjoyed a lot of nights out. He drank Guinness and I was on strong lager. I liked Vegard Heggem too. He was the smartest guy. You could have a good conversation with him. Dominic Matteo was there and everyone liked him. Boy, he could drink a lot for a young man. We went for a winter training camp in Malta and Dominic found a way of taping his door so the staff could not enter and check we were asleep. We sneaked to the casino for a beer. Didi [Hamann] was there. The night ended with Didi on the piano singing "American Pie". The song was his showpiece. Didi ate regularly at Jalons piano bar on Smithdown Road with me, Sander, Sami and Stéphane. We'd invite our wives. By the end of the night, Didi would be playing the piano, singing terribly.'

Living in Calderstones Park, Meijer made friends with people he still keeps in touch with.

'There is Ray Watt, who is a big Evertonian. He sells women's clothes in St John's Market. I met him on the golf course when I

242

was playing with Jørgen Nielsen, the Danish goalkeeper. Ray is married to Paula. They have three kids and to one of them I am the godfather. His name is Matty. As soon as I met Ray, I had such a warm feeling. Whenever I go back to see him, the whole family is there. They earn enough money. They share. Everybody sits in the back garden and there is food and beer. It is how life should be.'

When Meijer decided to sign for Hamburg, his wife, Sandra, who he is still married to after they met twenty-eight years ago as teenagers, did not want to leave Merseyside.

'We were very happy there. It is a place where I could have lived for ever if football had not intervened. The Scousers, they are my kind of people: hard workers, respectful of the past, determined to make history in the future; they won't put up with any bullshit. There is a healthy balance to their mind-set that other communities could learn from if they were not so ignorant.'

Meijer's departure from Liverpool was a gradual process. Frustration became a daily part of working life.

'In the second year, I visited every away ground as the number 17. There were sixteen players in the match squad. I am not the player who is willing to sit a lot. My contract was huge – nearly £50,000 a month after tax. I never believed I'd earn that much. The contract had everything: a car, a house, a membership to a leisure centre. But money and material things do not mean everything. So I went to Houllier and said, "You take me to every away match, I see every stadium in the country. But I wear my suit and sit in the stands. There will come a moment when I will kill somebody in training. I cannot handle this any more." I asked Houllier to leave me at home. He told me I was important for the team and the spirit. "That's nice for the others," I said. I was the one sitting up there in the stands like a melon. If Houllier told me I was not good enough, I would have respected it and left. But he never did.

'Now and then at Melwood I would train with that feeling. Patrice and Sammy had to calm me down a few times. We'd play small matches and the coaches would act as the referee. I would argue about whether a ball had crossed the line for a throw-in. I was in that type of mood. I would tackle people even harder. I did one on Heggem and he did not deserve it. He was in the wrong position at the wrong moment. I was so eager to achieve something and I thought the manager was not right, so I took my anger out on somebody else. Houllier called me into his office a few times. He told me off. I told him again that I did not feel part of the team.'

Meijer admits now that he fell short of Liverpool's standards.

'When I was a Liverpool player, I would tell everyone that I was good enough, that I had different qualities to the other players. I knew that whenever I started a game, Liverpool never lost. I tried to convince myself. I would go to the manager and tell him to play me because I thought I was right. Only after it was over could I admit that the step up from Leverkusen was too big. Robbie, Michael, Emile – they were all better than me. They were the strikers that Liverpool needed to be successful. I was not at their level. You do not want to admit it. But later I realized that my qualities were not the same as Liverpool's. I accept it. I went back to Germany and I said to myself, "Erik, you were just not good enough." I am proud that I can admit that.'

Before moving back to Germany, he signed a short-term loan deal with Preston North End, where David Moyes was manager. Within eighteen months, Moyes would be appointed at Everton – a job he would keep for the next ten years.

'He came to my house and explained that Preston had some bad injuries. Would I help him out? I liked Moyes. He was wearing shorts. He was one of the boys. The only difference was he had a whistle. We had a bad, bad pitch to train on. The facilities were poor. But after two days, I accepted it was not Anfield or Melwood. I realized Moyes had created a certain atmosphere. There were some good players. Sean Gregan was a good leader. [Gregan later played in the Premier League with West Bromwich Albion.] The team was near the top of the Second Division. I knew I had to make something of it.

At the end of my six weeks there, I think we were close to the play-offs.'

What happened next says much about Meijer's personality. He is not a bitter man. Joining Hamburg, he rediscovered his goal-scoring touch. Within six months, Liverpool had reached the final of the UEFA Cup final against Alavés in Dortmund. He acquired four tickets from Sander Westerveld and went along with three friends, starting the day in the Alter Markt.

'I had four match-worn shirts with "Meijer 18" on the back. I wore one and gave the other three to the boys. We set off very early in the morning, parked the car at our hotel and got the tram into town. There were Liverpool supporters everywhere. We decided to have a beer, so my friend orders at the bar. He is approached by this guy, "Hey, why are you wearing an Erik Meijer shirt? He was crap." My mate says, "Yeah, Erik's just over there." It was the beginning of a few funny hours.'

Meijer doesn't remember buying many drinks.

'The place was bouncing. The fans put me on a podium and started singing, "Erik, Erik, give us a song." It went very quiet. Then I sang "You'll Never Walk Alone".'

Meijer doesn't remember much about the match that followed either: a remarkable 5–4 victory.

'It was as special as my wedding day,' Meijer insists. 'I was there with a beer in my hand, celebrating all the goals like I'd scored myself. I had left Liverpool and I would never go back but these were my best moments.'

Meijer played until he was thirty-six years old, finishing his career with Alemannia Aachen, a twenty-minute drive away across the German border. 'My hobby became a profession – and a well-paid profession. I work now even though I don't need to. How lucky is that?'

Although he describes his time as Aachen's sporting director as 'the worst fucking time', explaining that he could not address the lack of commitment from some players on the pitch while he was sitting in the directors' box, it taught him to slow down and 'enjoy life' by walking away.

Meijer remains a cult figure at Anfield and he thinks he knows why.

'The favourite players are the ones who show their human characteristics,' he says, while walking me between a few of Maastricht's finest public houses later on.

'Robbie Fowler? He could have been the brother of any Liverpool fan. Me? I tried hard and looked like a guy you could have a pint with after a day in the factory.'

Meijer is a pole apart from the introverted, monosyllabic modern footballer.

'Now, players have the same personality. It's all one kind of soup. There is no chicken, tomato or spice. It's tasteless water. If you listen to an interview after a match, it does not matter which club the player represents or even whether he has won or lost. Many say the same thing. It's boring. Why bother speaking to these players? Come on, it's bullshit.'

CHAPTER TEN

cultzeros.co.uk

THE LEGEND WHO BECAME MANAGER,
Graeme Souness,
1978–84 and 1991–94

IT SHOULD NOT BE LIKE THIS FOR GRAEME SOUNESS, EXPLAINING where it all went wrong. Souness should be in line with Kenny Dalglish and Steven Gerrard whenever Liverpool's greatest post-war players are mentioned. Yet he took a risk on his reputation and, as he puts it, 'blew the chance'.

He dismisses my suggestion that he might regret accepting the role of Liverpool manager, 'No, no, no, not at all.' Yet he stresses the problems in 1991 were greater than anyone really appreciated. 'Listen,' he continues, 'it was a job that I felt I had to do.' Then, without any hesitation, he offers a caveat: 'Though I took it at completely the wrong time.'

Souness compares the situation he inherited to the one David

Moyes found at Manchester United after Alex Ferguson's sudden retirement.

'You've got a club with twenty-five years of success,' he says. 'The first manager in is a bringer of bad news, where he's telling players – in some cases legends – that their time is up. Nobody goes quietly. There's a period when you are not going to be successful because you are buying in players that are going to take time to settle down.

'You are asking supporters to be patient, and this is at a time when the expectation levels are still enormous. It has to be managed. For me, you don't want to be the first one to follow Fergie, because you'll be the one that gets all the flak for doing what would appear to be *everything* wrong, when it's not really the case.

'The second one [Louis van Gaal] comes in and maybe tries to achieve success too quickly by adopting an aggressive transfer policy without any real thinking behind it. Perhaps you could compare that to Roy [Evans] at Liverpool after me.

'Ideally, you want to be the third one in, when expectation levels are back at a manageable level. Then you can build it up again.'

The Liverpool move seemed like the dream appointment, both for the club and manager. 'I was blinded by my feelings for Liverpool,' admits Souness, who as a player at Anfield won nearly everything there was to win, both domestically and internationally. As an obdurate, iron-willed wall of muscle, he captained the greatest club in Europe before making a lucrative transfer to Sampdoria in Italy. His step up to management, at the hitherto struggling Glasgow Rangers, initiated a period of almost total dominance in Scotland.

'Since leaving Spurs as a teenager, everywhere I'd gone it was success, success, success; medal, medal, medal; trophy, trophy, trophy,' he says. 'I thought the pattern would continue at Liverpool. I didn't stop for a minute to think about what I was doing, to analyse the situation.'

He was not to know at the time, but his reputation would

spectacularly alter. Souness the player and Souness the manager are viewed somewhat differently. Considering his achievements as a captain – the swaggering style and spirit with which he led the team – I find it sad that he is not remembered with absolute reverence. He reminds me several times that although there are mitigating circumstances if people are willing to listen, only he is to blame for a blemished legacy.

'I know I made mistakes,' Souness says, immediately citing an interview he did with *The Sun* on the third anniversary of the Hillsborough disaster. The paper was hated on Merseyside after it printed lies about the role of Liverpool supporters on that dreadful April afternoon in 1989. 'I will regret the decision forever. I don't have a defence.'

Souness admits that also he took the wrong approach when dealing with players. 'I appreciate that I was too hard with every-one. I'd come from a generation where the attitude to problems was just to get on with it: to look at yourself in the mirror and sort it out. As players, we were treated like men and expected to act as men.

'The thing I miss most as a player is the confrontation and the rivalry, standing in the tunnel and waiting for the battle. If we lost, I found it hard to shake hands. I'd go home and sit alone for the evening. You see a lot of players now hugging each other. They swap shirts with the opposition at half-time. It's wrong.

'In management, I expected my players to feel the same as me. But the world was changing. Players were expecting a shoulder to cry on. The players were holding more power than the manager. I wasn't cute enough sometimes, or political enough.'

Souness speaks in the arrivals hall of Edinburgh Airport in his home city, where he is meeting with old friends for the weekend. I had interviewed him six years earlier at Anfield as he waited to go live on air for a Sky broadcast. He is an impressive individual. While Richard Keys and Andy Gray bantered away in an other-wise hectic room, Souness sat alone in a dimly lit corner amongst his own thoughts. I recall a lone sliver of bright light piercing through a tinted window and crossing Souness's tough-looking face. It made him seem like a prisoner in a war movie as he slowly, thoughtfully and confidently spoke about his experiences. He exuded an awesome aura that instantly commanded respect. I thought Souness – the only Souness in football – was made of granite.

I wondered whether he was born a leader. Like Irvine Welsh, the acclaimed and controversial writer of *Trainspotting* and *Filth*, Souness's family came from Leith – Edinburgh's industrial centre and dock area. Souness grew up, however, further inland in Saughton Mains, where the city's prison is a brooding presence.

'I had a very loving and caring family background,' he tells me. 'I was the youngest of three brothers, which meant I always had something to prove. When you're around kids that are older, they always tell you that they are better at everything. I didn't want that to be the case. It toughened me up.'

Souness's father was a glazier and the family lived in a prefab. Between the ages of twelve and fifteen, Souness would sleep at his grandmother's home in a tenement block a few miles away on Gorgie Road, where the air reeked of fermenting yeast from the nearby Caledonian Brewery.

'She was lonely,' he explains. 'My grandfather had died and my brothers had cared for her before they hit sixteen as well. There was no questioning; we just did it. It was our way of life.'

It did not mean Souness missed out on football. There was a big field outside his parents' home. 'I wasn't bothered about Hibs or Hearts really, because I was always playing football on a Saturday, although Tyncastle was closer to my home. For as long as I can remember, I never thought about doing anything else. From the earliest age, the thought never entered my head that I wouldn't become a footballer. Some people may have seen it as misguided confidence but I turned out to be right, didn't I?'

Although he'd been captain of his school team, Souness only took the role on for the first time as a professional at Liverpool, aged twenty-eight.

'I wasn't captain of the Spurs team that won the FA Youth

Cup. I wasn't made captain at Middlesbrough. I was a late developer, although I'd always played with arrogance.'

Coming from the same Carrickvale Secondary School as the great Dave Mackay acted as motivation in the early days.

'I occasionally stood on the terraces at Hearts and saw Dave play. He was a real warrior type. I was constantly reminded by my headmaster that I'd never be as good as him.'

After playing for Scotland Schoolboys against England Schoolboys at White Hart Lane, Mackay – who was Tottenham's captain and watching in the stands – recommended Souness to Bill Nicholson, Spurs' legendary coach.

'Dave was the only name ever mentioned by Bill Nic. He never mentioned John White, he never mentioned Danny Blanchflower – only ever Dave Mackay. It felt like I lived with him. I told him years later that I was fed up hearing his name. But I never set out to be like anyone else. I played the game as I saw it.'

Souness insists he was more impulsive as a teenager than he is now.

'I went to Spurs at fifteen and thought I was going to be a superstar,' he admits. 'I was headstrong and pretty soon I was knocking on Bill Nic's door asking why I wasn't in the first team.' At seventeen, Souness was suspended for two weeks by the club without pay for taking a leave of absence in Edinburgh, citing homesickness. He felt 'completely at sea with the London scene'. By nineteen, he was allowed to leave for Middlesbrough. 'It came as a real shock when Spurs agreed the deal. It made me more determined than ever to become a successful footballer and to prove them wrong.'

Souness's towering self-belief and desire to win brought him more medals than an army veteran. Yet his career was fuelled not just by what he describes as 'the unique taste of success' but also by the whiplash of a few failures. 'No person's playing career is full of highs,' he says. 'My one real low came right at the start of mine. It kicked me where it hurt and I had to deal with it. It shaped the way I was thereafter.'

His combative performances for Middlesbrough earned him

a record transfer to Liverpool in January 1978. On his first morning in the Anfield dressing room, he remembers asking Tommy Smith, Liverpool's most ferocious player, if he could borrow his hairdryer. 'Tommy turned to Phil Neal and commented, "Everyone is allowed to make one mistake."'

Liverpool had great managers. But Souness believes the team was driven towards triumph because of its senior players. 'I turned up at Liverpool when I was twenty-four. I was a bit of a Jack the Lad. At least I thought I was. Very quickly, I was put in place verbally by the senior pros. There were no prima donnas and no superstars. Any problems on or off the pitch, the more experienced boys would stamp it out.'

He was made captain upon Liverpool's 3–1 defeat to Manchester City at Anfield in December 1981, leaving Bob Paisley's team in twelfth place in the league. Dalglish and Neal were older than Souness and considered favourites for the role after it was revealed that Phil Thompson was being relieved of the responsibility. By the end of the season, Liverpool were champions, having toppled Ipswich Town by four points.

Michael Robinson, the striker who signed for Liverpool from Brighton & Hove Albion in 1983 before struggling to deal with the expectations of the club, said Souness approached every game exactly the same.

'The attitude throughout the club was that if we didn't do well, anybody could beat us,' Robinson said. 'If we did do well, nobody could beat us. It was humble. I remember once before a game against Brentford in the League Cup, Graeme had the dressing room buzzing like we were playing against Manchester United. There was no complacency – ever.'

Robinson also said that Souness helped him deal with his own insecurities about being good enough to play for Liverpool.

'Once you chipped off that varnish, I found Graeme a very personal, cuddly chap who was actually quite vulnerable about being a human being with emotions. To this day, he still tries very hard not to be this lovely cuddly person, when really he is.'

When asked whether he found any aspect of captaincy

challenging, Souness responds before I can finish the question. 'None, absolutely none,' he says. 'My attitude didn't change at all. Joe [Fagan] pulled me to one side soon after and told me to focus only on looking after my own game. I realized that if I set the example, the rest would follow.'

Souness says his greatest performance for Liverpool came in his last match before joining Sampdoria, against Roma in Rome in the European Cup final of 1984. 'It felt like we'd gone to the Coliseum and sacked the place. Nobody gave us a chance. But we had the most ridiculous inner belief. Had it been Barcelona in the Nou Camp or Real Madrid in the Bernabéu, we'd have done what we had to do to win the game and done a number on them.'

He believes, however, that captaincy did not prepare him for management 'one bit'. As captain of Liverpool, the responsibility was 'easy because of the calibre of person and quality of player you're sharing a dressing room with'. He reiterates that he rarely had to think about anyone else's welfare, only his own. Management was different.

'As a manager, I could not forget about the job – much to the irritation of my wife. It wasn't a case of leaving the stadium and thinking about something else. I'd be thinking about it driving home, I'd be thinking about it when I got home, I'd be thinking about it when there was an interval on a television programme I was watching, they were the last thoughts in my head before I fell asleep. I found it impossible to switch off. It's a roller-coaster ride. Not year by year, not month by month, not week by week, but day by day, hour by hour, result by result.

'If I was winning – like I was at Rangers – or if I was losing – like I was more often at Liverpool – my mind was only ever on the job. As a captain, you concern yourself with your fitness and form. When you're a manager, you think about the welfare of thirty players. Then there are the media and the board of directors that you are answerable to.'

Souness became the first player-manager in Rangers' history when he succeeded Jock Wallace at Ibrox in 1986, a month short of his thirty-third birthday. Financed initially by the club's then owner Lawrence Marlborough, Souness and chairman David Holmes embarked upon a bold strategy of reclaiming the footballing ascendancy that Rangers had been desperately seeking in Scotland after years in the wilderness due to the dominance of arch rivals Celtic and the emergence of the 'New Firm', Aberdeen and Dundee United.

At Rangers, Souness proved early on that he was not afraid to make difficult decisions. He capitalized on the banning of English clubs in European competition after the Heysel stadium disaster by signing numerous English players, in turn reversing decades of historical tradition whereby Scottish players moved south of the border. Not only did he revive the glory days, he succeeded in taking the most enormous and brave risks. After Mark Walters became the first black player to represent Rangers in more than fifty years, Souness made Maurice Johnson Rangers' first Catholic player. Souness claims the decision to sign the pair was made for practical rather than any profoundly historical reasons. 'They were two good players who I thought would serve us well,' he says.

A year after Souness's departure from Anfield, Joe Fagan retired as Liverpool's manager. For twenty-six years, Liverpool's management structure had been comparable to that of a mafia crime family. In Bill Shankly, there was the boss, Bob Paisley was the *consigliere* or councillor, then Fagan, the underboss. Ronnie Moran, Roy Evans and Reuben Bennett were the *capos*, who headed the crew of soldiers – in football terms, the players. The organization was put in place so that Liverpool would achieve long-standing success. Like the mafia, Liverpool was led by a group of old men who met in private in a smelly old room to discuss their plans. Nothing was ostentatious or above suspicion. There were simple and ruthless principles and no fancy purchases. In the Boot Room after games, Fagan particularly was well skilled at slapping beaten opponents on the back with one hand and extracting information for future reference with the other, much like a mafia priest.

By 1985, Shankly had died, Paisley had gone, Bennett had gone, as had Fagan – after just two seasons and sooner than anyone at the club had expected. Liverpool's response was to promote Kenny Dalglish from soldier level to boss. Dalglish sacked both Geoff Twentyman as chief scout and Chris Lawler as reserve-team coach and began appointing his own people. Sackings had not happened since before Shankly's appointment. Dalglish was under pressure to achieve results while the backroom staff were being restructured. By the time he was to depart, Moran and Evans were not considered ready to make the step up. Before Souness, some traditions already belonged to the past.

On Dalglish's sudden resignation in January 1991, Souness did not think of leaving Rangers, where he was the second biggest shareholder and had been promised a job for life under new chair-man, David Murray. There had been three Scottish First Division titles and four League Cups. Only once had he come close to a move away. Had Michael Knighton completed his takeover of Manchester United in 1989, Souness would have replaced a then struggling Alex Ferguson.

Knighton had agreed to buy Martin Edwards' stake for £10 million and appeared on the pitch at Old Trafford before a game dressed in a full United kit to publicize his proposed purchase. At a meeting in Edinburgh, Knighton discussed the project until the early hours of one morning with Murray, who planned to make a considerable investment in United. It was agreed that Souness should be United's new manager and Walter Smith would earn promotion at Ibrox from his role as Souness's assistant. Knighton's acquisition, however, fell through when Murray had second thoughts. The FA were cracking down on individuals having influence in more than one club after the mess created by Robert Maxwell at Oxford United and Derby County. Chelsea owner Ken Bates had put money into Partick Thistle and, with investigations taking place, Murray was reluctant to get involved in a similar controversy. Knighton also approached Blackpool's Owen Oyston but never completed the deal. He was later involved with Carlisle United, but the club entered voluntary administration in 2002.

Souness received two phone calls from chief executive Peter Robinson asking whether he'd be interested in replacing Dalglish but had been informed by someone close to the board that Liverpool's priority was to appoint from within, as they had done before. Moran had acted as Dalglish's temporary replacement. First-team coach Evans was another contender, as were Phil Thompson and Steve Heighway, who led the reserve and the youth teams. Alan Hansen, captain since the 1985–86 season, had just retired as a player but he ruled himself out almost immediately. Then there was John Toshack, the former striker with the most experience of management, having recently left Real Madrid.

Souness's bond with Rangers had grown because of the relationship with his chairman. 'David gave me a free reign,' Souness explains. 'He was a friend and our understanding couldn't have been any better. We lived near each other and socialized most nights of the week. These were good times: success after success. We'd turned it round there and the team was ready to have a good go of it in Europe. There was no reason to leave.'

Yet living in the 'goldfish bowl of Glasgow' had its difficulties. Rangers were always under the spotlight and so was Souness. There were problems on a personal and professional level. Having separated from his first wife, he was regularly followed along the motorway from his Edinburgh home to Glasgow by tabloid reporters hunting for scandal. By 1991, Souness was in the middle of a long touchline ban, while an incident with a tea lady had nearly led to a fight with St Johnstone's chairman after a league match. It proved to be a tipping point.

After the first brief talks at the start of February, Souness called Robinson back towards the end of March to try to establish whether an offer was still in place. Under Moran, Liverpool's results had faltered and the recruitment process had stalled. Within twenty-four hours, Souness was meeting with Walter Smith and first-team coach Phil Boersma to tell them about his plans to quit Rangers. Souness wanted both Smith and Boersma to join him. Kirkby-born Boersma had scored thirty goals in one hundred and twenty Liverpool games before joining Souness at Middlesbrough in 1975. 'Phil was a lifelong Liverpool supporter and could not have been any more excited.' Smith, who would later manage Everton, decided against it and replaced Souness at Ibrox on Souness's advice, even though Murray wanted a higher profile name. 'Walter had been my right-hand man and someone I trusted implicitly.' Smith was concerned that he might not be welcomed by Moran or Roy Evans, as their roles were similar. 'I was disappointed, because it was my plan for everyone to work together,' Souness says. 'But even without Walter, I'd made my mind up to go.'

. Murray made a final attempt to keep Souness in Scotland by offering a blank contract where he could fill in the details himself. 'The decision had been made,' Souness continues. 'David warned me that going back to Liverpool would be a huge mistake. I have to admit it, he was right.'

Souness was warned about the problems at Anfield by Peter Robinson, who had been a key administrator at the club for almost thirty years and remained loyal despite several offers to join the Football Association. Robinson's influence was so considerable that when Bill Shankly was offered the manager's job at Sunderland following one of his many arguments with the Liverpool board in the early sixties, Shankly discussed the possibility of taking Robinson with him.

Souness had tried to sign Jan Mølby for Rangers and planned to build his new Liverpool team around the Danish midfielder and John Barnes. Robinson advised that Liverpool's team had faded and only Barnes was capable of remaining in the long term.

'Tom Saunders was also a respected figure at Liverpool and he told me as well that the challenge was greater than anyone on the outside recognized,' Souness says.

Robinson warned of Manchester United's business potential if they ever married a successful managerial selection policy with positive results on the pitch. Within a month of Souness's appointment, United lifted the European Cup-Winners' Cup with victory over Barcelona in Rotterdam. A year earlier, Alex Ferguson's side had won the FA Cup in a replay with Crystal Palace, who'd beaten Liverpool in the semi. A new challenge was coming.

Souness believed Liverpool had to react quickly. It was his immediate view that many of his squad had 'lost their passion for Liverpool', and it came as a shock.

Not for the first time in this interview, Souness speaks about his expectations of 'senior players' during his time as captain.

'Bob Paisley and Joe Fagan were the managers and Ronnie Moran was the disciplinarian. But the real lessons came from players like Steve Heighway, Phil Neal, Ray Clemence and Emlyn Hughes. The staff deserve all the credit for selecting the right type of person to join the squad but once they were in place Melwood governed itself. You'd have three or four leaders showing the way and the rest following, whether that's in the match or socially. By the time I went back as manager, that culture had gone.'

Souness speaks of individuals more concerned by the value of their next contract. He refuses to name names, as he's 'made up with many of them since', but this was a time where wages were accelerating. Ageing pros did not want to miss out on one final payday. Souness says his relationship with many of them was strained after Peter Robinson asked him whether he wanted to take charge of negotiating players' contracts. Perhaps Robinson felt uncomfortable in dealing with the skyrocketing sums. Liverpool had long been notoriously tight with wages and used the history and position of the club as leverage. Robinson would enter discussions with a lower offer than the player expected. Often it meant a pay cut. Robinson would exit the room and leave the player alone with his thoughts. Then the manager, be it Shankly, Paisley, Fagan or Dalglish, would enter separately, informing the player he would help him by getting Robinson to raise his offer. This process would get the player believing the manager was on his side, immediately setting the agenda for their relationship, and leave the club paying roughly what they wanted to pay in the first place. Suddenly, however, the trusted routine was broken.

'Initially, I thought it was Peter's way of paying me a compliment but it was my first big mistake, agreeing to it,' Souness says. 'I couldn't understand why anyone would grumble with being paid what I thought was a decent sum to play for Liverpool. Whatever I offered, they always wanted more. Liverpool was the only team I wanted to play for and I would have stayed forever had the club not accepted a really good offer from Sampdoria for me. There was no place I'd rather have been.'

You can detect the anger even now when Souness speaks about the shift in attitude and the haggling that took place.

'I should have kept them on and waited for their replacements to bed in. Instead, I couldn't help it. I'd tell Peter [Robinson] on the phone, "You know what? Whoever it is, get them to call me this afternoon. They can go tomorrow as far as I'm concerned." That was a mistake. You're buying under pressure then. I should have been far cuter.'

Peter Beardsley, aged thirty, Gary Gillespie, thirty-one and Steve McMahon, thirty, were the first of the most experienced players to leave, ones that with hindsight Souness wished he'd kept longer. Others, like Ray Houghton, remained. 'Ray told me his wife was homesick and wanted to return to London, so I accepted a bid from Chelsea. Ray was halfway down the M6 when he called to tell me Ron Atkinson had made him a better financial offer. "You know what, Ray, do whatever you bloody want," I told him.'

Souness was happy to release Jimmy Carter, Glen Hysen and David Speedie, who were 'not up to it', though he did not want to sell twenty-two-year-old Steve Staunton, the Irish left-back whose future was influenced by a 'silly rule' that classified non-English players as foreigners and decreed that only three could play at a time. 'Steve had a beautiful left foot and could play in a number of positions,' Souness says. 'The regulation was withdrawn by the FA within twelve months and that really frustrated me.'

What also made it hard for Souness was that he was telling players who had developed an emotional attachment to Kenny Dalglish and, indeed, to Liverpool in the aftermath of the Hillsborough disaster that suddenly they were not wanted.

But ever since Bill Shankly had struggled with the idea of dispensing with key members of his 1960s team, leading to nearly seven years without a trophy and a humbling 1–0 defeat to Second Division Watford in an FA Cup quarter-final in 1970, Liverpool had never allowed sentiment to get in the way of decisive decision making.

'When your time was up, it was up,' Souness says. 'I was a case in point. It was a transfer record between two English clubs when Liverpool bought me from Middlesbrough for £352,000. Then they sold me for £650,000 to Sampdoria. Although it also suited me to go, nobody sat me down and tried to persuade me to stay using football reasons never mind financial reasons. I was thirty-one years old. Liverpool figured they'd had seven years of great service out of me and they were more than doubling their money for a player who had peaked. It was ruthless business.'

After Hillsborough, the policy of moving players on before their decline became too evident understandably slipped and Liverpool's team became a victim of circumstance.

Yet I suggest to Souness that Liverpool's transfer policy had altered under Dalglish long before Hillsborough. After missing out on the title to Everton in 1987, and with Dalglish under some pressure, he decided to spend big. John Aldridge, aged twenty-eight, Beardsley, twenty-six, Houghton, twenty-five and Barnes, twenty-four, all arrived for huge fees. For the first time in its history, Liverpool were outspending their rivals in an attempt to keep ahead of the game and nobody seemed to mind. The First Division championship was wrestled back in 1988 and won again in 1990. Yet behind the scenes, young players were either not good enough or had not been given the necessary exposure that would eventually enable them to secure long-term first-team football.

In Dalglish's five and a half years in charge, he signed seven players under the age of twenty that would play for the first team, promoting only Gary Ablett from the youth system. Of the seven, four left impressions that ranged from reasonable to good: Mike Marsh, Don Hutchison, Jamie Redknapp and Staunton. It meant that by the time Souness returned to Merseyside, Liverpool's squad was made up of old players almost past their best and youngsters not ready to represent Liverpool on a regular basis. Souness was the first manager since Shankly unable to make signings and give them time to get used to the demands of the club by playing them in the reserves first.

'Only Kenny will be able to tell you why he made certain decisions at certain times,' Souness says. 'All I know is, when I arrived the team wasn't good enough and neither was the squad. There was a need for urgent reconstruction. The ability wasn't there and the attitude was bad. I oversaw three or four testimonial matches in my first two years and that shows you how old the players were and where their priorities lay. In my six years as a player, only Emlyn Hughes was granted a testimonial. [It was actually four: Steve Heighway, Phil Thompson and Ray Clemence were also granted testimonials.] This was a period where the hunger was always there even though we won the league most seasons. Ronnie Moran was always telling us we weren't as good as the old teams under Bill Shankly. That motivated us to prove him wrong. I wanted my Liverpool team to be like this.'

Souness recalls the afternoon Liverpool hosted Joe Kinnear's notorious Wimbledon side and Vinnie Jones scrawled 'Bothered' across the famous 'This Is Anfield' sign that hangs over players as they enter the pitch. The reaction inside Liverpool's dressing room was to laugh it off rather than seek retribution, as they probably would have done a decade earlier. It summed up the attitude.

'We were too soft,' Souness says. 'Where were the leaders fighting our corner? In the eighties, we could beat a team by playing football. If the other team wanted a fight, we could beat them by fighting. We could deal with any situation. Things had changed.'

Souness believed he would be the manager that would take Liverpool into the twenty-first century. He wanted to make his own mark on the club by transforming the way the football staff operated.

'I'd been in Italy and I'd seen how all the big clubs were run there. Since the days of Bill Shankly, Liverpool's players had always changed at Anfield and got the bus up to Melwood. I recognized it was part of the routine – the banter in the dressing room and on the bus – but I wanted one base at Melwood, mainly because it would shave an hour off the working day and allow us to focus on other things rather than dodging the traffic in West Derby. Anfield was becoming a tourist attraction for out-of-town and foreign supporters and I felt it would be better for the club if they opened up the stadium. They could make more money and also guarantee the safety of supporters milling about in the car park by not having buses going in and out. Anfield would have been used by the players on a match day only. Yet there was great resistance.

'We used to put lager on the bus on a Friday for an away game. It was a particularly strong lager. I was happy for the players to have a drink but I thought it was better if they had a lighter lager. There was also resistance to that. I wanted to change their eating habits. There was great resistance there as well.

'I'd done all this at Glasgow Rangers and because they hadn't won anything in nine years everybody was buying into it. When you go to a club where there has been non-stop success and go to the players, "By the way, you shouldn't really be eating fish and chips straight after a game," it wasn't easy to convince them.

'It was never going to be an easy transition. It is natural for people to resist change, especially when a method is in place that is tried and trusted. It's a hard argument. But had the players listened, Liverpool would have been the first club in England to implement it. We'd have been ahead of the game. [Arsène] Wenger came into Arsenal in 1996 when Arsenal hadn't won a league title in five years and he was able to do it. But, hey, did I try to change things too quickly? Yes.'

Contrary to popular belief, Souness says he did not order the Boot Room to be destroyed.

'That's a rumour still doing the rounds today but it's absolute rubbish,' Souness insists. 'It was the club's decision to demolish it. They wanted to expand the press room. The Premier League said the old one was too small, so a decision was made above my head.'

Souness cannot deny he made errors in the transfer market, especially with those he bought. He remains convinced some would have been considered good signings had they been integrated into the team when it was winning rather than struggling for form.

'I would say Michael Thomas, Mark Wright, Rob Jones and David James all gave the club good service. You know, I liked committed players. Neil Ruddock, if managed properly, I thought, was a real asset because there were few left-footed centre-backs as powerful as him. He was a better footballer than people remember but he struggled with his weight. I liked Julian Dicks too. He was aggressive and rugged but wanted to play and had a will to win. I think I made a big mistake in selling Dean Saunders. I should have stuck with him. His goalscoring record was decent. He scored more than twenty in his first season. But I listened too much to players who told me they didn't like playing with him. I foolishly agreed when I should have stuck to my principles and told them to get on with it.'

When Souness is criticized, the signings of Paul Stewart and Nigel Clough are usually mentioned.

'Both of them came in for big fees, so I can understand it. Paul came in because I wanted us to have a bit more physicality in midfield. It was a department where we were lacking. I'd seen him play as a striker for Manchester City when I was manager of Rangers but he was better at Spurs in the middle of the park. He was man of the match in the 1991 FA Cup final against Forest and was desperate to do well at Liverpool but it never worked out.

'Nigel was very quiet but I thought he'd be able to supply the passes for Rushie. But it didn't work out between them.'

There was also Danish defender Torben Piechnik and Hungarian midfielder István Kozma, two individuals clearly out of their depth.

'They were relatively cheap signings and both were intended

to be squad players. Because of injuries, they had to play more often than I would have liked. Some of these you get right, others you get wrong. Both were low risk. But when the team is losing, players like this get highlighted a lot more.'

Souness had the opportunity to sign other players that could have made a difference. The first was Peter Schmeichel, who as Manchester United's goalkeeper would win fifteen trophies.

'I hadn't been at Liverpool long. Ron Yeats was the chief scout and he came into my office one day and showed me a letter. It read: *I am a Danish goalkeeper who has been a Liverpool supporter all my life. I am willing to pay for my own travel expenses. Can I come to Melwood for a week's trial?* I was trying to edge Bruce [Grobbelaar] out. But it was proving difficult. I thought that if another goalkeeper turned up, we were going to have more problems with Bruce. So it never happened.'

The next was a striker later voted as the greatest player in United's history.

'We played Auxerre in the UEFA Cup. We lost 2–0 in the first leg in France, then won 3–0 at Anfield. Jan Mølby scored a penalty after about two minutes and that set us on our way. After the game, Michel Platini knocks on my office door and comes in. He said that he had a player for me. "A proper player." He told me that he was a problem in France but would be perfect for Liverpool. The player was Eric Cantona. I said, "Listen, I'm fighting lots of fires here at the moment; I don't need any more trouble." It was another situation where I should have been more open-minded.'

A deal for Alan Shearer was closer.

'I had a conversation with him on the phone while I was sat outside McDonald's near Stockport railway station. I was really confident of getting him and I told my wife-to-be, Karen, that I really believed we'd push the deal through. Whether it might have been a woman's intuition I'm not sure, but she told me that he'd go somewhere else. And she was right. When I later became Blackburn's manager, I spoke to Tony Parkes, who'd worked for the club over a number of years. Tony told me that all the people at Blackburn recognized whoever got Shearer would end up winning the league. They were right too. I later managed Alan at Newcastle and I have to say he was the best English centre-forward in post-war history.'

Souness is more frustrated that he did not get to see young players like Robbie Fowler, Steve McManaman and Jamie Redknapp flourish in the mid nineties. His problems at work, though, were nothing compared with his problems at home. Souness faced not only a bitter divorce, the death of his father due to natural causes as well as the death of his two German Shepherd dogs who were shot by a farmer herding sheep on a field near his former home in Knutsford, but also the sudden news that he required urgent open-heart surgery, although he swears his health had nothing to do with the pressures of football. 'I had two uncles that died of heart attacks in their thirties. I've got the dodgy gene.'

A triple-heart bypass operation for a then thirty-eight-year-old man would scare most people but he insists he took it all in his stride. 'I was determined to be the hospital's best-ever patient and get back into football as soon as possible, so I pushed myself.' Souness was due to be released but collapsed, resulting in a second operation, and spent twenty-eight days in bed rather than ten.

The ordeal of coping with so much should have worked for him like it did for Gérard Houllier years later but instead it only served to further alienate him from the fans at a time when league results were not in keeping with expectations. He does not blame the stress of the time for the gross misjudgement that followed.

Souness shared a professional working relationship with the *Sun*'s Merseyside reporter, Mike Ellis, a journalist who eventually wrote his second autobiography in 1999. That Ellis was on holiday during the week beginning Monday, 13 April 1992, Souness says, was significant.

He'd agreed to sell the story of his hospital ordeal to Ellis. After his operation, the interview appeared in *The Sun* on 'the 6, 7 or 8 April'. Initially, there was no angry reaction, with Souness claiming Ian Rush and Tommy Smith, both Liverpool legends, had had public dealings with the newspaper before him and post-Hillsborough without a public fallout. Souness was approached again on 13 April by a photographer from *The Sun*, asking if he could take a picture for the following day's edition, a picture that would reflect his road to recovery. Liverpool were playing Portsmouth that evening in an FA Cup semi-final replay at Villa Park. With Ronnie Moran and Roy Evans in charge while he was in hospital, Souness told the photographer that he could take a picture providing Liverpool progressed, as it would be bad if he was seen smiling in his hospital bed the morning after a defeat. Eventually, Liverpool did win but only on penalties. Because the photograph was taken so late – beyond the 11 p.m. copy deadline – editors decided to use the picture a day later instead and included a short caption. Rather than appearing on 14 April, Souness's photograph was printed in *The Sun* on 15 April 1992 – the third anniversary of the Hillsborough disaster.

'Mike would have advised the paper not to print it on that day, there's no question about it,' Souness says. 'Instead, it looked terrible: me smiling and confident of recovery on the same day a lot of people were still in mourning.'

As he was in Scotland at the time of the disaster, Souness maintains he did not appreciate the depth of bad feeling towards the newspaper.

'I have nobody to blame but myself, though,' he adds. 'I gave all the proceeds from the interview to Alder Hey Children's Hospital. I knew I'd got it wrong. Ignorance is no excuse.'

The episode made Souness's position at Liverpool 'impossible'. Merseyside reporters, who had always worked as a pack, were annoyed that they had been left out of an exclusive story and were unsympathetic towards Souness in their column inches when the public tide turned against him. Souness sat on the bench during Liverpool's FA Cup final victory over Sunderland and looked ill.

'What I should have done is resigned after the FA Cup final both because of the mistake I'd made and because of my health. Looking at pictures of myself, I shouldn't have been there, because I was still fragile.'

Somehow, Souness continued for another eighteen months. He even survived a period where Liverpool slumped to seventeenth in the Premier League table as late as March – just three points above the relegation zone. Though the team finished the 1992–93 season in sixth, in a congested table, it was a mere ten points above the bottom three.

'I lost the dressing room and that hurt me, because it started with some of the players I'd worked with and looked after as young boys,' he says. 'I was disappointed in a lot of people but I was far from blameless. I went into Liverpool probably believing I knew everything there was to know about management because I'd been successful elsewhere. The setback at Spurs served me well for the rest of my playing career but that was twenty years earlier and as a manager it felt like I could win everything in a rush. I'm not blaming anybody but myself, because if I did it again now, I'd do a lot differently. I would hate to think this is coming across as me not holding my hands up.'

To hear this admission from someone who appeared outwardly indestructible as Liverpool's captain is quite humbling. Souness is seen as a cold and uncaring type of person but he clearly regrets the errors made in his life and the opportunities missed.

Souness realized his time was up at Anfield before Liverpool's FA Cup replay with Bristol City in January 1994. While he was eating his pre-match snack of toast and tea at the Moat House Hotel, Souness could hear the visiting manager holding a team meeting in the next room.

'Russell Osman had seen enough of us in the first game at Ashton Gate to tell his players that if they matched us for effort we'd bottle it in front of our own supporters. I knew he was right. This was coming from Bristol City in the old Second Division.'

After a 1–0 defeat, Souness tendered his resignation in person to chairman David Moores as well as Peter Robinson and, with that, he was gone.

'The bottom line was I didn't feel I was getting the full support of the players,' he says. 'After the *Sun* thing, the supporters inside Anfield could have turned on me in a big way. I was aware attendances went down but verbally they were always very encouraging to the team.'

Souness continued his management career and there were some achievements. After winning the Turkish Cup at Galatasaray, he planted the flag of his club's colours in the centre of the pitch at city rivals Fenerbahçe.

'One of their board members had called me a cripple earlier in the season, so I thought it was the right thing to do,' he reasons. 'I loved it in Turkey and would have stayed much longer had the president that appointed me been elected again.'

Abroad, he also managed Torino and Benfica, and at home, Blackburn Rovers (where he was happiest) and Newcastle United. Yet the drive to improve himself and get results meant he could rarely enjoy the moment.

'There have been far better players than me that have won nothing,' he concludes. 'I won a hell of a lot. I've had the most fantastic career in football when you consider where I started off to where I ended up. I have twenty-six medals to my name. I'm deemed as a failure as a manager of Liverpool. But I won eleven trophies in three countries after moving on. There are far better managers than me who haven't won anything. So I'm proud of what I've achieved.'

CHAPTER ELEVEN

cultzeros.co.uk

EVERYMAN,
Roy Evans, 1963–98

ROY EVANS' PUPILS NARROW SOMEWHAT, ALTHOUGH NOT IN A hostile way. There is a sense of acceptance. He appreciates the subject matter is near, the one he has discussed during every interview since leaving Liverpool in 1998 following thirty-five years' service to a club where he filled nearly every staff role.

I have been leading to this point. We have spoken about his childhood, his brief playing career, becoming a successful reserve-team manager, first-team coach-cum-physiotherapist, then Graeme Souness's assistant. And now here we are, arriving at the inevitable, discussing a term that ended up defining his entire managerial career, possibly his life – the Spice Boys.

'I knew we'd get there eventually,' he shrugs, taking a quick sip of his coffee before answering the question I'd just posed to him: did you feel let down by the players in any way?

'Listen,' he begins matter-of-factly, sinking into the couch behind him. 'You can call them Spice Boys or whatever you want, but when they played football matches, they wanted to win.' A pause. More coffee. 'The attitude was always good when it came to the game. They had a great ability. Did we fulfil our promise? Probably not. On our day we were as good as anybody but our day didn't come quite often enough. We got caught out too many times believing we could attack any team and outscore them. It was my choice to go that way. Attacking was our strength. Just look at the players we had. But you could also say it was our downfall. The outside stuff – when players went home – it was irrelevant.'

There is a curious mix of positivity and stoicism in Evans' tone. He is clearly proud of managing Liverpool. Yet there is pain. Surely it annoys him, being asked repeatedly about those white suits worn at the 1996 FA Cup final before losing to Manchester United, with people believing it was symptomatic of the fact he was too nice to impose the discipline supposedly required to achieve success?

'I don't see what the problem is with being a nice guy,' he responds swiftly. 'I hope I am a nice guy. Other Liverpool managers before me were nice guys too. We tried to do things in the right way.'

Evans insists that there were situations when he couldn't be, as he puts it, 'Mr Friendly'.

'Like when you're standing there in front of twenty lads doing a team talk and someone starts giggling at the back, you have to be on it. When Don Hutchison started sniggering about something I'd said in front of the group, I ripped straight into him and the room fell quiet pretty quickly.

'You don't have to like all of your players as people. You don't even have to like all the staff you work with. But you have to make sure you have a relationship that works for the benefit of the group and the club. I was never one to stay angry. I brushed things off. I got on with things as normal after telling someone off. If there was a confrontation, I'd get over it quickly. Maybe some people saw that as me not being tough enough. Any manager will tell you, though, you can't afford to hold grudges.'

He did not set out to be Liverpool's manager anyway. Evans was no careerist.

'I never wanted to be a coach, you really must understand that,' he explains. 'I'd played a few games for Liverpool's first team. I was twenty-six. Bill Shankly had just retired and Bob Paisley and Joe Fagan approached me, asking whether I wanted to join the staff. "No way," I told them. I felt like I had plenty of games left. It became a bit of a myth that I had problems with injuries. I just wasn't playing much because there were better options than me. In the end, Bob and Joe nagged for a while. They wanted me to take charge of the reserve team. "Why not take the chance?" they kept asking. Tommy Smith was my best mate and best man at my wedding. He thought it was a good idea. So, after a lot of persuasion, I took it.

'Individual ambition amongst the coaching staff wasn't particularly encouraged at Liverpool. There wasn't any clear policy but you had a job and you did it. You didn't look for the next guy's job. If it came along, great. As time went on, I progressed. I became first-team coach, running on to the pitch with the sponge. Then I became assistant under Graeme [Souness]. When Graeme left, I was offered the [manager's] job by the chairman at his house and I'd accepted it within an hour. It was all done in a day. I didn't ask him how much the contract was worth or anything like that. Until that point, I'd never really considered it – being a manager. But I realized that I had a lot of experience, having worked under some great people. I figured it was my turn.'

Anfield had been his place of work for his entire professional life. He knew of little else. Between 1994 and 1998, he was the gatekeeper to all Liverpool's hopes and dreams. Yet he is the man on the street with the ordinary-sounding name: Roy Evans. His marriage to Mary is halfway through its fifth decade. He left school without many qualifications. He says he doesn't read books. He wears a tank-top and when he meets me he is rattling a set of keys like an off-duty caretaker. He is short and has cropped silver hair. He speaks in old-school Scouse: fast, hushed and often from the side of his mouth. You have to listen closely. You could imagine him being the voice of reason in a lively football debate amongst punters at a darkened Dock Road tavern.

Evans was originally appointed after Souness's departure because Liverpool wanted to return to tradition. Evans considered himself as the 'spokesman' for Liverpool. Yet he was the one with everything to lose.

When Evans took charge, only four years had passed since Liverpool's last title. During his era, Liverpool were expected to be champions. They never were. Whenever Liverpool lost, the radio football phone-ins were clogged with listeners wanting to be listened to, talking about Evans' position. Even when Liverpool drew or conceded a soft goal, there was a jam, the same people taking part, the same topics being discussed.

'Of course I'd hear them,' Evans says. 'It's very nice to get patted on the back. But most of the time as manager you're taking stick. The good times don't last very long. I'm always saying to people, "Hey, you might have an opinion but yours will never get put to the test." My opinion was being tested week-in, week-out; day-in, day-out.

'I'd supported Liverpool since the 1950s. I can remember when we were in the Second Division and struggling to get out of it. By the 1990s, there was a generation of supporters who'd been brought up on nothing but success. They wanted more of a say about what was going on. It might have been better if some of them had gone through a period of lean years. Then they'd understand what football is all about.'

Evans felt 'an unbelievable pressure' of expectancy. Before him, Souness underwent a triple heart bypass. Bill Shankly died a sad and lonely man. Bob Paisley and Joe Fagan were unable to communicate to a wider audience and their successes made them even more nervous as speakers in the public arena. Kenny Dalglish admits he lost the ability to make decisions, later referencing in the first of several autobiographies a Shankly quote about a 'lifetime of dedication' that 'follows you home, follows you everywhere, and eats into your family life'. Evans had been there for all of this. He was aware that being in charge of Liverpool came at a price.

'I'm not sure that being a fan of the team you manage is necessarily a good thing,' he continues. 'The doubts start the first time you get beaten. Only then do you realize what it means to so many people. You take the job, you say to yourself, "This is great – I'm managing Liverpool, the club I love, I know what this is about." But your heart rules your head. When you're winning, life is rosy. When you lose, you realize how it can spoil a person's day or week. It's your feelings multiplied by forty-five thousand people at Anfield and those watching it on TV or listening on the radio. Liverpool is a club where you've got people waiting outside the training ground every single day. It's not just kids, either. Fellas are there; they're twenty, twenty-five, thirty-five or forty years old. These people, they're dependent on the result. It breaks their hearts when that doesn't happen.

'That's the difficult part. It hit me hard. You obviously need to have some sort of social life yourself. If you haven't seen the wife all week, which was regularly the case, you'd go out for a meal on a Saturday night. It wasn't nice if we'd lost. You felt like you'd let people down, there was a horrible feeling deep in your stomach. You didn't want to be there. There was a level of embarrassment to it. Whenever you were beaten, it felt like there were no positives. I'm certain it hurts even more when you support the team you're managing. It hits you two ways. Like any person, you take a pride in your job but it also hits you as a fan. It's a double whammy. The key is not to show any of this to the players.'

It took him weeks to even think about watching a replay of the 1996 cup final. 'Would you want to watch that first half again? Fuckin' hell . . .' he pauses again. 'But look, I came through the system, I'm probably the luckiest Liverpudlian ever, to be able to be there as a kid, a player, do every job and end up as the manager. I don't think there will be another person who does that.'

Evans was born on 4 October 1948 and grew up three miles

north of Anfield in Bootle, an area that had suffered serious bombing during the Second World War due to its close proximity to Canada Dock and Gladstone Dock, a pair of significantly sized maritime landmarks that provided cargo links with North America and West Africa. Although Bootle is now virtually politically impregnable as one of the safest Labour seats in the country, at the start of the twentieth century it had been a Conservative haven – a reasonably prosperous suburb of boulevards and towering Victorian houses owned by rich merchants who once elected Andrew Bonar Law as their MP, a future Tory Prime Minister. After 1945, with the borough in need of rebuilding, those with money moved up the Mersey coastline to neighbouring Crosby or further to Blundellsands, Formby and then Ainsdale, Birkdale or Southport. Bootle took on a new identity. On the flattened land, new cheaper homes were built.

Out towards Netherton, an inland tangle of featureless council estates, the Evans family lived on Masefield Crescent before moving to a terraced house close to the large Mons Public House in the mid fifties. The Evanses were workers, his mother for English Electric and his father, Bill, on the production line at the nearby Dunlop rubber factory on Rice Lane in Walton. Bill's income was supplemented through football. After playing for Liverpool's youth team before the war, he signed for Cardiff City. It led to a decade playing semi-professionally for a series of clubs in the Welsh Football League.

'Every Saturday, he'd be driving a few hours for a decent wage, £8 a week or £10 a week,' Roy says. 'It was a decent standard; there were no mugs. The teams were full of Liverpudlians with the same idea. Even when he stopped earning, he continued playing in the Business Houses League across Merseyside. It meant my mum saw more of my games than my dad did, because he'd be out earning money.'

On Sunday mornings, Evans remembers seeing matches at a public playing field over the road from his house. 'Sport was on my doorstep. You could see all the men getting angry. You'd have fisticuffs. But at the end of the game, they'd shake hands.'

His football education was furthered by watching Liverpool and Everton play home matches on alternate weekends. At Anfield, he stood in the boys' pen. This was an area of the Kop reserved for pimply faced urchins, where other 'extras from *Oliver Twist*', as an observer from the time once described them, would shriek swear words all afternoon. Evans recalls the sense of achievement when he invaded the pitch to celebrate Liverpool's promotion from the old Second Division in 1962 as a thirteen year old.

By then, he'd already become the best player successively at St Robert Bellarmine primary school and then St George of England secondary school. 'I always seemed to be two years younger than the lads I was playing with and against.' Progress was marked by selection for Bootle Schoolboys, Lancashire Schoolboys and then England Schoolboys. Offers came to join Chelsea and Wolverhampton Wanderers. Yet it was Everton who were most determined. 'The scout was on my doorstep every Sunday morning.'

Evans waited. Finally, Liverpool approached. Not for the last time, he went with his heart, even though it meant giving up cricket, a sport in which he again excelled, representing Lancashire. 'I went to Shanks and asked if I could go on tour with them. It was just a simple "No. It's football or nothing."'

On Monday, 16 March 1970, Evans made his first-team debut in Liverpool's 3–0 victory over Sheffield Wednesday at Anfield. A stand-in for Ian Ross at left-back, he kept his place when Ipswich Town were beaten the following weekend. But after a 1–0 defeat at West Ham United, that place was lost.

Evans says he was plagued by a feeling that he was not quick enough for First Division football. 'It had never been a problem when I was younger but suddenly I felt a couple of steps behind everyone else. In my mind, I knew what I wanted to do but my body wouldn't really let me do it.'

Between August of the same year and December 1973, Evans played just four games before another chance came against Manchester United. Wearing the number 3 shirt, he kept George Best quiet during a 2–0 win. 'At the final whistle, Besty came

over and thanked me for not kicking him off the park.' Four
days later, Evans played his last match, a 2–1 loss at Burnley.
Alec Lindsay, virtually ever-present previously, returned to the
side and six months later Evans was offered the post of reserve-
team trainer. He says those in the Boot Room had spotted his
ability to 'follow instructions and pass information on with a bit
of enthusiasm'.

Evans was hired by a group of five men with a combined age
of 259. Bob Paisley, Liverpool's new manager, was fifty-five;
his assistant Joe Fagan and head of youth development Tom
Saunders were both fifty-three. First-team trainer Reuben Bennett
was nearly fifty-nine – the same age as Bill Shankly when he
retired a few months earlier – while Ronnie Moran, promoted
from reserve- to first-team duties, was the youngest at forty but
had nearly a decade of coaching experience behind him already.
Evans was just twenty-six.

These were people who since 1959, when Evans was eleven
years old, had helped take Liverpool from eighth position in the
old Second Division to the cusp of European greatness, men old
enough to claim a pension, avuncular types with so many creases
on their foreheads it seemed as though their knitted hats had been
tacked on. In normal circumstances, they would be travelling
around Liverpool on reduced-rate bus passes, yet here they were
at Melwood wearing Gola tracksuits, heavy black jumpers and
muddied football boots, showing professional footballers half
their age how it was done in five-a-side matches.

The Boot Room was a shabby space, twelve feet by twelve
feet, that reeked of dubbin, liniment and sweaty boots. There
were no windows. Almost-empty bottles of Glenfiddich stood on
a few wall ledges and the floor space was taken up by crates
of Guinness Export and cases of Harp lager that doubled up as
chairs to complement the two real ones by the old wooden door.
It was staff-only. Every day of the week, Paisley, Fagan, Moran,
Bennett and Saunders would gather to discuss what had gone
well in training and what had not. Any player found lurking
outside suffered the wrath of Moran. After matches, the doors

were opened and stars like musician Rod Stewart, opposition coaches and managers were invited in. Although the premise was for 'a cup of tea or a beer', as Moran puts it, in the true spirit of Liverpool, kidology conversations were geared towards gathering information that might lead to another Liverpool victory some time in the future. Evans calls it 'interrogation by feather duster'.

Bill Shankly, who had his own office and other duties to attend to, rarely ventured into the Boot Room, only occasionally showing his face. In his absence, the other staff members would even gather for a debrief on a Sunday morning from ten o'clock until twelve, after those of a religious persuasion had been to Mass. Boots were washed and hung back on pegs – first team first and reserve team second. Kits were absent, however, having been transported home in wicker baskets after the match. The staff did not trust external laundrymen after several kits had been shrunk or gone missing. The responsibility was now shared between Evans and Moran, who passed the duty of washing shirts and shorts on alternate weekends to their wives, Mary and Joyce.

'Imagine being so young and being welcomed into a place that at the time was *the* place to be. It was like being invited on tour with the Beatles. But what made the Boot Room wasn't the room itself; it was the people inside it – the clever minds. In reality, it was a pokey little space underneath the Main Stand, filled with cases of beer, bottles of whisky and boots.

'My biggest input initially was a *Playboy* calendar on the wall,' Evans laughs lightly. 'People would send them through the post to us. If Liverpool ever lost, which wasn't very often, Bob would look at the calendar, point at the pair of tits and go, "Those two up there could have done better today." Then, despite the defeat, we'd chuckle along with him.'

Although he took no notice of the comment at the time, Evans was earmarked more or less immediately as a future Liverpool manager by chairman John Smith. 'We have not made an appointment for today but for the future,' he said. The grooming process was under way.

'Reserve-team matches were played on the same day as first-team matches. When the opportunities were there, like a European game, they'd tell me to come along. The message was always the same. I can hear Bob telling me now, "If you've got something to say, say it." For my first year, I thought, "Hang on a minute, I'm twenty-six, I was a bit-part player at best not so long ago; what can I offer?" So I asked them why. I went to Joe. "It's nice you're giving me the right to speak and have an opinion, but . . ." Joe stopped me. "You might just see one thing we don't, a little gem one day that we've all missed. If you think we're wrong, tell us. And if we think you're wrong, we'll tell you. But never take offence if that happens. It's only opinion."

'With the reserves, I could do it my way. Bob, Joe and Ronnie would come to our games when they could and sit on the bench. They wouldn't interfere. I was the one making the decisions, telling players off when it was necessary. It gave me tremendous confidence.'

Evans was his own man. 'The trick was to put your personality into it. I was never going to be a Ronnie Moran, someone whose work can't be underestimated. He made sure everyone fell in line and gets called the sergeant-major, but he was much more than that. Joe was the glue. Bob wasn't great at speaking in front of a crowd but everyone on the staff knew what he meant. Then I was the fella that put the arm around a few, hence the reputation as Mr Nice Guy. There was a great balance, all good people, nobody went after anyone else.

'I remember going to Man City once and we won convincingly. Joe was manager. Afterwards, we went into their Boot Room for a drink and one of their coaches comes in going, "Our manager picked the wrong team today." Joe looks at him and responds, "What are you telling us for? If you think that, go and tell the manager to his face, not us." That kind of thing never happened at Liverpool.

'When I was in charge [as manager], I'd discuss the team with the staff a few days before. "This is what I'm thinking of." Then we'd go round the table, each person offering their own ideas.

But once I'd made the decision, I'd insist they backed me. You should never, as staff, go behind the manager's back and try to be clever after the event. When you're part of a coaching team, you back the fella in charge.'

Paisley won more trophies as Liverpool manager than Shankly. Yet without Shankly, Evans believes Liverpool would never have moved forward, offering Paisley the opportunities he exploited. Although Shankly was asked by Paisley not to turn up at Melwood following his retirement, with Paisley feeling undermined by players still referring to Shankly as 'Boss', Shankly's influence at the club remained.

'Really, the Liverpool way is Shanks's way,' Evans says. 'The man came and changed the whole outlook of the club. It was all about good players doing the simple things well. He wasn't the greatest coach in the world. Joe, Bob and Ronnie took most of the training. Shanks would throw a little bit in. But he was the best manager, the best motivator. You certainly can't coach a team to win. There is no manual that says: "This is how you win football matches." There are training techniques and tactics that can help you win. But the art of winning is something you can't teach.

'Shanks was great at making people feel good and brilliant at making people feel awful as well. With one word, he could make you feel ten foot tall or bury you deep into the ground. He was like an actor doing a job. I thought of him like I thought of John Wayne. Other days, he'd be like a mafia mob boss. He made it fun; he made it all about the ball. He also trusted players to make big decisions on the pitch. Above all, it was geared towards getting the result at the end of the week.'

Although Shankly was gone, his ideas helped Evans establish himself as reserve-team manager. For example, on Monday afternoons Shankly had instituted the tradition of six-a-side games, with the sides made up of two first-team players, two from the reserves and two juniors.

'You'd get a sixteen year old playing up front with Roger Hunt. Other weeks, it'd be Cally [Ian Callaghan] or Gerry Byrne. The interaction was great. If one of the senior players thought a youngster had a chance, they'd take them under their wing and push them forward to the management.

'Being so young, sometimes I had to deal with players that were older than me, players that had been better at football. But the culture of the club was well established: if you didn't play for the first team, you played for the reserves. It was the accepted norm. We also had a very strong team. We played winning football and aimed to win the reserve league every year. The more experienced lads knew, coming with us, they weren't playing with a bunch of nuggets, because they'd already trained with us too. We really wanted it.

'Shanks had instilled the idea that the second-best team in Liverpool was the Liverpool reserves and not Everton. It resulted in reserve matches being seen as important. If a player wasn't in the first team, his only way back was by playing well for the reserves. I think every player treated the reserve matches seriously. At the end of the day, they were pulling on the red shirt of Liverpool. It mattered.'

Evans admits that he did not have the 'charisma' of Shankly, the 'ruthlessness' of Paisley nor necessarily the tactical mind of Fagan. He believes his main strength was common sense.

'I understood what a lot of the boys were going through, because a few years earlier I had been in the same position. Some of them needed delicate handling, so there were times when you'd put your arm round their shoulder and then other times when you needed to give them a bollocking.'

After the turbulent Souness regime, Liverpool needed a steady hand at the helm. The summer before his appointment as manager, Evans became assistant. The board were preparing for Souness's departure. Having tampered with the hereditary line, Evans was a return to what the board once knew. It was never admitted publicly but, within, there was a hope that Evans could create a new Boot Room.

Souness's era had left Evans without any natural successors. With Moran becoming assistant, he approached Tottenham Hotspur's Doug Livermore, an old teammate from the reserve days, and made him first-team coach. Livermore had left Anfield to coach Norwich, Spurs and the Welsh national team. Sammy Lee, another home-grown and hard-working disciple of the Liverpool way, was charged with managing the second string.

Evans also realized that there was a need for specialists. In the past, even the great goalkeepers like Ray Clemence did not have a coach directing them. Clemence always trained with the outfielders, improving his reading of the game so that he was able to sweep up behind the defence. For a short period at the start of the 1970s, Shankly allowed Tony Waiters, who had appeared as goalkeeper for Blackpool on more than three hundred occasions, to work with Clemence and the defence. Yet Waiters – a clipboard-and-whistle type of a coach – clashed with the other staff and within a few months he'd left for Burnley. When Clemence later admitted to Shankly that he was a nervous goal-kicker, Shankly's response was to remove the flags at the top of the Kemlyn Road Stand. If there was no sign of wind, there was less to worry about.

Evans realized such a basic approach amounted to neglect of a crucial position. 'Graeme toyed with the idea of getting someone in but Bruce [Grobbelaar] had been our first-choice goalkeeper for so long and he actually preferred training as an outfielder,' Evans says. With Grobbelaar on his way out of Liverpool and his successor David James needing guidance, Joe Corrigan, who'd played more than six hundred times as Manchester City's number 1, was named goalkeeping coach.

The next move was to appoint a full-time physiotherapist. With Mark Leather's arrival, there was an end to the running-repair jobs carried out by a succession of unqualified coaches mid game. Regularly injured players had long been treated with suspicion at Liverpool. Shankly maintained his side were the fittest in the league, with pre-season geared towards building stamina and therefore preventing muscle tears. It was a difficult theory to argue against. Liverpool won the 1965–66 title using just fourteen players all season. Anyone who suffered an injury was almost bullied into feeling better. 'Otherwise you really were *persona non grata*,' Alan Hansen said. Leather's recruitment meant that Moran could focus on drilling the first team in the Liverpool way rather than writing what Evans describes as 'little scribbles' on an old ledger, charting training patterns.

Evans recognized that the squad was not up to previous standards. He admits advising Souness against making certain signings. But he also reaffirms, 'Once the manager has made his decision you have to back him.'

Evans believes Liverpool's deterioration began before Souness's arrival. 'It wasn't the best team around in 1991,' he says, explaining that it was understandable if Dalglish had lost his focus after the Hillsborough disaster. 'Football did not seem to matter any more.'

Evans regrets waiting six months before starting his own rebuilding process. 'There had been so many changes under Graeme, I wanted things to settle down and give everyone a chance to prove themselves. Maybe that was the wrong thing to do, maybe it was a bit of naivety. If I had my time again, I probably would have got rid of people sooner, bringing others in; enabling us to hit the ground running the next season. In my mind, I knew what needed to happen.'

With Evans as coach of the reserves, Liverpool had won five successive Central League titles and numerous regional cups. It was no coincidence that when Evans succeeded Souness as manager in 1994, having achieved excellent results with young players, the average age of Liverpool's first team dropped by three and a half years.

Although given a debut by Souness, Robbie Fowler flourished, scoring nearly one hundred and twenty goals in four seasons. Evans had first seen the forward as an eleven year old putting a hat-trick past his own son, Stephen, who was goalkeeper, during a schoolboys' game in Burscough. 'Afterwards, I checked that Liverpool had already signed him and fortunately we had,' Evans remembers, adding that he felt lucky to be walking into a job that would involve working with some of the most exciting players in the country.

'They were all different: different lads with distinct personalities. Robbie was a natural finisher. Maybe he didn't have great pace but upstairs he had it going on. Then Michael [Owen] came into the situation. Nobody could deal with his speed. It was unreal. He gets a lot of criticism now, Michael – a bit like Steve McManaman and Jamie Redknapp, who was on the same level as anyone else in the Premier League in terms of passing ability. But these players gave the club nearly a decade of service. Joining Man United wasn't the best thing to do but please don't forget how brilliant Michael was.'

Evans would have preferred to use experienced players. 'But when the young boys are better already, you can't ignore them. Really, you want the senior lads to be forcing the issue – like when I was reserve-team manager, giving Bob no excuse to change the side.

'Robbie was regularly in the starting eleven at eighteen. A bit later, you had Michael [Owen] starting games at sixteen. I know Michael has since said that it would have been better for his career if he was in and out a bit more. But Michael, for instance, would never stop asking to play. He was desperate. And with good reason. You try to balance it the best you can. Whenever I left Robbie or Michael out, they went crazy. They'd be knocking on my door and stopping me before training. That's what made them top players. They were as keen as mustard. They wanted to play every game. I want players like that – not ones that didn't seem bothered. There were a few of them about.'

Evans does not name names. But it is clear who he is referring to. Julian Dicks was the first to go: too fat and too slow. Then Torben Piechnik: just not good enough; Don Hutchison: too much trouble; Bruce Grobbelaar, Ronnie Whelan and Steve Nicol. In getting rid of the last three, it shows Evans was prepared to remove the old guard if he felt they were past it.

In his early years as reserve-team coach, Evans had worked closely with Fagan. Later, he spent more time with Moran. He says both had a knack of being able to pass on their knowledge without being overbearing – to teach a player to take on his responsibilities with confidence but to be true to his own personality. Their example of a more hands-off style led Evans to take a step back from coaching during his time as manager.

'It was a bit of advice every now and then. I'm a great believer in encouragement. I hear people saying that Fergie liked throwing cups but he probably only did that once every blue moon to shake things up. You get more out of people in any job in any walk of life if you say, "Hey, good job, you did well today." You have to treat people fairly and as human beings first. On the flip side of that, when things aren't right you have to let players know too. You have to go for them no matter how important they are to the team. It doesn't matter if you're Kenny or a young lad, you have to meet the level. If you let a bad performance slip and say nothing, it's an unhealthy precedent.'

What infuriated Evans most was a player being unable to make a decision on the pitch. He'd rather someone had the courage to make a mistake and even someone who was then prepared to argue with him about it. 'I expected the team to win every week but if they didn't have an opinion about how the game should be played, then we were the daft ones, asking for the impossible.'

In training, Evans kept things simple – the Liverpool way.

'Players need to enjoy what they're doing in the long term. OK, in the short term there would be sacrifices in terms of fitness but you have to look forward to your work. Usually one unit of a training session would involve running and the rest would be with the ball. Sessions would be longer earlier in the week then shorter but more intense as you got closer to the match. The emphasis was always on the ball. We'd mix the rules up. The most important thing was to get a good tempo. There's nothing worse than watching a game where everything is slow. If you play passing football at speed, it frightens the opposition. You can't play against it. So the intensity of training was important. I wanted it to be intense, so the players didn't have to flick a switch on the Saturday to get it right.

'If you enjoy yourself, you play well. Now, kids see a lot of the antics that go on. I ask them why they want to become a footballer. It scares me how many say, "Big car." I'll tell them it's the wrong answer. Fewer are saying it's because they love football. Those that do are the ones you want. They'll go further. For me, life isn't about material things. It has always been about enjoyment.'

He concedes that maybe the players were 'too free' to make their own decisions in an era where wages meant any 'material thing' was available to them by outlaying only a small percentage of their weekly wage. These young footballers were different to the ones Evans had managed before. In an interview with *Goal* magazine in 1997, Evans gave some insight into the mindset at the time:

Week in, week out, our team talk is, 'It's great when you've got a talent but the most important thing is how the team plays and how you play for the team.' Trying to get that into their minds [is tough], because the younger ones are all a bit Roy of the Rovers. Someone like Jason McAteer is always playing up to the crowd, and sometimes it distracts him. Yeah, he's Liverpool daft but he's got to concentrate on the game.

Undeniably, however, there were distractions. Due to the influx of television and revenue streams for the newly revamped and globally marketed Premier League, footballers were earning more money than ever. Lifestyles were being portrayed as more significant than jobs. Look back through the autobiographies of players from the time and many of them read like guides to the London club scene. In his, Dominic Matteo – not even one of the stars – admits he thought nothing of following an all-night drinking session with a 10 a.m. champagne breakfast, or water-skiing across Lake Windermere while still drunk. On becoming Liverpool's most expensive player, Stan Collymore recalls being invited to Liverpool's end-of-season do, meeting up in a London hotel near Lord's Cricket Ground and walking into the room of a new teammate without knocking only to find him being treated to oral sex by not one but two mystery blondes. This was before the night had even started. He considers it a moment that summed up the attitude of the players at the time: partying before there was anything to party about. Managing these players was Evans, a man who blushes at the racy recollection of placing a *Playboy* calendar on the Boot Room wall.

The Spice Boys label had not been invented when Evans won his only trophy as Liverpool manager in April 1995, beating Bolton Wanderers in the Coca-Cola Cup final 2–1 at Wembley largely thanks to an inspired performance by Steve McManaman. Progress was marked by a final league placing of fourth, a jump of four positions from the previous season. A year later, Liverpool finished third and memorably beat Newcastle United 4–3. It was the type of spectacle that Rupert Murdoch must have dreamed of televising when Sky started pumping money into the game.

Liverpool's football was sometimes breathtaking, with Fowler, Collymore and McManaman as a three-pronged attack, capable of scoring at any moment. Yet while this was happening, the players were being written about for their off-field antics. Jamie Redknapp married a pop star from Eternal. He and David James were on the front of magazines and involved in modelling for Armani. The photogenic duo jetted to Milan for catwalk shows and fashion shoots. Jason McAteer was the first footballer since Kevin Keegan to appear in a hair shampoo advert. His work with Wash & Go led to an appearance in the Top Man catalogue. It might seem a normal thing for footballers now but this was a brave new world.

Fowler and McManaman gave interviews to raunchy magazines like *Loaded*, where their faces appeared under such headlines as 'BIRDS, BOOZE AND BMWs'. In February 1996, the pair were invited to the Brit Award music ceremony by McManaman's agent, Simon Fuller, who also represented the Spice Girls. Surrounded by magnums and balthazars, Fowler was pictured with Emma Bunton, perhaps the most understated of the pop group. Even though Fowler claims Bunton was just a friend, the *Daily Mail* was the first on to the supposed non-story, labelling Fowler, McManaman and the rest of the players featuring regularly in the newspaper's gossip columns as the 'Spice Boys'.

Evans admits he was not prepared for any of this. Previously, Liverpool's footballers had drunk themselves silly, gotten in fights and even ended up in prison. But, Jan Mølby aside, it had never affected the actual football: the appearances; the performances; the results.

Evans admits that some of their 'behaviour' was 'a bit daft'. But he remains adamant that in the 1990s, the focus was always present when it came to matches.

'Football was changing and I chose to embrace it freely rather than take a tight rein,' he says. 'They were young lads; Christ, they were young lads with a life to live. I wanted them to self-govern and that involved the staff too. I didn't want to hear about every single little indiscretion. If someone comes in five minutes late for the first time, I didn't want to deal with it, even hear about it. I had bigger things to do. I trusted the staff to deal with it, dole out the discipline. Give them a bollocking and then move on. But, hey, if it happened time and time again then I wanted to know, of course.'

Self-governance had always been one of the Liverpool squad's greatest strengths. There was a rank and file. Any player had to work his way up the chain. Barely a few months after first signing, Ian Rush considered moving to Crystal Palace due to a lack of first-team chances as well as the remorseless nature of verbal stick that came his way for speaking in a Welsh accent and wearing the wrong clothes. He was persuaded not to leave by Joe Fagan. In the 1990s, Rush stood as Liverpool's all-time leading goalscorer. By traditional Liverpool standards, the responsibility was on him and others like John Barnes and Mark Wright to pull their juniors into line if necessary. That they did not appear to might be considered a neglect of duty, although Evans does not see it the same way.

'First and foremost those boys were there to do their own job,' he says firmly. 'They wouldn't have been there if I hadn't felt they were capable of that. In a team situation, they tried to help the younger lads as much as they could. But the lads have got to listen too. It's not as simple as saying, "Hey, you, control that." The lads are who they are because they've got personality. You try not to quash that. I didn't want robots. Sometimes I see the players in modern football and I want to hide behind the couch. You want personalities, people who are streetwise. But you also want people who are accountable – people who will admit when they're wrong. I have no regrets at all about the way we went about our business. The only regret I have is that we never won the league.'

Evans believed the signing of Collymore for £8.5 million from Nottingham Forest had the potential to capture the title for Liverpool. Six months earlier, Andy Cole had moved from Newcastle to Manchester United for a British record. The Collymore deal suggested one of two things: a) Liverpool were capable of competing with their greatest rivals in the transfer market at least, or b) Liverpool had panicked and felt it necessary to respond. Had Frank Clark, Nottingham Forest's manager, replied to Alex Ferguson's telephone call quicker than Kevin Keegan's – who had fallen out with Cole at Newcastle – there is a chance Collymore could have ended up at Old Trafford and Cole at Anfield. 'We liked Cole,' Evans says. 'We realized Rushy was nearing the end and we needed to find a replacement. We eventually got Stan but it was nothing to do with United spending money. I felt we really needed him.'

Collymore was twenty-four and still a few years away from his prime. His path towards Liverpool had not been easy. He was brought up by his single-parent white mother as the only black kid in a ferociously Caucasian working-class area of southern Staffordshire. Aged eighteen, he'd asked to be released from Walsall because he didn't like the pugnacious coach Ray Train – a person he still blames for his aversion to training. Soon, despite scoring eighteen goals in twenty youth-team games, he was given the boot by Wolverhampton Wanderers for an inconsistent attendance record. Collymore then found a home at Stafford Rangers in the GM Vauxhall Conference, where John Griffin,

Steve Coppell's chief scout at Crystal Palace, remembers seeing him for the first time after initially travelling north to check out a goalkeeper. 'The keeper didn't impress me but the 6 ft 2 in lad built like a brick outhouse playing up front certainly did,' Griffin told the *Mirror* in 1997. Collymore was substituted at half-time due to an injury but by then Griffin had seen enough. 'I went back to Palace and told Steve I had just seen the best non-league player ever. He had two great feet, super skill and great strength. I couldn't find a fault.'

Palace had taken Ian Wright from park football and the plan was to eventually replace him with Collymore. Yet Collymore never felt a sense of belonging at Selhurst Park, where the Palace squad was split equally between black and white players and he was the only one from a mixed-race background. At Southend United, first-team opportunities were there straight away and in the 1992–93 season Collymore scored fifteen times to keep the seaside town club in the old Division Two. Those feats earned him a move back to the Midlands with Forest and over the next two campaigns his development was marked by another forty-one goals. Forest, meanwhile, won promotion before finishing a place above Liverpool in the Premier League during their first campaign back in the top flight.

Evans claims Collymore's ability was equal to that of Ronaldo, who, having been part of a Brazilian World Cup-winning squad, had finished as the top goalscorer in Holland during his first season at PSV Eindhoven after moving from Cruzeiro.

'On the face of it, there wasn't much of a difference [between the players],' Evans says. 'They both had power, pace, skill and a great finishing ability. I'd considered Ronaldo, just as I'd considered a lot of players at home and abroad. But it boiled down to Stan being English and knowing the demands of the country and the Premier League.'

For the first eighteen months, Collymore was successful without being prolific, developing an understanding on the pitch with Fowler, be it an understanding that did not extend off it. Collymore tells a story where he and Fowler argue in their first game together, a 5–0 friendly defeat by Ajax. It ends with Fowler telling Collymore to 'fuck off'. After that, Collymore states he chose never to speak to Fowler again, perhaps illustrating what a sensitive and complex individual he was and probably still is: the type who would have either had all of his insecurities exposed and then flourished in his earliest days as a Liverpool player under the old dressing-room regime based on one-upmanship; or simply not have fitted in and gone elsewhere sooner rather than later.

Evans' explanation is rather more superficial than that, suggesting Collymore had an ego. 'Stan had always been the big fish in the small pond elsewhere. When he came to Liverpool, he was just another player. After eighteen months, I hoped he'd get his head around it. It was a waste of his talent, because he had loads.'

Evans is more open about Collymore than he is about any of the other players that represented him. The striker has been scathing in his assessment of Evans too. In his autobiography, Collymore pins many of Liverpool's failings on the manager of a club that he suggests was stuck in a time warp.

At Forest, Collymore admits he was the focal point of the team. At Liverpool, he claims Evans used him improperly, asking him to drift wide and drop deeper. He insists that Liverpool clung on to its links with former glories. He is critical of Rush and Barnes, stating that they were not worthy of their places but remained because nobody had the courage to tell them to go (Evans did, in fact, during the summer of 1997, just before Collymore's own departure). He saw Melwood's four wooden training boards as a metaphor. The boards were 'rotting away' but, acting as monuments to a time when Liverpool ruled English football, they remained in use as well.

Then there was the lack of discipline in the squad. Players could walk on to the training pitch eating toast and on one occasion after a quip, Fowler allegedly got Evans' head in an arm-lock, messing his hair with the free hand. Collymore asks what would have happened if Gary Neville had tried something similar on Alex Ferguson.

Most significantly, perhaps, Collymore recalls how Ronnie Moran took to calling him 'Fog in the Tunnel' because of the number of times he was either late or did not turn up for training. Collymore lived in Cannock, a one-and-a-half-hour drive down the M6 on a morning without traffic. It was a journey he made most days.

Evans understood that, for a period, Collymore's mother was not well. He was prepared to make allowances. But then the pattern continued. He asked him to move to Merseyside on numerous occasions. The request was ignored. Collymore continued to be late.

It is at this point that Evans suspects his own future began to unravel. Collymore was not the most popular player in the Liverpool squad anyway. Living far from Merseyside, he was not a regular on the social scene. He was not really one of the lads. Now Collymore wasn't turning up for work while others were and resentment built up towards him for, as one member of the team puts it, 'taking the piss'.

There is a feeling from Evans that he felt lumbered with Collymore. Because of his financial outlay, he had to be patient with him. But it prompted a spiral of problems. There are other stories: of players taking shortcuts at training and not taking the football seriously enough. It has been said that David James once missed a session for one of his Armani photo shoots, although James himself denies this.

As for Collymore, he eventually found himself in the reserve team. 'Stan was one of those who raised his nose,' Evans says. '"I'm not doing that," Stan would say. But I'm not sitting having a go at Stan. I think we'd blame Stan for everything if we could. He wasn't the only one with that attitude but he may have been the first. He argued that he didn't sign for Liverpool to play in the reserves. I told him that we didn't sign players to play in the reserves. I felt he needed to be sharper – match sharp. It would have helped him. I can't understand why players complain about playing in the reserves. It was only for their benefit. It was never a punishment. You can't punish someone by asking them to play a game of football. You punish someone by leaving them out altogether.

'Stan let himself down in the last six months, when I felt he lost his concentration. It's sad because he was one of those guys you feel could have gone on to be a really great player. His ability was natural: pace, power, technique – everything. But for some reason, he started making things difficult for himself. The other players would ask where he was when he didn't turn up. You can only make excuses for a short period of time. It starts causing problems within your camp. I'd like to sit down with him one day in private, now we're both a bit older, and discuss what really went wrong.'

Under Evans, Liverpool were becoming predictable and relied too heavily on Steve McManaman. And when he was absent, there was criticism that Liverpool had five defenders and a huddle of midfielders who played too deep and passed too short, missing a vital link with the forwards and instead feeding the play to the overworked wing-backs.

Evans wanted to sign either Jari Litmanen (who later joined Liverpool under Gérard Houllier) or Teddy Sheringham.

'The Finnish lad [Litmanen] was a very, very clever player. We had people who could score goals and needed a few more who could create chances. We were playing in a friendly against Everton and Peter Robinson flew out to Amsterdam to speak to him. Again, he wanted the Champions League and went to Barcelona instead.

'We then looked towards Teddy. The deal was a long way down the line and I was confident of getting it signed. The only problem was that the board's policy was to buy younger players. It always had been at Liverpool. Lots of other clubs were signing foreign players on the wrong side of their thirties. Teddy was twenty-nine. We were paying big money for him. Teddy really wanted to come; we'd chatted all about it. But the board pulled the plug. It frustrated me because he spent four years at United and helped them win everything before moving back to Spurs until he was in his late thirties. I realized Teddy was no angel off the pitch – he liked a drink and a night out. But he was one of those guys who knew when and where. I figured he'd guide the younger boys.'

Then there was an argument that Liverpool were a ball-winner short of a title-winning team. Evans believed that in the prevailing refereeing climate, tigerish tacklers were a liability, though he was eventually persuaded to sign Paul Ince from Inter Milan, a midfielder in the tough-man mould. 'Paul was in the world-class category and few of those were available,' Evans says of the former Manchester United player. 'He wasn't just a competitor. He was a leader and could pass, otherwise he'd never have been a success in Italy. We played with wing-backs and Incey had been schooled in a 4–4–2 system. In the end, it was a formation that we decided to return to.'

A new breed of lithe, agile midfielders was emerging, epitomized by Patrik Berger, who became Evans' first foreign outfield signing for £3.25 million from Borussia Dortmund in the aftermath of an impressive Euro 96 campaign with the Czech Republic.

British players at other clubs claimed the presence of foreigners helped improve their own technical abilities. While Evans admired Alen Bokšić, then of Juventus, and Fiorentina's Gabriel Batistuta as well as AC Milan's Marcel Desailly, he was not tempted to emulate a Ruud Gullit-type signing in the transfer market just for the sake of it.

'I didn't want to go and get someone just to put more bums on seats. We filled Anfield anyway. You saw Gullit and Vialli, they were both well into their thirties and cost a lot of money. How long did Chelsea get out of them? If the chance had come to sign an older player – maybe in his late twenties like Teddy – I would have done it. But I wasn't someone who wanted to fill the place full of foreigners. I thought there was enough talent in this country at the time.'

Eric Cantona's legendary status at Manchester United did not help.

'OK, a lot of people did not like Cantona because he kicked a fan [at Crystal Palace in 1995] and got banned. But his supporters loved him. And so did the media. He was this foreign fella, different. Everyone wanted one like him. It didn't mean players like that grew on trees.'

The distrust of foreign footballers harked back to Shankly and Liverpool's peculiarly Celtic insularity. Yet Evans did not have a single Scot in his first-team squad, a far cry from the glory days when Hansen, Dalglish and Souness led the fight. Instead, Evans allowed John Barnes a significant influence, someone who translated his thoughts on to the field.

'John had some interesting points to make. He was another coach on the pitch. He was desperate for the team to succeed and that was the thing we really had in common.'

There is certainly more of Paisley than Shankly in Evans. He uses that term again – 'spokesman' – when I ask him whether he might have been more forceful with the players rather than continue the tradition of self-regulation. The cult of the manager has grown since his departure, with coaches like José Mourinho imposing their characters on the identity of a club, attempting to command respect.

'When the club you manage is high profile, that makes you high profile because you're in the public eye on a regular basis. But as far as my own personality being bigger than the club, I don't see the point in that. I was there as their spokesman, really. It's only part of the job but if you've got one voice then there's no mix-ups, and we tried to keep it that way.'

Evans could sense the demands in football were shifting. He was prepared to listen to whatever the board of directors suggested when he was called in for a meeting by chairman David Moores in the summer of 1998.

'I agreed there was a need for something different. The game was turning very European. The idea was to bring someone in who knew more about that side of it. We spoke to John Toshack and several other people about the idea of appointing a director of football. We needed someone who could help build a bigger scouting base and improve the training ground. John rejected the opportunity because he wanted to be a number 1, and I should have learnt from that.'

Evans believes Liverpool 'ended up' with Gérard Houllier.

'Arsène Wenger had revolutionized Arsenal, and France had just won the World Cup. It seemed like a sensible idea to get Houllier in as joint manager and work together. I let my heart rule my head. Deep down, I knew it wasn't right. I still regret going along with the idea of the board meeting him a few days before I did. I was on holiday in Barbados.

'[When we did meet] on the football side, we got on. At the end of the meeting, it came to roles, responsibilities and titles. I said something about not having an ego and that I'd do whatever was better for the club. It was a massive mistake. I should have been sharper or brighter than that. I wasn't strong enough to insist that he would only be a director of football. I should have said that under no circumstances can two men do the same job. The board should have known that too. It had been tried at other clubs and it hadn't worked. At the end of the day, you can sit down with your best mate and talk about football and you don't have the same opinions. There's always going to be a clash. And that's what happened.'

Evans says he and Houllier did not disagree over 'big things'.

'It was silly things, like what time the bus left – stuff that erodes the confidence in the squad. Gérard's a cleverer man than I am, that's for sure. I don't hold any grudges against him. But he knew this was going to happen, although he later admitted he didn't think it'd be so quick. He was quite happy to bide his time.

'I felt it was starting to get to the players. While I was still there, all of them still called me "Boss". I picked the team – the final decision always fell to me. Most of the players were on my side when it got into a bit of a war towards the end. The lads who weren't in the team were always going to go with Gérard. It was messy. Should I have stayed and fought it out? Because I was a supporter of the club, I realized somebody had to go. It was never going to be Gérard; it was going to be me. Regrets? Of course. About not being the guy that pushed himself forward.'

Evans did not find the separation easy.

'You leave Liverpool and you're bitter. I'd been there my entire working life. I had six to nine months when I wasn't interested. I didn't care whether Liverpool won or lost. The wife would tell me the result and I'd grumble and walk away. I realized I couldn't live that way. It was ridiculous. So I decided to become a fan again. Why spend the rest of your life hating something that you loved for so long? It wasn't healthy.'

Evans hoped another top job might come his way. But Liverpool took their time settling his contract, meaning he missed out on opportunities elsewhere.

'It took a fair while to pay me off, which didn't help in terms of going to another club,' he says. 'I always believed I had the best job I was ever going to have at Liverpool. But my record stands up today against any English manager in the Premier League. Maybe it warranted another shot. Maybe because I didn't have an agent and, again, maybe because I didn't push certain issues as I should have done, I was out of the public eye.'

In the years that followed, Evans took roles at Swindon Town, Fulham and the Welsh FA.

'They were always jobs for other people, doing favours as a coach or an assistant. Sometimes in life you have to be a selfish bastard and I wasn't.'

He despairs now at the state of management generally.

'Everybody wants to move into the top job straight away. Top players feel like they should go into management at the same level. I'm not quite sure that's the way to go. Management is very different to playing. Players have to serve some kind of an apprenticeship and so should managers.

'You have too many coaches in management positions. Sometimes I feel they try to dictate too much of what goes on during games. They want to kick every ball of every game. Shanks, Paisley and Fagan set the team up and made it clear what the intentions were. But at the end of the day, it's about people making decisions on the pitch. That's what footballers are paid to do. Coaching, to me, is about making little points, tweaks. If you played for Liverpool, you were expected to know what to do. But there was nothing wrong with giving bits of advice, offering the right guidance.'

He remains adamant that his approach at Liverpool was the right one.

'I wanted players to be free to make their own decisions. There was trust. Maybe I gave a bit too much. If it goes wrong, the buck stops with the manager.

'But you can't coach winning. Before my team went on the pitch, I'd finish the team talk with a simple message, "Enjoy yourself." After that, they were away. I trusted them to do the business.'

ACKNOWLEDGEMENTS

Thank you to all of the footballers interviewed in this book. Thank you to Ged Rea for his remarkable eye. Thank you to John McDermott for his proofing skills. Thank you to Paul at Cult Zeros for his generosity and patience. For being a good gang of lads, thank you to Mark, Matthew, Ian, Andy, Andrew, James, Billy and Paul. Thank you to Peter Hughes for his financial assistance. Thank you to David Luxton for guidance, Brenda Kimber for encouragement and Ailsa Bathgate for being a brilliant editor. Thank you too to David Cottrell. Rosalind, the dedication is yours.

BIBLIOGRAPHY

Blows, Kirk, *Terminator: Authorised Julian Dicks Story*, Polar Print
    Group, 1996

Carragher, Jamie, *Carra: My Autobiography*, Bantam Press, 2008

Collymore, Stan, *Tackling My Demons*, Willow, 2004

Dohren, Derek, *Ghost on the Wall: The Authorised Biography of
    Roy Evans*, Mainstream, 2005

Fowler, Robbie, *Fowler: My Autobiography*, Macmillan, 2005

Gerrard, Steven, *Gerrard: My Autobiography*, Bantam Press, 2007

Hughes, Simon, *Red Machine*, Mainstream, 2013

Matteo, Dominic, *In My Defence*, Great Northern Books, 2011

Mitten, Andy, *Glory Glory!*, Vision, 2009

Mølby, Jan, *Jan the Man*, Gollancz, 2000

Owen, Michael, *Off the Record*, HarperSport, 2006

Ruddock, Neil, *Hell Razor*, Willow, 2000

Rush, Ian, *Rush: The Autobiography*, Ebury Press, 2009

Souness, Graeme, *The Management Years*, Andre Deutsch, 1999

Yates, Michael, *Steven Gerrard, Michael Owen and . . . Me*,
    Independent Publishing Network, 2013

ABOUT THE AUTHOR

Simon Hughes is a journalist and author. He writes for the *Daily Telegraph* and the *Sunday Telegraph*, as well as Liverpool Football Club's official magazine. His book *Red Machine* won the Antonio Ghirelli Prize for Italian Soccer Foreign Book of the Year in 2014. His other title is *Secret Diary of a Liverpool Scout*. He lives in Liverpool.

CW 6115

CW 6115